Animals
on View

Weidenfeld and Nicolson London

Animals on View

An Illustrated Guide to Britain's Safari Parks,
Zoos, Aquariums and Bird Gardens

ANTHONY SMITH
in collaboration with Jill Southam

House editor Esther Jagger
Designed by Sheila Sherwen for
George Weidenfeld and Nicolson Limited,
11 St John's Hill, London SW11

ISBN 0 297 77379 8

Printed in Great Britain by
Cox & Wyman Ltd,
London, Fakenham and Reading

Colour separations by
Newsele Litho Ltd.

All the information given in this book was, to
the best of the author's and publisher's
knowledge, correct at the time of going to press

Contents

Foreword

The aim of this book is to help you find your way through the current jungle of animal collections within Britain. So many have sprung up in the past 15 years that there are more to choose from than ever before; but, as we do not know what they are like until we see them, and then wish we had known beforehand, this book aims to provide that necessary information.

There are four sections. The first examines the so-called (by us, if not by the collections themselves) safari parks. In these a car or bus is crucial for travelling through one or more of the enclosures. Because I have talked about the history of the safari parks, I have dealt with them not alphabetically, as in the other three sections, but in order of seniority. The second section, estates, lists those other animal collections in large areas of the countryside that do not have to be seen from a vehicle. Section 3 is a vaguer assortment. As the fourth – town zoos – describes all major collections closely connected with a city or town, those that used to have a monopoly over our desire to see exotic animals, it is a relatively straightforward group. The third section details places neither sufficiently major to be in town zoos nor sufficiently extensive to be in estates. The purpose of all four sections is to give a broad picture of the kinds of animal collection now available to us.

The policy throughout has been to give many of the basic facts about each place in box form, to have maps for the first two sections (plus drive-round maps for the safari parks) and also to provide general descriptions. These vary greatly in their length, as some places plainly merit more words than others, but the overall wish has been to tell something of the flavour of each collection, of its uniqueness, its charms (or horrors) and of

its particular animal offerings. Not every creature can be listed, partly because a zoo's population is forever changing but mainly because (with several hundred kinds of resident in many places) the prose would much resemble a telephone directory. Therefore items and species have been selected in the hope that a subjective assessment will give a better picture. After all, that is the sort of opinion you get from your friends when they have been somewhere and you want to know from them what it is like. They can tell you far more than the brochure will ever do.

This personal approach has extended to names and spellings. To some it may be the Blackfooted Penguin. To others the Black-footed, or even the Cape Penguin, or the Jackass Penguin, but it is all the same bird. In this book just one name is (usually) used for each species. Similarly all specific animals have been capitalized. It is the White-faced Whistling Duck, and not the white-faced whistling duck which could confuse if the white-faced part (or even the whistling part) looks like an adjective rather than a portion of its name. Other awkwardnesses have been encountered. If the place looks like a zoo but is called a park, which word should best be used? 'We are not a Zoo Park; we are a Park Zoo,' said one zoo-keeper (or park-keeper or park-zoo-keeper); but is it right to pass confusion on to gentle readers? Once again a personal preference has been adopted. It is Harris' Hawk, not Harris's. It is Laggar Falcons, not Lugger; Red-shouldered Hawks, not Red-shouldered Buzzards. It is the Wild Cat and a Sealion, the Sea Horse and a sea-bird, a Lung Fish and a Catfish.

So, enough, enough. Sufficient to say that others have their prejudices and I have followed mine.

A.S.

Introduction

The safari parks, now 11 years old, revolutionized the observation of wild animals in this country. They permitted a sense of involvement and excitement quite different from any zoo experience because the visitors, however much within a car, were also within a cage. The novelty of the new situation took time to sink in. Drivers would leave their cars, open the boot or check the oil if a minor hold-up offered opportunity, thereby offering major opportunity to the Lions for checking their own prowess upon a human. A short sharp cuff with a paw and the motorist would be as dead as the dipstick now wrapped around his hand. The safari parks were a novelty and people were delighted with the drive-through idea, but they did not appreciate sufficiently, notably in the early days, that Lions, however penned for their pleasure, are no pussy cats. At all times, whether soporific in the sun or even fast asleep, Lions must merit respect.

Longleat had been the first stately home to open its doors to the public, and even that act had caused criticism, but this was nothing to the roaring which followed the announcement by Lord Bath and Jimmy Chipperfield of their joint wish to keep 50 Lions in Wiltshire. Their plan was that motorists should drive through this reserve as if on safari in Africa. All the media attacked the idea in their varied fashion, with *The Times* being among the most strident. A leading article concluded:

Cattle, sheep and deer ought to be good enough for a Wiltshire man. The proper place for lions in an island that is spared them in the wild state is in heraldry. Although some planning permission has inexplicably been given, there is still time for wiser counsel to prevail. Lord Bath's dangerous folly is not due to be open to the public until next Easter. Ordinary citizens who seek to make modest changes on their property are often checked by a miscellany of planners with power. Here if ever is a just cause for official intervention – if necessary from Whitehall.

Whitehall did not intervene. The Lions did not escape, live wild in the Welsh hills (as some had predicted) or eat the visitors who came to look at them. There was some damage to cars but initially most owners were proud to possess these combat wounds. The really extraordinary fact, which took even the promotors by surprise, was the colossal popularity of this new form of entertainment. Within half a dozen years, and after another half-dozen estates had been dedicated to the same theme of cars and animals, the number of annual visitors to them was around eight million. Much of the money spun off, for example, to repair the roof and every window of the Longleat stately home. Who would have believed beforehand that the ailing finances of an inherited estate could be so bountifully set to rights by the majestic indolence of a group of Lions?

It was not all plain sailing. None of the Longleat animals came from the wild but they proved to have lost none of their wildness when the assorted collection was introduced to itself in the 100-acre compound. That particular section of oak forest was vast by zoo standards, with an average of two acres per animal and a great advance on traditional confinements, but the size was inadequate to prevent the slaughter of Lions by Lions as various hierarchies were established. Land Rovers broke up the fights; so too shotguns and other forms of noise; but Lions did die. One particular male killed six in a night, and he too had to be killed. The situation was resolved by fences being built between the groups that had established their independence, and by having manned checkpoints at the gateways. Cars could subsequently pass between each region but no Lions could do so.

It had long ago been learned that people in cars are curiously safe from wild animals, and it had been assumed that British Lions would disregard car-borne Britons just as African Lions pay no attention to their motorized tourists; but there were unforeseen differences between Wiltshire and the Serengeti. Many a British car, dusted off in the springtime and cranked into life after a winter of idleness, does not compare too well with the kind of machine confidently expected to travel on schedule through the heat and dirt of Africa. The British vehicle, notably when confronted with a day of modest warmth and a slowly moving jam, will often despair. It will

AN EXPERIMENT IN ACCLIMATISATION: IMPORTED AMERICAN ELK (WAPITI) AT OSMASTON MANOR, DERBY

1894 and 1965. *Above* Wapiti recently imported to Osmaston Manor, Derby. *Below* The first fence going up to house the Lions of Longleat.

boil. Its clutch will fail to grip and its hoses will show their age. In Africa it is up to each driver to fix any breakdown. On a British safari, where Lions crowd in more closely, the driver has first to be towed from the scene. Consequently, the wardens and rangers, decked out in bush hats and jungle gear, had to spend more time removing dead vehicles than caring for their living animals.

Those early days were difficult. Queues of cars stretched for miles just waiting to get into the reserve. The warden–breakdown teams learned how to hook chains to failed buses, keep an eye on the Lions, instruct all foolhardy drivers to go back to their cars, insist upon windows being closed, pacify those who had seen only oak trees, collect roof-rack baggage pulled down by tooth or claw, pray gently as soft-top sports cars went through the area, and speak by radio with other wardens in other sections who believed they too had problems. There were other more fundamental setbacks. The early roads were far too narrow; cars could not pass each other. The early landscaping was wrong; dead ground often hid the Lions from the eyes of visitors. Nevertheless, despite the confusion and the roaring and snarling from unhappy car loads, people did flock to see this brand-new show.

They also flocked to almost every other new form of country zoo. The safari parks collected the lion's share of attendance and publicity, but they were not alone in giving people a destination for their beloved motor car. Many private collectors, struggling with the finances of an overgrown hobby, realized their salvation might be down at the gate. If motorists could be induced to enter it there would be a steady supply of ready money. Large estate owners, sorely wounded by new taxes, began to appreciate that a walled garden crackling with Macaws could do more for their income than west wing ghosts or rows of Gainsboroughs. Quite suddenly, most exotic animals living in Britain were no longer quartered in urban zoos but in the countryside. In the 1960s in particular, dozens of new animal collections were initiated and they all relied, more or less, on car-borne visitors.

This leads to an unsatisfactory truth. The foreign animals are here, by and large, only because we pay to see them. They are not here, like Magna Carta, green fields or the Tower of London, because history put them here. If we were to cease visiting zoos, and to stop leaving money at the gate, the animals would swiftly disappear. One or two zoos receive state aid but 99 per cent of the money comes directly from our pockets and not indirectly from our taxes. Animals do not have the status of museum exhibits or art gallery paintings. If a zoo has a bad year – and many

have had recently – the cages soon empty, by saie, by unreplaced death or merely (as the simplest expedient of them all) by using one animal to feed another and thus reducing two food bills at one stroke.

An equally unpalatable corollary is that the kind of people we are affects the kinds of animals put on show for us. We are, it would seem, hooked on Lions. Therefore the safari parks have concentrated on them. Apparently we prefer the males, liking their maned arrogance more than the sleek female lines. The parks often give us great groups of males only, a most unnatural phenomenon. We also like the manes to be black, and therefore a greater quantity of such Lions are to be found in Britain than anywhere in the wild.

This may seem harmless, but if all animals flourish here according to their popularity we will end up with an appealing but unrepresentative selection. There are over 4000 species of mammals, over 8000 of birds, and yet we see only a fraction of that number. In the safari parks, the places most adept at winning our cash, we find an even smaller number. Animals with minority appeal are therefore being excluded. There is no difficulty in finding Lions, Tigers, Giraffes, Elephants (almost always females, since the males are 'difficult'), Bears, Camels, Zebras; they are easily recognizable, expected in every zoo and part of our story-book folklore. Not so the Margay, Paca, Cacomistle, Fossa, Aardwolf, Woolly Tapir, Gaur, Anoa, Oribi, Goral, Serow, Markhor, Bongo, Babirusa, Manatee, Zorilla, Grison, Olingo, Tucotuco, Mara, Souslik, Pika, Pangolin, Tamandua, Douroucouli, Angwantibo, Aye-aye, Sifaka, Tenrec, Wombat, Cuscus and Pudu. How many of these mammals can we pronounce, let alone recognize?

In the world there are 248 different kinds of marsupial, but in a typical zoo there are probably just a couple of Kangaroos representing this sort of animal. There are 981 different Bats and 1729 rodents, but Bats and Rats are not popular. As a consequence we see few of them, although these two orders provide more than half of the kinds of mammal alive in the world today. We like Lions and there are 700 of them now in England. That is a density of one in every 70 square miles, a far greater proportion than on the continent of Africa. Even a place like the Serengeti National Park, famous for its Lions and with a few million prey animals for them to feed on, has only about one lion to each square mile.

We do not have that number in Britain, but we have a glut none the less. At the time of writing the price tag for a good Lion is £50 or even less. They breed well and zoos have no difficulty in acquiring them. Therefore many British Lions must be killed, either when young or as soon as

Zoos frequently feel obliged to display animals that people expect to see, but it can be more rewarding when they show us creatures whose names we are not sure how to pronounce, let alone identify. Try with this assortment. Their names are on page 12.

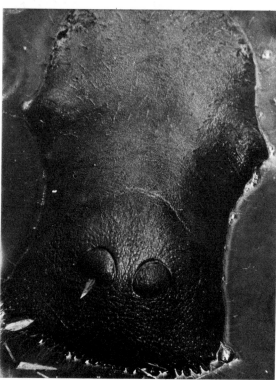

6

7

8

9

10

11

age makes them less attractive. What a pity that
we have them in abundance but a shortage of so
many other mammal types. I would swap a Lion
for a Slender Loris or Golden Mole any day.

In fact, it is this kind of personal idiosyncrasy
that partly helps to save the day. Zoo-keepers are
about as mixed a bunch of human beings as could
be found. They do not conform to a pattern.
They each have their preferences – for species,
for animal orders, for disregarding the prevailing
public wish. Philip Wayre has concentrated on
Pheasants and Otters. Leonard Williams has
focused on Woolly Monkeys, Peter Scott on
wildfowl, Molly Badham on primates, John
Knowles on ungulates, John Aspinall on Gorillas
and Tigers, Philip Glasier on birds of prey,
Robert Goodden on butterflies. Those are all
general preferences but animal people also have
more specific feelings. For no comprehensible

There are 981 kinds of Bat in the world, but very few are exhibited in animal
collections even though they represent about one-fifth of all mammal species. *Above*
and *below* The Greater Horseshoe Bat, showing its 14-inch wingspan and powerful set of teeth.

reason they adore or suffer some particular creature in their collection. They can no more explain this predilection than we can comprehend why we like our friends, particularly the ones who never speak, but do smell and eat our cupboard bare. To go round a zoo with its director is to realize these idiosyncratic fondnesses. We wait and wait and finally marvel, not so much at the boring little protrusion but at the ecstasy simmering from our guide. Long may such preferences prevail. They give us more to see, more variety. We do not have to settle for the so-called ABC animals, the Antelope, the Bear, the Camel and down to Z for Zebra. We welcome them, but not to the exclusion of the Aardvark, the Binturong, and the Cururo down to Zagouti and Zebu.

Despite the mixture of zoo directors (and a guide to them would be a fascinatingly libellous book to write) there is one aspect of considerable uniformity: they are happy to tell scurrilous tales about their rivals. I say this, not in order to be equally outspoken about the lot of them, but to explain that it has often been difficult to collect the facts for this book. I naturally wished for wholesome accuracy and all too frequently met slander, malice or mere packs of lies. 'Are male Elephants difficult to keep?' I asked X. 'Why not ask Y for the answer to that one,' came the reply, 'because I know from one of his sacked keepers that he shot/castrated/maimed/buried/drowned all his males a couple of months ago.' 'Nonsense,' would say Y, when questioned later, 'I sold them all to Cuba. And for good money too!'

On my own personal safari of every major collection in the British Isles – a necessary precursor to the writing of this book – I was told extraordinary tales. I heard of men disguised as women poisoning chicks to put the blame on someone else's wife. I was told of 22 Cheetahs being killed by one Lion. (A basis existed for this story but the number grew with every telling.) I learned how wire can be cut to make it seem as if the animal has engineered its own escape, and how that same creature would be on display one week later 12 miles down the road. On a lower level, I was told again and again of males being sold as females, of crosses being described as pure stock, of infertile animals going as a breeding pair. It would seem that the second-hand car business is, by comparison, a model of propriety and fair trading.

My opinion is that much of the dishonesty in the zoo-men's world (I did not accept all the stories but do believe that a high degree of untruthfulness prevails) has its roots in the hypocritical nature of the zoo business. In this instance I think the public is largely to blame. Everyone knows that animals are either prey or predator. They are likely to be eaten, or to eat

"We never catch the visitors at it, M'Lord."

Both before and after its opening Longleat received considerable publicity, a much needed ingredient of any new venture. Cartoon by Thelwell, reproduced in *Punch*, 20 September 1967.

others, or both. Visitors to zoos do not wish to be reminded of this fact, or so it is said. They do not like to see one animal catching another, and can complain of cruelty. They do not even like to see one dead animal, however it was killed, being fed to another; they say their children will suffer nightmares (although children, I find, are remarkably resilient to such events). People only want to see carnivores eating meat, something no longer resembling the animal it came from. Only in one zoo did I see recognizable hunks of cow lying in a cage. I saw lots of dead day-old chicks serving as food, a sight now becoming commoner, but not once did I see a living creature being given *au naturel* to another. This may be as we wish it, but it is hypocrisy.

So too is the way that much animal behaviour is curtailed. Many species live in groups. This often means that a single male or female becomes dominant and maintains its dominance by killing potential rivals. A Wolf pack is one example. In the struggle for the hierarchy animals can die, both in the confines of a zoo and in the wild. Visitors do not, in the main, like to see this happening. They hate death or injury before their very eyes, and proclaim most vehemently what damage this will do to their children. What is the zoo-keeper to do? He can reduce the pack to two, and witness the ensuing listlessness in the eyes and lives of his animals, or let the pack grow naturally. He will then have Wolves alert to the constant demands of aggression, submission, dominance and all else as they replicate their wild behaviour. He will hope that the bloodiest fights happen when no violent visitor is in the audience, immediately eager thereafter to involve editors, initiate litigation and make fur fly in every possible human way. The zoo-keeper is torn. If he attempts to simulate the wild his visitors may resent the subsequent savagery, with cubs eaten or left to die. If he opts for simplicity his own standards suffer, and a pair of Wolves is never so good as a pack.

One solution is to be more informative. Visitors cannot know that a single Wolf caged by itself has been cast out from the group, but a notice could inform them. They cannot know that creatures often lead solitary lives, such as many Bears, Cats and the Giant Panda, and will breed better in zoos if the males and females are only intermittently brought together. Once again a notice could stop much public complaint about loneliness, but not all such extra information may be well received. Large male Elephants are rare in Britain because such Elephants have frequently killed their keepers. Chester Zoo recently achieved the first Indian Elephant to be conceived and born in captivity, but its father had already been put down. The notice providing this information could create criticism and a general feeling, not expressed before, that Elephants should not be kept in zoos if breeding units cannot be arranged.

In the long run it is plainly best to be informative, but a shorter expedient is to say nothing People do react strangely, partly because sentiment rather than reason is often in command. The British people are possibly more considerate towards animals than those of any other nation, but are probably more illogical as well. They complain loudly at seeing British birds in cages, even to the extent of prising open a release for them, but do not mind about foreign birds equally trapped for life. Pairs of Golden Eagles receive more cluckings of shame, more expressions of dismay at their captivity, than far larger birds perched on either side of them. We long to feed each beast with food, and readily do so whether or not such feeding is allowed, but we rarely consider the food we proffer to each animal. Are sweets good for Elephants, or Monkeys, or Bears? Moreover, if feeding is allowed, we do our best to destroy the animal hierarchy, calling the dominant male 'greedy' and making every effort to feed his underlings when he knows and they know (but we fail to know) that he should have the prime choice of food.

It must be unpleasant to be on the receiving end of much public criticism. The rebukes can be right; they can also be very wrong. I remember seeing my first Lion in Africa. Its fur was a mess. It had several wounds. There were flies by the thousand which buzzed briefly whenever that angry head came round to snap at them. It was not a dying Lion, nor even old, but was living a natural life within its habitat. Had it been transferred in its condition to a British zoo there would have been an outcry. Soon afterwards, as

the simplest remedy of them all, there would have been no Lion. It is always best to keep sick or apparently sick animals out of sight, and it is also best to have young beasts. The elderly can look old and therefore invite censure. But do we want euthanasia for every ageing beast? Do we never want to see that animals, like us, get sick and age and die?

Once again it is the gate money that dominates. If people have no wish to see geriatric Lions they will not pay that entrance fee. The aged animals must therefore die to keep the zoo alive. It even sounds reasonable, much like the law of the jungle, with the cash till rather than natural selection ordering events. Nevertheless, there is a most unhappy ring to all such happenings. Whether an animal is imported, kept alive and permitted to breed, or merely killed, is largely a matter of show business. Does it attract? Is it top of the bill or an act that no longer pays? Fortunately there are the zoo directors who do not behave equally. Certain animals, for each of them, can never be sold or killed. However uneconomic, and however capable of inducing outside criticism, these will survive whatever the consequences. They may eventually be put down, just as Dogs and Cats are, when the pain becomes too great; but until then they live, come what may.

Survival in zoos used to be the sole consideration. All was well if an animal could be kept alive. Provided it was there, day after day or even year after year, the zoo was doing its job. An animal was more likely, generally speaking, to remain alive if it remained alone. The introduction of a mate or of a partner might create extra risk. The two animals might fight, might wound each other and one or both might subsequently die. Consequently the business of breeding within the zoos remained at a low ebb for a very long time. The London collection in Regent's Park, initiated in 1826, was the first of its kind in the world and the first to be called a 'zoo', but breeding was not among its priorities for a very long time. There was, for example, amazement and delight when, in the royal jubilee year of 1935, its first baby Chimpanzee was born and reared. In 1950 the zoo's first-ever Polar Bear was born and a million *extra* visitors came that year to look at the infant Brumas.

Quite suddenly, much of the world changed course in its attitude towards wild animals. By the end of the 1950s various voices crying in the wilderness began to be heard. Their message was conservation. The World Wildlife Fund was started. In 1961 Tanzania was host to the largest meeting ever held on the subject of saving wildlife. The subsequent Arusha Declaration, a kind of charter for nature, was the most dramatic

Safari parks are not entirely new. *Above* An 1851 print of Eland in the Earl of Derby's menagerie at Knowsley, and *below* an Eland of today at the Lambton Pleasure Park.

There are 36 members of the Cat family and the Serval is one of the most gracious.
Found in Africa south of the Sahara, it eats widely, being able to catch large birds, Rats
and even the smaller Antelopes. Fortunately it also 'does well', as the saying goes, in captivity.

appeal there had ever been. Simultaneously, the zoos began to take their task more seriously than ever before. In Volume I of the *International Zoo Yearbook*, an excellent publication also started in the late 1950s, Sir Solly Zuckerman of London Zoo wrote that 'one of the most important and vital functions of the modern zoo is its role as a living museum – as a repository of the world's fauna'. If this was to be the case, and if zoos were actually to be producers and maintainers of animals rather than the consumers they had always been, it was up to them to improve their skills in breeding animals *and* realize the urgency for doing so. The fact became common knowledge that, of the 250 species vanished from the earth since the beginning of the Christian era, two-thirds had become extinct during the previous 50 years. Zoos had helped in a few instances to prevent the number being larger, but could have done much more. In 1972 the first international conference on the breeding of endangered species was held, and delegates were shocked to hear how badly, according to an American who had added up the figures, the zoos were doing in breeding animals. They were still net consumers rather than producers of their stock. This was no way to be a repository.

Events have since moved rapidly. Many 'difficult' animals have become breeding animals.

The Gorilla is one example. Twenty years ago zoos congratulated themselves if they could keep this tropical animal alive, as most perished speedily. Many even died on the journey out of Africa. Then, in 1956, a Gorilla at Columbus, Ohio, actually gave birth. The offspring, Colo, had to be hand-reared, but happily survived. The world's zoos were amazed at this coup. Basle Zoo in Switzerland determined to produce the second Gorilla. They had possessed the species since 1948 and for the first four years were proud of the male Achilles. Then, showing up their ignorance about the ways of Gorillas, an operation (for a swallowed pen) demonstrated a gross injustice. The awkward name of Achilla was immediately contrived for this undoubted female and, on being given a more suitable partner, she was able in return to provide Basle with a Gorilla baby. No less important was the fact that Achilla reared her offspring on her own. By 1970 not only had Colo, the pathfinder, produced a baby of her own but 18 other Gorillas had been successfully born in captivity. The total is now well past three figures.

This is not to say the problem is solved, even for Gorillas. The majority of this species in zoos today were captured in the wild (and this probably involved the slaughter of others of their tribe) but the proportion of zoo-born to those

16

taken from the wild is improving all the time. So too is the proportion of many other animals inside the zoos. About 70 per cent of the Regent's Park inhabitants were born there. At Longleat all but one of the mammal species in residence has produced offspring. The question 'Do more living animals enter your zoo or leave it?' is often met these days by the assurance that more leave.

Unfortunately, it is only the general picture that is improving. Scores of animals breed only rarely, such as the Bottle-nosed Dolphin and the Cheetah. We still dip into the sea whenever we have need of performing Dolphins, and no one knows their ocean numbers, but it is known that the Cheetah is more of a rarity than ever before. There are over a thousand of this superb cat in the world's zoos and 10 per cent of them are breeding. The Cheetah is no stranger to captivity – the first reference to hunting with the animal is dated 856 BC – but it was not until 1966 that Cheetah offspring were both conceived and reared within a zoo. A total of 2822 years must be some kind of record for non-productivity, but even now no one understands why some Cheetahs breed and others do not. There was a theory that the male had to be kept separate for most of the time, but some breeding Cheetah pairs live permanently in the hurly-burly of a group. There was a theory about cage size, as Cheetahs roam widely in the wild, but big and small cages have been successful. John Aspinall has green fingers when it comes to breeding, but not with his Cheetahs. If it is not known why certain animals become parents no one can know why others do not. It is sad, and may be catastrophic for the species, if the non-productive still exceed the productive individuals by a margin as wide as with the Cheetah.

Curiously, it can also be difficult for the zoo-men when the technique of breeding an animal suddenly proves successful. Very soon there is abundance, initially within the particular zoo that developed the technique, and later everywhere else. Let us say that the average litter of an animal is four, that two litters are born each year and the young reach maturity after one year. Many mammals readily achieve this kind of productivity. The original pair will therefore produce eight young in their first successful year, making a total of ten animals of that particular species. The zoo itself will be delighted at this burgeoning as eight youngsters romp for the delight of all. However, by the end of the second successful year, there will be a total of 26 animals as eight more young are born to the original pair and the first-born litter will itself produce eight young. (For arithmetical convenience I am assuming not only incest, a frequent feature anyhow of zoo – and wild – life, but also equal numbers of each sex in every litter.) By the end of the third year, if the original animals are still alive and still breeding, the total population will be 72 and this will rise to 234 by the end of the fourth successful year.

In short, possibly by the simple addition of vitamins in the diet, or a different cage, or keeper, or routine, or luck, an infertile problem can become 234 animals within four years. What does the zoo-keeper do? Initially he is overjoyed. Not only do his visitors like the exhibit but the young can be sold at good (rare animal) prices. By the third year the visitors are less pleased ('Look, Dad, here's the same animal again!') and the selling price is falling dramatically as an uncommon animal becomes a glut. One solution is to permit the animals to exercise their own form of population control, to let (if that is the way of this species) the dominant male kill off the young sired by other males, to let the weaklings starve as they would in the wild and to let nature keep numbers down (and prices high). Needless to say, not a word of this appears in the zoo's brochure or on its notices.

Visitors, so I have been told, do not even like to be informed that animals are bought and sold. Certainly I have rarely seen a price stated publicly. The animals are 'acquired' rather than 'bought', providing one more example, to my mind, of hypocrisy with regard to animals. We are no strangers to commerce, and buy and sell virtually everything, even plots upon the moon, but we seem to shy from the fact that animals are also in the market place. On a dealer's list there is no such reticence. The facts are printed as clearly as on any catalogue: 'Stump-tailed Monkeys (adult) £85; Kinkajou (two years) £150; Llama £125; Puma (breeding pair) £300; Puma (ditto) £250; Lions (eight months) £100; Bengal Tigers (pair) £1500; Crowned Crane £130; Hamster 40p; Peacock £35; Green Monkey £75.' There is a distasteful element to such lists, and one wonders what was less satisfactory about the second Puma pair (older, scarred, disagreeable?); but, of course, there is trade in animals. The creatures that we see in zoos, and pay to see, are as subject to supply and demand as second-hand motor cars, pop-up toasters and works of art.

All zoos are commercial, however much those that are non-profit-making by their statutes like to condemn the others that are able to make money. The visitors do not get a rougher deal when they enter a commercial rather than a non-commercial zoo. Nor do the animals suffer, in my opinion, just because an owner can cream off profits for himself. It is a nice sentiment that any trust or charity will care for its creatures more than ordinary commercial ventures will ever do, lavishing money upon the inmates whenever there is need, like a dowager showering care upon her pampered pekingese; but this cannot be the case. The trusts have to pay as much for their cages, employees, foodstuffs and fuel as anyone else. Should they disregard the normal economic laws of income and expenditure, and should their books fail to balance, it will be the animals who suffer as they are sold off or killed to appease the creditors. A dowager's Pekingese does not have to pay its way.

Nevertheless, British animal collections fall, by and large, under two headings. Either they can make a profit or they are owned by trusts or societies. They also (almost all of them) fall into two other camps which are possibly more divisive. There is the Federation of Zoological Gardens of Great Britain and Ireland on the one hand and the National Zoological Association of Great Britain firmly on the other. The former could be called the establishment list while the latter, containing almost all the safari parks, could be considered anti-establishment. The Federation inspects its members from time to time to check their worthiness for membership, but the Association members resent this Federation inspection and have banded together for their common good. There is a conflict, frequently expressed, and a resentment of the other side. Scurrilous tales are told and it is as if there are two oppositions but no government. Only in Scotland do the two sides meet as a natural course of events to discuss common problems. It would be good, both for the animals and zoo management in general, if the rest of Britain could persuade itself to follow suit.

A trouble is that zoo-men are, apart from the similarities already expressed, extreme individualists. There is no conventional route to the directorship of a zoo, and each man or woman seems to have taken a wildly different course. Moreover, the best zoos are generally run by individuals holding such power that they are dictators. There may be committees also at the top, but these work best when they are either weak or happy to favour the advice of the man in charge. Consequently, a community so full of autocrats is unlikely to weld itself into a harmonious whole.

It has frequently been said, notably by the Federation, that there ought to be minimum standards laid down for the animals. I personally welcome the idea but have no idea how it could be made to work. One man may feel that concrete is clean, easy and safe. Another may think (and loudly proclaim) that grass, or deep litter, or earth is the only suitable flooring. How much space is necessary for this species, and how much height, and running water? And what about those creatures that like to hide, either from each other

or from the all-paying public? Should they be allowed to? To what extent is naturalness to be encouraged, like the aggression of the dominant, the wounding of the weakest? Are the public's wishes, say for large enclosures, to be gratified even though some animals prefer and do better in a small area that mimics their modest territory in the wild? What about apparent cleanliness? An unkempt cage is rich with nesting material; a tidy, sterile cage is not. Science can provide a balanced diet via pellets and other artificial feeds; but many zoos will use only natural food, whatever the dietary consequences. An otter likes a waterfall; should one be obligatory? Should herd animals be disallowed in ones and twos? Birds of prey can do more damage to themselves in large enclosures; should only small cages be permitted? I personally doubt if a set of zoo-keepers could agree about the design of a safe, cheap, simple, spill-proof, bird-proof, rat-proof rubbish bin, let alone the fundamental needs of 4000 kinds of mammal and 8000 kinds of bird.

There is also the largest question mark of all. Should animal collections of every kind be permitted only if they are able to breed their stock? In the past the question would have been irrelevant. Not only was it difficult to breed the animals but there was a steady flow to Britain of suitable replacements. Today that flow is drying up. The animals are becoming less abundant at their place of origin. The exporting countries are restricting the removal of their precious heritage. (To get a marsupial out of Australia is about as easy as getting Giant Pandas out of China.) Even the laws governing import have multiplied enormously in recent years. Australia, for example, refuses entry to any bird and any hoofed animal from its native land. Britain is not so severe, but more and more animals are coming on to more and more restrictive lists. Rare animals are now particularly protected, with the extremely rare only allowed in if *not* for commercial purposes, and the fairly rare only permitted if a licence has been issued. All birds of prey, including Owls, need a licence. Many creatures have to be quarantined. The list of possible rabies carriers is very long. Quarantine for hoofed animals can be even longer, and there are more regulations than ever before about the actual transit from one country to another. For many groups of animals the ship transporting them cannot call at any intermediate port. (The number of vessels sailing directly from, say, Mombasa to the United Kingdom is minute.) An animal man these days needs not only the ability to keep his animals well, but the greater skill of handling all the paperwork that now goes along with them.

The increasing power given to various government departments, like the Home Office and the

There are 18 kinds of true Seal in the world, but most common in British zoos is the Atlantic Grey, one of the two kinds that live around our coasts. Both pictures were taken at London Zoo where, as anywhere else, a Seal pup is a sure crowd-puller.

Ministry of Agriculture, Fisheries and Food, has inevitably led to increasing evasion of the subsequent strictures. Not every regulation makes sense, particularly in the eyes of those whose freedom has been trimmed. Therefore animal smuggling, false declaration and evasion of the law is more rife than ever before, if only because there are more laws. Many animals reach our zoos that should not, by current right, be doing so. For example, Crowned Pigeons come from New Guinea, or rather they did until that country's government forbade their export. Not many of these beautiful blue birds are yet being bred in captivity; the reported number is about 15 a year and the actual total may be nearer 30. Whatever the figure it could not possibly account for every bird, 500 in all, that passed through Heathrow alone in the past four years. Traffic in stolen goods cannot be the most truthful business in the world, but trade in animals may equal it from time to time for deception and skulduggery.

Having, up to this point, accused zoos and zoo-men of a wide variety of colourful drawbacks, such as dishonesty, hypocrisy, in-fighting, secrecy and mere illegality, I should hasten to add that I am entirely on their side. I love to see exotic animals. I think it would be appalling if legisla-

tion or hard times forced zoos out of business. The loss would be immeasurable if people could not learn in this way about the wildlife with which they share this planet. I do not believe that any instruction can compare with seeing, smelling, hearing and touching an actual creature. Books, talks, television and photographs all help, but they are nothing like the real thing before one's very eyes.

There are those who do not like zoos, who

resent even the best kind where breeding groups flourish within the protective benevolence of a man-made sanctuary. They say all animals should be sent back where they belong, and we should see them there if need be. These people hate cages and dens (or pens and paddocks as the zoo-men call them) and they want freedom for all creatures. It is a lovely thought, a Garden of Eden of a thought. Unfortunately, it cannot everywhere apply. If the Bengal Tiger was restricted to India there would soon be no Tigers. If all the animal species alive only in zoos today had been banished to their homelands there would be no living representatives of their kind. The ancient habitats are not what they were, and never will be again. Animals, generally speaking, cannot go back where they belong. The few reserves dotted around the world are but microcosms of former empires, and there is no guarantee that these can maintain either their status or all the kinds of living form that used to roam nearby. Besides, all the world is a cage. Animals leave the Serengeti, Tsavo, Manyara, Amboseli at their peril. Within those unfenced enclosures they are safe, or relatively so. Without man's protection they would go as the rest of their kind have gone in Africa. We can both destroy and protect, and animals are at our mercy wherever they may be.

In the third *Zoo Yearbook* the editors wrote:

The word 'zoo' was first used in the 1840s, but did not become well known until the Great Vance popularized it in the 1860s with a song called 'Walking in the Zoo'.

'The policy of zoos all over the world must surely be conservation; whether rare species of animals are preserved in a natural or captive environment is of secondary importance.' In the old days there was a great gulf between captivity and freedom, between the bear pit and the wilderness. Now the wilderness has shrunk pitifully whereas the cage has, not before time, improved enormously. The zoos can often do what the wild places are no longer able to achieve: they can prevent extinction. The European Bison, Mongolian Wild Horse and Père David's Deer are only alive through the medium of captivity. There is even talk (and occasional action) about reintroduction, with zoos repopulating areas empty of their former inhabitants. Whether it is Pheasants to Taiwan or Geese to Hawaii it is quite an amazing turnabout, to give and not to take.

The people who dislike zoos and who state that animals should only be seen in the natural world, should appreciate that such lonely areas cannot be visited by most of us and, if they were, would rapidly cease to be lonely. Those who wish to see animals must seek gratification nearer home. Many a British zoo receives more visitors each year than all the East African game parks added together. Similarly the Nairobi National Park, a mere 40 square miles conveniently located on the outskirts of that city, sees more visitors than the sum total who go to all the other bigger but more distant parks in eastern Africa. If we wish to see wild animals, the exotic and the most extreme examples of their kind, it is plainly more convenient for us to have them near at hand.

Do we need to see foreign animals? After all, we have plenty of our own. There are 52 kinds of mammal free in Britain. On a good and energetic day it is possible to observe a hundred kinds of bird, and the determined can seek out some of our few reptiles and amphibia. These statements also mean, if they are turned around, that even the most diligent Briton can observe a mere 3 per cent of the world's birds, 1 per cent of its mammals and an even smaller proportion of its reptiles. A single day at London Zoo permits a visitor to see almost four times as many mammals as he could ever discover within a lifetime of searching all of wild Britain. Should he learn of prosimians, Lemurs, Lorises, Tarsiers, Anteaters, Sloths, Armadillos, Hyenas, Bears, Monkeys, Apes, Camels, marsupials, big cats, Elephants and all the odd-toed ungulates (save the tame Horse) only through books and pictures? Should he never see a Giraffe, a Gazelle or a single primate? What loss occurs if he cannot ever look into the face of another Ape to see the distorted image of his own?

For many people the zoo is a giggle, a place to go when other spots are stale, an entertainment

If there were no zoos we would never be able to look into the faces of our primate relatives. *Above left* A Baboon, and *above right* Colobus Monkeys.

on the list like Big Ben or the Tower of London. 'What'll we do? We'll go to the Zoo!' It can mean nothing, beyond a chance to laugh, to throw a rock or two, to peer and sneer at some unfortunate. However, there are other people, or those same people on other days, for whom the zoo can provide revelation, a sudden comprehension of biology, of living things, of our place on this earth, of families and maternal bonds, of aggression and care, humility, curiosity, evolution, life. It is not reality or normality any more than is a library, but it can teach and we can learn.

Of course the modern zoo is not perfect. There is still concrete, iron-work of the grossest kind, poor husbandry and much of the old menagerie. Indeed there are many of the old cages, even scheduled as ancient monuments (London, Dudley), but there is progress. Not even every advance is satisfactory – glass can form a barrier between observed and observer just as rigidly as

bars – but there are several steps forward for each one back. Exploitation of the country, first by Whipsnade, then by other collections and the safari parks, has at least given space to the animals. The new ideas of conservation have pushed vague thoughts about breeding towards a determination that breeding must occur. After 150 years of existence almost three-quarters of London Zoo's mammals were born within its premises.

I do believe people should see zoos, sanctuaries, aquariums, zoo parks, bird gardens, animal kingdoms, wildlife wonderlands and all the rest. To this end I have visited a very large number of them, criticized, questioned, admired and enjoyed their varied offerings. The following pages are a distillation of all that talk, time and concern. So, over to them now and to that fraction of the wild world they each have to offer; provided, of course, we have the entrance fee.

1 Safari Parks

Lions of Longleat

Address	Warminster, Wilts
Telephone	Maiden Bradley (098 53) 328
Open	All year 10.00–18.00 or dusk if earlier
Acreage	300
Station	Warminster (5 miles)
Facilities	Guide book and information leaflet Guided tours Safari buses Bar, licensed restaurant and snack bar; self-service cafeteria and kiosk; children's menus Picnic area Gift and camera shops
Other	Longleat House Pets' corner Pony, Donkey and Camel rides Pony and Donkey traps Playground Safari boats Giant slide Dr Who Train Nature trail and woodland walk Garden centre
Shows	Chimps' tea parties in pets' corner every afternoon in summer
Feeding	Sealions, with purchased fish

Jimmy Chipperfield – the man who started it all.

Previous pages The Woburn Lions have learnt to treat
our cars with complete disdain.

Longleat has been the great innovator. Lord Bath
was the first peer to open up his stately home (in
1949). He and Jimmy Chipperfield then jointly
dreamed up the first drive-through 'safari' outside
Africa. They thought Lions would be ideal and
amazed everyone with their announced plan 'to
introduce 50 lions and a number of hippopotami'
to Wiltshire.

Rarely before can a fairly simple extension of
an idea – after all, there had been zoos here for a
long time – have received such publicity. Protesting letters were written to *The Times* and that
paper considered the proposal 'one of the most
fantastically unsuitable uses for a stretch of England's green and pleasant land that can ever have
entered the head of a noble proprietor'. 'One
stunt leads to another,' wrote the Bath *Weekly
Chronicle*; 'After the lions – what then? His lordship will be advertising for Christians next!'

The general newspaper anxiety does seem
remarkable. A Lion escaping from Regent's Park
would be more hazardous than a similar breakout between Frome and Warminster. Perhaps the
drive-through aspect scared everyone, even
though the African continent had given ample
proof of the extraordinary immunity provided by
a car for its occupants. People are not hauled out
of their vehicles in the game parks, even by
wounded, starving, desperate animals. For the
visitors who wish to sleep out at night in such
places the traditional method of ensuring protection against Lions is to be beneath a mosquito
net. Just what was likely to be so lethal about the
British Lions? Their meals would be more regular, their wounds would be treated and they
ought to be more docile than their African
cousins. Nevertheless there was considerable
reservation, objection, protest, rumpus, complaint, fury and furore as opening day
approached – just as there had been at virtually
every other novelty, from balloons to bicycles.

All this noise ensured the one essential ingredient for any new venture – publicity. Longleat
had never been so famous throughout its 400
years. There were jokes about the Lions, and cartoons, and no wonder there was a queue on opening day. In fact, people were the main problem in
that first year of 1966. They came in their hundreds of thousands. Their cars stretched for
miles, proving that the single lane through the
reserve was most inadequate. The striped Land
Rovers, driven by 'white hunters' wearing bush
hats, rushed about like anxious sheepdogs keeping the cars on the move. Not every visitor saw
the Lions – which often hid out of sight – and
not everyone felt the £1 per car was money well
spent, but there was general delight at the idea.
Lord Bath and Jimmy Chipperfield had dreamed
up a financial winner.

It seems that we like the Lion best of all. Without its idle, powerful, thick-maned presence the safari parks would assuredly not be the winner they have proved to be.

Those days now seem long since gone. Nearly a dozen similar 'safari parks' have started here since then, and many more abroad. The world's captive Lion population has multiplied dramatically. People in their tens of millions have now driven past Lions and seen them from the security of their family motor car. The Lions may have been idling, or dozing, and just once in a while they may have been snarling with all the tooth and claw at their command; but, whether lucky or unlucky in the timing of their visit, the humans have enjoyed the excitement of the new experience. It is not just another cage. It is a drive among Lions, a slice of Africa beneath the oak trees and upon the lush grass of ordinary countryside.

Success helped, as it often does, to stir up resentment. There had been criticisms beforehand and these did not vanish when it was shown that 12-foot fences could contain Lions, that people were not eaten (despite much encouragement given by occasional visitors) and that the Lions themselves, once they had established distinctive power groups, could live in harmony at a density of one or so to the acre. The considerable

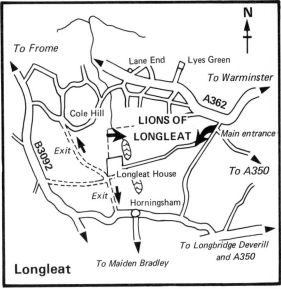

financial return per Lion was huge, and therefore irksome to those in the same line of business who thought they had a better show to offer, more animals, and a greater variety of species at less cost to the visitor. Without doubt Longleat made a packet – and therefore made some enemies along with the rich rewards.

The trouble with any novelty is that it ceases,

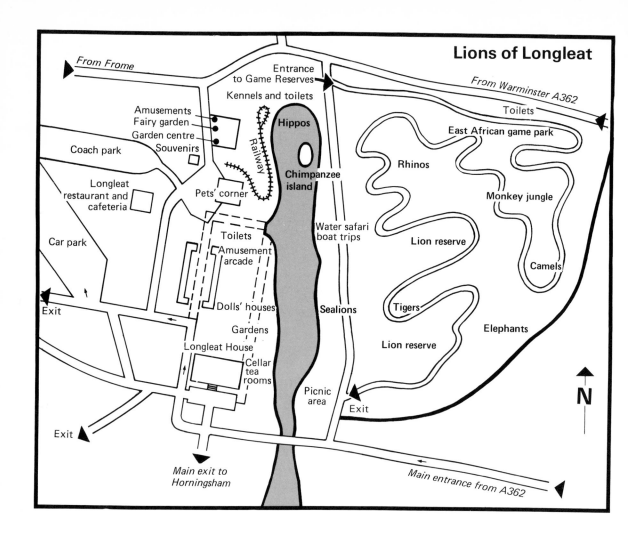

Lions of Longleat

after a while, to be novel. The safari park peak was probably reached in the early 1970s. The thrill of seeing Lions through wound-up windows, and of paying increasing sums for the privilege, began to wane. With a dozen safari parks, and Lions looking much the same in all of them, people had ample opportunity to savour the experience – and then to want something new.

Once again Longleat was an innovator. It had been quick to realize that Lions, although kings of the cash flow, would be insufficient. It brought in Baboons to make a drive-through 'Monkey jungle', Sealions to give zest to a 'safari boat-trip', and Giraffes and Zebras to provide greater excitement and interest in, of all things, a walkabout picnic area. This last experiment is one of Longleat's greatest triumphs. A beautiful hollow of land is now peopled by the largest herd of Giraffes (Masai and Rothschild's) outside Africa, many Zebras (Grant's), Ankole Cattle – and people. There is a great intermingling and a kind of proximity impossible anywhere in wild Africa. It was a courageous step to take, as a Zebra could despatch a child with the ease of a

rugby footballer kicking between the posts.

It has been said that Longleat provides a fuller day's entertainment than any similar park. Apart from the animals mentioned so far, there are White Rhinos (which have bred), African Elephants (which may be the first in Britain to do so), Cheetahs, Siberian Tigers, Wildebeest (sometimes called Africa's most 'successful' animal), Chimpanzees (which breed on a lake island and which also, in another group, give tea parties), Hippos, Eland (said to be the best-tasting of all Antelopes), Ostriches, Pelicans, Crowned Cranes, Grévy Zebras, and Bactrian and Arabian Camels. It is not just Lions any more, even though it is still called Lions of Longleat and has no intention of dropping this principal attraction. In fact, it is particularly proud of its so-called Longleat strain, a silver-maned variety fathered by a Sudanese Lion which had itself a strikingly black mane.

Longleat is a leader among safari parks in that most crucial aspect of extracting money graciously from visiting pockets. Pay for the boat ride. Pay for the fish to feed the Sealions on the boat ride. Pay for the film to picture the feeding of

26

For most of the time the Big Cats in the safari parks are relaxed and indolent (*above*). But every so often, particularly when hierarchies are being established, visitors can encounter a more dramatic display of tooth and claw (*below*).

fish to the Sealions. There are Pony rides, Pony traps, Donkey rides, Donkey traps, Camel rides. There is a pets' corner, a giant slide, gift shops, a guide book, and all such items bring in more money than is collected at the entrance gate. There is also the most exceptional house which, even in the days before the Lions, attracted 150,000 visitors a year.

Longleat is a beautiful place. Most of the commercialism that might be unsightly is hidden away behind the house. Capability Brown, who had a hand in landscaping the estate, would be amazed by the transformation but not, I think, entirely displeased. He did not plan for 125,000 visiting cars a year, let alone 10,000 coaches, and yet they are absorbed without overwhelming the place. He did not allow for 300 animals of 30 mammal species and 10 kinds of bird, but they too have been fitted in, along with the 700,000 or so people who now come each year to have a day at Longleat. The individual for whom there is no room any more is Henry Frederick Thynne, the tenth Viscount Weymouth, the thirteenth Baron Thynne, and the sixth Marquess of Bath. He now lives down the road near Warminster. Jimmy Chipperfield, his partner, also lives elsewhere, but he firmly asserts that, of all the wildlife reserves around the world in which he has played or plays a part, Longleat is still the one he favours most.

Windsor Safari Park

Address	Windsor, Berks
Telephone	Windsor (075 35) 69841/2/3
Open	April–September 10.00–19.00; winter 10.00–dusk
Acreage	160
Station	Windsor and Eton (2 miles), Windsor Riverside (2 miles)
Facilities	Guide book Information leaflet (for schools) Lectures and guided tours Safari bus Bar and self-service cafeteria; snack bar and kiosk (summer) Gift and camera shops
Other	Aquarium Dolphinarium Pets' corner Playground, roundabouts, children's rides Pony rides Prehistoric forest Woodland walk
Shows	Dolphin show (at intervals throughout afternoon) Seals fed 12.00 and 15.00
Feeding	Visitors may feed certain animals with purchased food

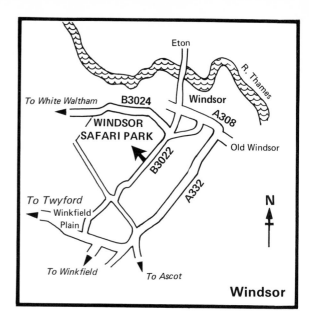

Windsor

Hard upon the heels of Longleat came the Windsor Safari Park. The circus family of Chipperfield had plainly scored a winner. The circus family of Smart were quick to follow suit. They found and bought a large piece of land amazingly and conveniently placed, being 28 miles from central London and two miles south of the M4. It is also near Windsor Great Park, Royal Windsor and the royal residence of Windsor Castle, and the safari park has undoubtedly benefited from its high-class location. It was even opened (in 1970) by Princess Margaret.

Having such a good catchment area, owning its own land, and pulling in, for instance, 800,000 visitors during the central seven months of 1976, must mean it is the most prosperous of all the safari parks. It also feels the most crowded, with cars never far away. On a hot summer's day the grass is as tired and the litter as abundant as in a city park. However, without any doubt whatsoever, it does have goods on show and the people flock to see them.

The safari side of things, the drive-through animal reserves, is similar in its style to Longleat. But, despite the Windsor location (more people living nearby, more possibility of vandals letting Lions out), the opening of this second Lion park did not cause the furore that Longleat had experienced. It is pioneers who suffer most. At Windsor the first enclosure contains Hamadryas (or Sacred) Baboons, well displayed upon a heap of old building stones taken from a demolished London bridge. There is a nursery to one side containing young and pregnant females and all individuals are caged at night.

Enclosures two and three contain the Lions. There used to be double the number, but the current total of about 40, with more males than

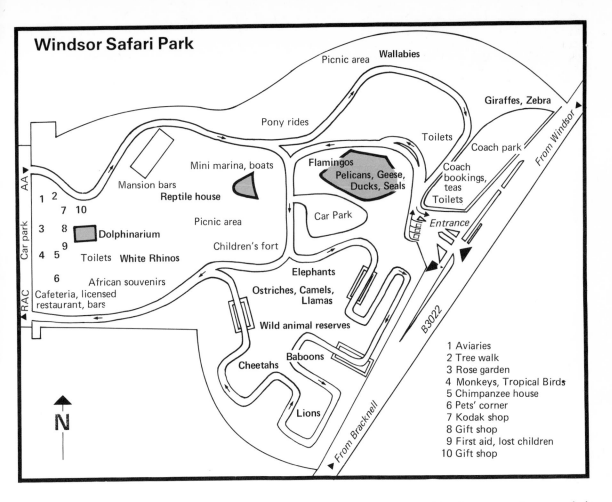

Windsor Safari Park

Picnic area

Wallabies

Pony rides

Giraffes, Zebra

From Windsor

Toilets

Coach park

Mini marina, boats

Flamingos
Pelicans, Geese,
Ducks, Seals

Coach
bookings,
teas

Mansion bars

Reptile house

Car Park

Toilets

AA

Picnic area

Entrance

1 2
7 10
3 8 **Dolphinarium**
9
4 5 Toilets **White Rhinos**
6 African souvenirs
Cafeteria, licensed
restaurant, bars

Car park

RAC

Children's fort

Elephants

**Ostriches, Camels,
Llamas**

B3022

Wild animal reserves

Baboons

Cheetahs

Lions

From Bracknell

N

1 Aviaries
2 Tree walk
3 Rose garden
4 Monkeys, Tropical Birds
5 Chimpanzee house
6 Pets' corner
7 Kodak shop
8 Gift shop
9 First aid, lost children
10 Gift shop

females, is considered adequate. The fences are roughly five yards high with one yard of overhang but, like the Baboons, the Lions are housed at night, not so much because they might escape as because people might enter and cause them to escape. It may be profitable having animal collections near urban centres, but there are disadvantages. Vandalism is one.

The fourth enclosure contains Windsor's extraordinary collection of Cheetahs. In the wild this is a fairly solitary species, with females bringing up their cubs on their own, and the male being independent except for the period of mating; but at Windsor there is a great group of Cheetahs all living together. Plainly such a disruption from normality should cause a total lack of progeny, but the Windsor animals have helped to disrupt current opinion. Several litters have been born and most of them have been raised successfully. Captive Cheetahs usually do not breed, despite strenuous efforts by their owners who, for example, introduce the male only when the female is on heat (as in the wild behaviour), but the Windsor Cheetahs seem to break all the rules – successfully. Nothing is being done to stimulate their mating and Kiki, the first ever to be bred,

is now five years old. Anyway, whatever their breeding abilities, the sight of a Cheetah herd (there is, of course, no collective noun) is excellent.

Thereafter the visitors are on their own, able to visit and do and watch the enormous variety arranged for their pleasure and money. Quite the most sensational offering was the Killer Whale which, when aged ten, ate 175 lbs of fish a day, weighed three-and-a-half tons and put on a virtuoso display of power, speed, agility and (belying all those stories of a 'killer's unfailing ferocity') friendliness. Alas, but Ramu was getting too big for the pool when still only half-grown – a big bull can reach six or seven tons. Therefore this superb animal was sold to California, making the journey by air and slung in a special stretcher. A Pilot Whale is Ramu's replacement and will live with the Dolphins in the Windsor dolphinarium.

Other species to be seen include Giraffes and Zebras (which breed plentifully), Ostriches (which produce a dozen eggs a year, but none have hatched), Elephants, Camels, Llamas, White Rhinos (which mated in 1976 and should therefore breed in 1977), Chimpanzees, various kinds of Monkey (such as Rhesus, Crab-eating,

Two creatures that few of us could name. *Above* The Margay, a Central and South American Cat, and *below* The Common Wombat, a Koala-like marsupial that burrows rather than climbs.

Pig-tailed), Penguins (Humboldt's), Flamingos (Cuban and Chilean, which have actually made nests, laid eggs and hatched a few), Wallabies, Seals (in the large lake), Pelicans, Black and Mute Swans, some eight species of Geese, nine of Duck, and a host of farmyard animals. There is a 'Tree Walk' with cages on either side of the pathway containing Eagles, Vultures, Hornbills, Owls, Parrots and Cockatoos. Elsewhere are Budgerigars, Canaries, Guinea and Jungle Fowl. There is a reptile house, whose rarities include Spectacled Cayman, False Gharial, Indian Python and Mississippi Alligator. There is also a pets' corner and a small aquarium. Some of these animals can only be seen by paying extra money.

Windsor seems to have suffered most from accidents. A Dolphin died after eating a plastic bag. A rubber ball with nails embedded in it was once found in their pool. Two Camels died after being fed packets of crisps. A keeper was killed recently because he bent to tie a shoe-lace and a Tiger leaped at the chance. Three wardens have also been mauled by Lions. Vandalism has been troublesome and is a permanent worry, not just because London is down the road (a mixed blessing), but because people are in the park grounds after normal closing time on their way to the disco and the bars.

Although Windsor charges for each car, and for each occupant over the basic number of four, more than half its income arises from other sources, such as the guide books, gift shops,

A Cheetah spraying urine and thereby marking a treetrunk.

A Common Zebra foal.
The Common Zebra, one of the three Zebra species, has markings unique to each individual and there are also broad differences between the several races.

restaurants, bars, cafés, kiosks, roundabouts, pony rides and extra entrance fees. There is much for children to do, beyond eat and look at animals. There is an excellent Fort Windsor, a moon rider, safari trains. A considerable effort has been made to set up a decent lecture centre, aimed particularly at schools, which will provide from six to eight talks a day, and a museum. As with practically everywhere else there are all-inclusive rates for schools.

It is possible to spend a very pleasant day at the Windsor Park but not to receive the impression that conservation is a dominant consideration. This is, of course, true of many other animal collections, even if they pay lip-service to the ideal by mentioning it from time to time. Without doubt Windsor is a 'plum site', as Ronald Smart phrased it, but the 160 acres can look very tired on a crowded day. There is no' noble lord to worry about his trees and his inheritance. How-

ever much of a nuisance this may be to the safari operators it can have its rewards in a better-looking place. The directors of Windsor Safari Park Ltd are: R. Smart, D. G. R. J. Smart, S. Smart, Mrs Billy Smart, Captain L. V. Phayre, G. Smart and C. Smart. The place was never a stately home, and the extremely undistinguished house (first built in 1760, but almost entirely rebuilt in 1932) within the grounds is now full of bars and so forth. It had as its most distinguished owner Horace Dodge, the motor car manufacturer. For many people quite the most amazing inhabitant of the Windsor Park was the Killer Whale. What a great shame it was that Ramu had to go.

Woburn Wild Animal Kingdom

Address	Woburn, Beds
Telephone	Woburn (052 525) 407/8
Open	All year 10.00–18.00 or dusk if earlier
Acreage	300
Station	Flitwick (5 miles), Bletchley (8 miles)
Facilities	Guide book and information leaflet Safari bus Bar, snack bar, kiosk (summer); self-service cafeteria with children's menus Picnic area Gift shop
Other	Woburn Abbey and its many attractions Dolphinarium Pets' corner Camel rides Cable cars Waterboat
Shows	Dolphins, daily from 12.30 at approx. 45-minute intervals

When Longleat proved that stately homes and Lions could be satisfactorily mixed it was inevitable that other places would try this new recipe. The Duke of Bedford, who had opened up his ancestral deer park to paying visitors in 1955 and who had publicized Woburn with a wide variety of attractions (including his signature at half a crown a go), must have watched the Longleat experiment acutely. Certainly he was quick to follow suit. In 1970 the Woburn Wild Animal Kingdom was opened with Jimmy Chipperfield, in Bedfordshire as in Wiltshire, a partner to the enterprise.

In many ways it was pertinent that the home and grounds of the thirteenth Duke of Bedford should become a new location for Britain's 'safari' motorists. The place had long been a reserve. Its

Lions at Longleat. There are now 30 other kinds of mammal at this safari park, but Lions are still the major attraction.

principal distinction lay in providing sanctuary for Père David's Deer. First seen in 1865 by Armand David, a French missionary, the animals then lived in a park outside Peking. A few were brought to Europe and scattered throughout its zoos before every animal remaining in China was slaughtered during the wars around the turn of the century. The eleventh Duke gathered these European survivors, brought them to Woburn and established a breeding herd. There are now 300 in the park, while other smaller herds have been established elsewhere. Without that Duke's prompt action this attractive Swamp Deer, with its backward-pointing antlers and long tufted tail, would be extinct.

However, the ancient deer park, with its attendant stately home, is quite distinct from the 300 acres of 'wild animal kingdom' also set within this largest private park in Britain. The winding safari road takes the visitors first through an

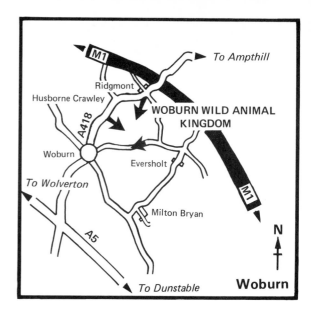

Rhesus Monkeys have generally taken the place of Baboons in the safari parks, as they are less destructive to our precious motor cars.

African plains area, stocked with Wildebeest, Eland, Ostrich, Zebra, a couple of Hippos (behind a ha-ha – a kind of sunken, invisible fence – around a pond) and a group of White Rhinos who crop the grass with the precision of weighty lawnmowers. The road then enters the Tiger enclosure, a small forest zone, predominantly oak, and leaves it for 'Lion country'. Excellent use has been made here of the slope of the land; whether they are below or above their visitors the Lions seem well placed.

There is then an opportunity for opening windows, most necessary in crowded cars on summer days, before the road reaches the Bear and Monkey area. There used to be Baboons but they grew too adept at wrenching off vinyl roofing, dissecting windscreen beading, extracting rubber strips, making corkscrews from aerials, opening boots, removing hub-caps, bending wing-mirrors and generally giving the once-over to our beloved motor cars. It was fun having them ride on board, warming themselves (on cold days) above the engine and scampering (on any day) over our roofs, but it was tedious (on wet days) observing windscreen-wipers fashioned into figures-of-eight never to wipe again. Alas, but the animals did do damage and they have been replaced by Rhesus Monkeys, still fun to watch but gentler creatures without the swaggering strength and bombast of the Baboon.

Cohabiting with the skimpering, scampering, tree-climbing Monkeys are some lumbering, lolloping, tree-climbing Bears. They can be quite hard to spot when they lie in the crotch of a tree, but the black lumps up there *are* Bears and not some kind of growth, a point dramatically proven in 1976 when one of the animals fell unaccountably to the ground and killed itself. Beyond this

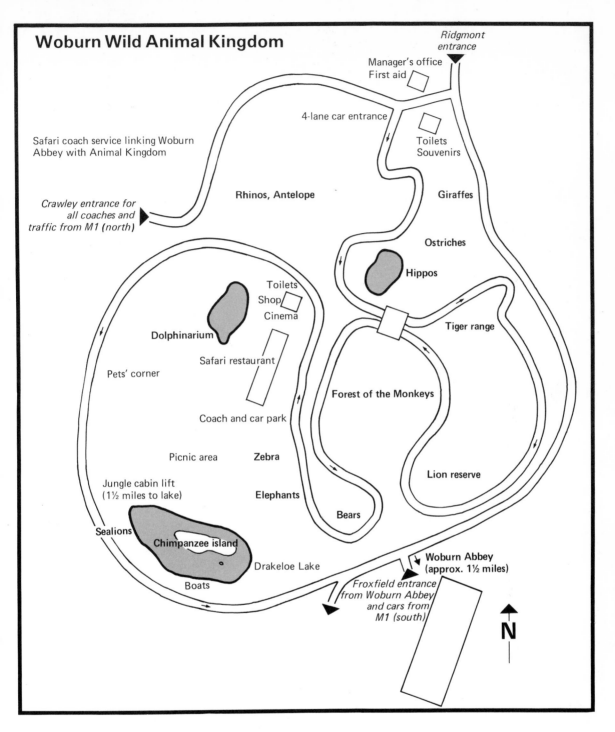

Woburn Wild Animal Kingdom

Ridgmont entrance

Manager's office
First aid

Safari coach service linking Woburn Abbey with Animal Kingdom

4-lane car entrance

Crawley entrance for all coaches and traffic from M1 (north)

Toilets
Souvenirs

Rhinos, Antelope

Giraffes

Ostriches

Hippos

Toilets
Shop
Cinema

Dolphinarium

Tiger range

Safari restaurant

Pets' corner

Forest of the Monkeys

Coach and car park

Picnic area   Zebra

Lion reserve

Jungle cabin lift
(1½ miles to lake)

Elephants

Sealions

Bears

Chimpanzee island

Woburn Abbey
(approx. 1½ miles)

Drakeloe Lake

Boats

Froxfield entrance from Woburn Abbey and cars from M1 (south)

N

enclosure the road goes past (probably, but they may be elsewhere and have been seen beforehand) a Giraffe group, originally from Uganda but now breeding well in England.

The most exciting Woburn animals for many people can easily be missed. In the same wood but farther along from the Bears and Monkeys are the Bongo. It is necessary to stroll to the wood from the car parking area to see them but, for lovers of the exotic and of Antelopes in gen-

eral (nowhere else in Britain can Bongo be seen), they are always worth the walk. They traditionally live high up and most secretly in Africa's equatorial mountains – such as the Aberdares of Kenya where the Woburn stock originated. Therefore few people see any in the wild, let alone a family group. The first two Bongo babies born at Woburn died but the mothers were promptly pregnant again and their next two offspring, happily both females, survived as the

Above Arabian Gazelles at Chester Zoo – a rare sight in Britain but becoming commoner.

Right Scimitar-horned Oryx are also rare in zoos, but most appealing wherever they are found.

WARNING
ALL VINYL TOPPED CARS PLEASE STOP HERE FOR ADVICE

Safari parks have problems. Giraffes (*opposite*), here with a two-week-old baby, eat every leaf up to 18 feet or so. Baboons have a habit of removing vinyl, wipers, wing mirrors and hub caps.

first British Bongo births. With luck (and skill, as all captive animals need care) there will be two more baby Bongo in 1977.

The Woburn visitors can leave their cars after reaching either the car park or a convenient spot on the grass near the kiosks and refreshment area. There are boats, a gift shop, a dolphinarium, a picnic area and, farther down the hill, a pets' corner possessing most of the Woburn animals not already seen. This is also the spot where the cable cars begin before whisking their occupants over Camels, through woodland rich with Pheasants and over a lake, the home of raucous Sealions. There are boats on this lake, and birds, and its banks are steeped with trees. All in all the 'wild kingdom' possesses 30 kinds of mammal, ten of bird, two of reptile and, throughout each year, 900,000 humans go to visit them. It is a prosperous park.

A tremendous boon for places like Woburn and Longleat is the love, care and management that has been applied to them over the centuries. Trees have been well planted. Open water has been suitably arranged. The lie of the land has been considered at every juncture. Consequently, those planning for the animals and all their visitors have been able to take advantage of the skill and foresight of earlier generations. That ride in a cable car would be far less exciting if it were over, say, Forestry Commission land. There would, probably, not be a lake at the end of it, with islands, a folly of a temple, a perfect setting. It is wrong when trees are allowed to be destroyed by the new animals, and both Longleat and Woburn have let this happen to some extent, but the estates are still beautiful and the losses have been minor. The visitors, despite their numbers and their cars, can still absorb much of

the beauty of these old stately grounds. Animals may be the big draw, and Lions may be the biggest draw of all, but it is probably the look of the estates that brings people back to Woburn and Longleat, time and time again.

Scotland's Safari Park

Address	Blair Drummond, by Stirling
Telephone	Doune (078 684) 456
Open	March–mid-October inclusive from 10.00
Acreage	120
Station	Stirling (7 miles)
Facilities	Guide book and information leaflet Safari bus Bar and licensed restaurant; self-service cafeteria and snack bar with children's menus; kiosk Picnic area Gift and camera shops Petrol station
Other	Dolphinarium Pets' corner Playground Safari boats Astraglide and astrabounce Amusement area Children's cars
Shows	Dolphins, usually on every hour from 13.00 during peak season
Feeding	Sealions, with purchased fish

Originally called 'Scotland's African Safari Park', re-named 'Scotland's Safari Park' and generally referred to as 'Blair Drummond', the place – whatever you call it – was opened in 1970 as yet another successor to Longleat. It is 50 per cent

Above Shy forest Antelopes, the only Bongos now in Britain are alive, well and breeding at Woburn.

Opposite Looking more like a Hare than the rodent it actually is, a Mara from the south of South America.

Orang-utans (*above* and *below*) are having a rough time in the wild, but fortunately they now breed well in zoos. If habitat destruction continues the day may soon come when all Orangs are in captivity.

owned by Jimmy Chipperfield, the circus and zoo-owner who dreamed up the Longleat experiment; 25 per cent by Sir John Muir, businessman (tea and insurance) and one-time inhabitant of Blair Drummond; and 25 per cent by Keir and Cawder estates.

Location is all-important for the safari parks. Blair Drummond is most neatly sited, being 35 miles from Glasgow, 35 from Perth and 35 from Edinburgh. Consequently, although it is a small park, it is one of the biggest tourist attractions in Scotland, pulling in over 350,000 visitors a year. Many of these are from abroad, with the Irish and the Scandinavians predominant. Unlike the all-the-year-round parks this one closes for the winter from the end of October to the middle of March. But, like so many of the others, some of Blair Drummond was laid out by that beaver of activity, everywhere at once, Lancelot (alias Capability) Brown.

Whether because the park is small, or run by a woman, or Scottish, there is a more intimate flavour to Blair Drummond than the bigger English reserves. The theme of the collection, as with the rest, is mainly African, and the Lions are just as large and potentially dangerous as elsewhere; but the park does have a less impersonal feel. Perhaps the names help: Mandy and Stubby, the African Elephants; Ernie, the four-year-old Hippo; Slipper and Slapper, the Sealions; Flipper and Scottie, the performing Dolphins.

Blair Drummond has a good breeding record. Seventy Lions have been born in its grounds, a suitably large number for a country with a Lion as its royal crest ever since King Robert II adopted it in 1370. Fifteen Giraffes have been born in the past six years, along with Pumas, Eland, Baboons and Rhesus Monkeys. A Chimpanzee made the mistake of arriving during a January snowstorm but happily survived.

Various changes have been made to the animal

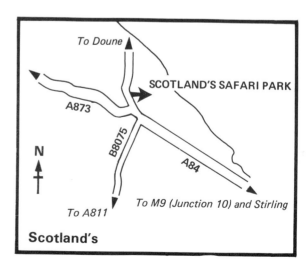

Scotland's

population over the years. There used to be Cheetahs but these have been replaced by Siberian Tigers, certainly a more appropriate species for Scottish winters. The Baboons, adept not just at wrecking cars but at getting out, once even attending a nearby funeral, have had to yield to gentler and less ambitious Rhesus Monkeys. Each winter, when the park is closed, there is further change. The Sealions are taken from the lake and moved to Plymouth Zoo. The Dolphins, whose indoor pool would require considerable heating, are flown to Malta or Gibraltar to perform their tricks down there.

Just around the corner from the dolphinarium is a 'pets' corner'. It is a spacious and well-stocked series of exhibits but that word 'pets' is somewhat invidious. There is a Goat tower, an aviary merry with birds and various other creatures which, although not in the Hamster class of pets, would at least not mutilate their human owners. However, there are also Leopards,

Pumas and Tigers, securely housed but either adult or as near full-grown as makes no difference. Pets? The Tigers, for some reason of their own, would snarl at the keeper most violently whenever he walked by. Pets' corner?

In 1977 White Rhinos and Cape Buffalo were added (not in the pets' corner) to the Blair Drummond community, making a total of 24 mammal species and 9 bird species on show. As with other safari parks the animals, notably the Lions, may be the big attraction but there are many sideshows to partner them. There are boat trips on the lake along to Chimp Island (and you are allowed to buy the Sealions food). There is an amusement centre, lunaland, trains, a pool table and a four-lane astraglide. There are shops and 'zoovenirs', an astrabounce (which should tire them out) but no stately home. Blair Drummond House looks down in its Scottish-baronial fashion but is not open to visitors. Nevertheless, there is history nearby, such as Doune (very near) and

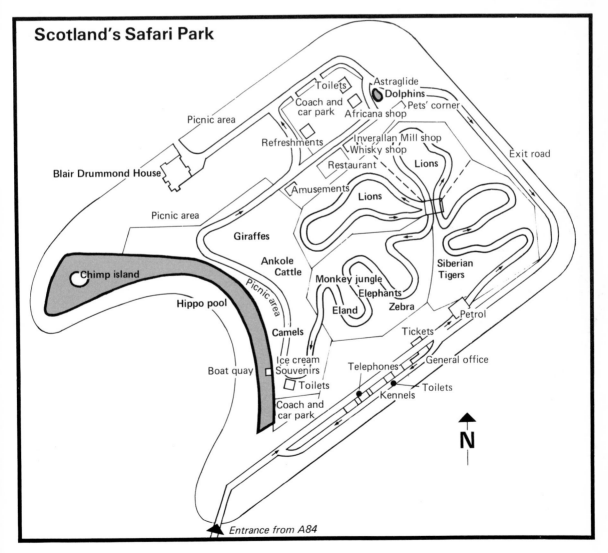

Overleaf A pair of Meerkats from southern Africa. These Mongooses live colonially in open grassland.

Stirling castles, a local motor museum and the Bannockburn and Wallace monuments.

Those who have difficulty finding Scotland's Safari Park may wonder why such major attractions are not better signposted. The truth is that every such establishment has difficulty with the local authorities who have strict and complex rules. It is easier to acquire permission for 'temporary' signs, however much they then stay there all year round. It is also easier if the name of the attraction is the name of a genuine place: all the RAC signs for Scotland's Safari Park therefore read Blair Drummond (which should confuse all the Scandinavians and Irish trying to get there). One woman, coming from Ayr with a car full of children, was at Perth before she realized the error of her ways and eventually arrived in 'fighting mood' asking for entrance free 'at the very least'.

If it is a hard place to reach it is also a hard place to leave. The picnic spots beside the lake are pleasant. There is a large area for strolling in, swings and seesaws, and animals are never far away. On a summer Sunday 3000 people turn up and all arrive shortly after noon. Therefore it is probably just as well that the manager of Blair Drummond used to be an airline stewardess and is accustomed to crowds of people turning up simultaneously expecting to be swiftly and expertly entertained.

Knowsley Safari Park

Address	Prescot, Merseyside
Telephone	Liverpool (051) 430 9009
Open	All year: summer 10.00–18.00; winter 10.00–16.00
Acreage	450
Station	Prescot (1 mile)
Facilities	Guide book and information leaflet Lectures and guided tours (by arrangement) Safari bus Bar; self-service cafeteria with children's menus; snack bar and kiosk (summer) Picnic area Gift shops Petrol station
Others	Dolphinarium (March–end of September) Pets' corner Camel rides Playground Children's amusement park Boating lake Miniature railway Astroslide Woodland walk
Shows	Dolphins, hourly from 12.00 in summer

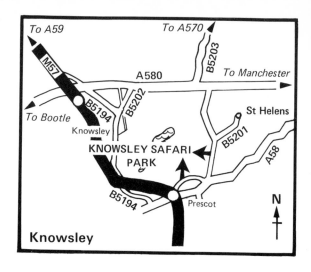

Knowsley

The most amazing thing about Knowsley Safari Park is that it exists at all. By whatever route visitors reach it they are bound to have travelled past much of Lancashire's industrial landscape. Then, suddenly, they find themselves among wild animals in a setting which is quite the most African of all the drive-through parks.

It was the fifth such place to be opened (after Longleat, Windsor, Woburn and Scotland's Blair Drummond) and was therefore able to benefit from earlier experience. Even so, by initially sending the visitors straight into the Lions, there were tremendous queues in the early days (of 1971). It is now arranged much more satisfactorily, with huge enclosures along a five-mile road containing Rhino, Deer, Giraffe, Camel, Baboon, Cheetah and others before there is a suspicion of a Lion. By the time the visitors do reach the all-important Lions, set largely in a forest of many different kinds of tree (Spanish chestnut is preferred for rasping claws), they no longer clog the roads as they used to do. In the third Lion enclosure there are Tigers as well, an odd mixture of India and Africa which, as an even odder point, is both appealing and amicable.

Knowsley's stars are the big African mammals, such as the Greater Kudu (the largest of the antelopes), African Elephants, Rothschild's Giraffe (which breed frequently, often dropping their young in full view of fortunate car-loads) and African Buffalo. The Knowsley group is probably the best gathering of African Buffalo in captivity. Many a hunter insists he is more wary of the Buffalo than any other animal, partly for its unpredictable temper which can switch from placid idleness to full speed without any of the warning signs given by other creatures. One bull at Knowsley occasionally upholds this particular tradition, and his existence probably helps to promote the excellent rate of breeding.

*Visitors to safari parks can see sights they could never
hope to observe in the wilder parks of Africa. This
Giraffe at Knowsley is dropping her calf in full view of
the fortunate visitors.*

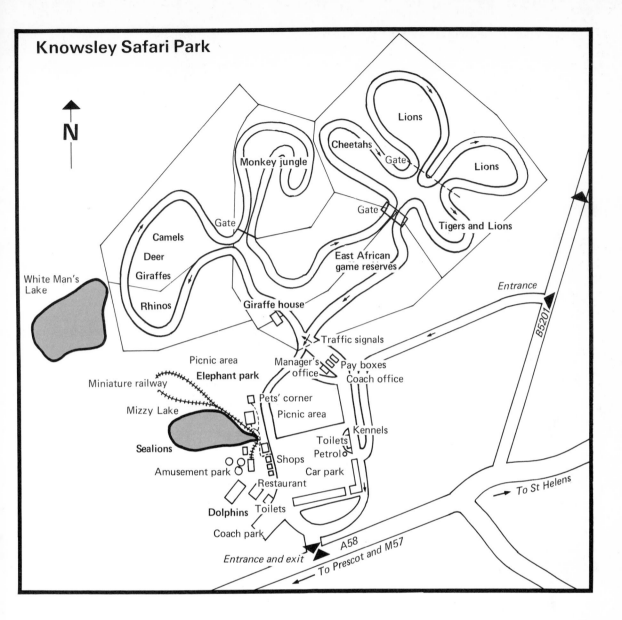

Knowsley Safari Park

N

Lions

Cheetahs
Gate

Monkey jungle

Lions

Gate

Gate

Tigers and Lions

Gate

Camels

Deer

Giraffes

East African
game reserves

White Man's
Lake

Rhinos

Giraffe house

Entrance

B5201

Traffic signals

Picnic area

Manager's
office

Pay boxes

Elephant park

Coach office

Miniature railway

Pets' corner

Mizzy Lake

Picnic area

Kennels

Sealions

Toilets

Petrol

Shops

Amusement park

Car park

Restaurant

To St Helens

Dolphins

Toilets

Coach park

Entrance and exit

A58

To Prescot and M57

There used to be 20 African Elephants here, but it was subsequently felt that 7 – one bull and 6 cows – would be a more manageable number when they got bigger. African bulls have caused many zoo accidents in the past; principally with their keepers. There would undoubtedly be less potential risk if only cows were kept. But, at a time when every effort is being made to breed exotic animals because the wild supply is drying up and restrictive legislation makes animal import so much harder, it is no longer correct to keep single-sex groups. Besides, there is a growing feeling that, with better care and better knowledge, safe mixed groups are feasible. Certainly

Opposite The Red Squirrel, Britain's native kind, is frequently said to be more attractive than the Grey that has taken over so many of its former habitats.

there is no more docile sight at present – the animals are still immature – than all seven of the Knowsley Elephants wending their way, single-file, through the cars and past the people along the two miles or so separating their sleeping quarters from their feeding area. Long may this remain possible and may Knowsley succeed in pulling off the greatest Elephant coup of all – the conception and birth of an African calf. Never yet has this been achieved in Britain.

Other star animals include the Cheetahs. They have bred at Knowsley – always a triumph with Cheetahs – but they tended to become remarkably invisible in the grass of their paddock and are now penned in a run beside the road. There are Hippos in a large excavated pool, and it is hoped they will breed in 1977. The Sealions have bred but the principal problem with this species

Eight miles from Liverpool and 28 from Manchester, Hippos bask at Knowsley in the most African of all the safari parks.

is not so much the breeding as the keeping alive of the offspring for more than a year or so. The Chinese Geese have bred, and so have the Eland (although the young ones can be skittish and break their legs). The Dolphins have not bred (no one in Britain has pulled off this feat successfully) but at least the same animals live and perform here as were originally brought in when the dolphinarium opened in 1972. In total, and on the 450 acres, are 248 mammals, 95 birds and hundreds of wildfowl which fly in to make use of the new ponds.

Knowsley exists as an oasis among the industrialization of Lancashire – it is 8 miles from Liverpool and 28 from Manchester – because the estate survived in the possession of the Earls of Derby. The eighteenth Earl arranged for the safari park (in partnership with Jimmy Chipperfield) but it was the thirteenth Earl who first and most assiduously linked the name of Knowsley with that of exotic animals. His private menagerie, which cost him £10,000 a year 150 years ago, included 94 kinds of mammal and 318 kinds of bird. He was the friend and patron of Edward Lear who, originally employed to draw parrots there, was undoubtedly influenced by all the other creatures so near at hand. He wrote *The*

Book of Nonsense for the children of the house and they were the first to hear of the

> . . . Old Man with a beard,
> Who said, 'It is just as I feared!
> – Two Owls and a Hen,
> Four Larks and a Wren,
> Have all built their nests in my beard!'

Their grandfather, Lear's patron, achieved further animal fame by being the one whose name was given to Derby's Eland, the giant Eland of the Sudan and West Africa.

Once again, as with Longleat and Woburn, a gracious estate worked over by the ubiquitous Capability Brown has provided a beautiful setting for the modern wish to see wild animals in more exotic surroundings than a cage. There is a superb feeling of elevation at Knowsley, of being above the world on every side. This feature is strongly emphasized on a windy day when a gale comes from the Atlantic with no stopping it on the way. It keeps the Elephants indoors, ruffles the Lions' manes, bends the trees and whips up waves upon the huge lake which separates the animal park from the Derby home. There are few visitors on such days, for they visit most at hot and sultry times when the Lions are idle and exhausted, much like the humans sealed into their cars; but wild days are the best.

The amusement area, with a variety of entertainments (Dolphins, Camel rides, children's zoo/pets' corner, boating lake, astroslide, miniature railway, gift shops) is distinct from the safari area. Unlike many it is well designed, with a sense of harmony despite its disparate offerings (for taking cash). These, of course, are about as African as black pudding and Eccles cakes but do not prevent Knowsley from being quite the most African experience of all the parks. It is also excellent that so many wild birds fly down to make use of the new lakes, despite their occupation by such exotics as Hippos, Buffalos and Pelicans. The mixture looks well and did so all those years ago to Edward Lear:

Ploffskin, Pluffskin, Pelican jee!
We think no Birds so happy as we.
Plumpskin, Ploshskin, Pelican jill!
We think so then and we thought so still.

Cameron Loch Lomond Wildlife Park

Address	Cameron, Loch Lomond, Dunbartons
Telephone	Alexandria (0389) 57211/2
Open	Easter–mid-October
Acreage	225
Station	Balloch (1 mile)
Facilities	Guide book and information leaflet Self-service cafeteria and snack bar Picnic area Gift shop
Other	Cameron House Pets' corner (recently renamed Zoo garden) Playground Giant astraglide Helicopter for children Commando-type course Boating Woodland walk
Shows	Seals and Otters fed 16.00

The Cameron Loch Lomond Wildlife and Leisure Park (as it was originally called) got off to a shaky start. In 1972 it opened up as a Bear park, a brave attempt to break the stranglehold of Lions upon the safari business. Unfortunately, although Bears are as big and potentially lethal as Lions, they do not have the same box-office appeal. Also, although Jimmy Chipperfield was well experienced in turning stately parks into animal enclosures and their owners into partners,

there were management disagreements. The triumvirate of Chipperfield, Patrick Telfer-Smollett (who owned the land) and Muir (of Blair Drummond) disintegrated when the Loch Lomond Bear Park was declared bankrupt not many months after its inception.

In 1975 there was another opening, this time under the control of Cameron Loch Lomond Ltd (directors: P. Telfer-Smollett, G. Telfer-Smollett, D. Telfer-Smollett) and everything is running much more smoothly. Bears are still the major animal exhibit, and live in the largest enclosures, but there is considerable diversification, with plenty of other animals, things to do and things to see. Currently, it only receives about a third of Blair Drummond's total of visitors, but it is just up the road from Glasgow (20 miles distant) and just off the A82, that much-used artery heading for the Highlands farther north. If the park can lose its reputation of being 'nothing but Bears' it is sitting pretty just by that road and Loch Lomond for far bigger attendances.

Or perhaps Lions will lose some of their appeal and we will start to see a similar magic in wild Bears, making every other safari park wonder if it is backing the wrong beast. The Loch Lomond Bears can look a delight, particularly when they are bathing in the pool. The first enclosure contains Brown Canadian, Brown European and Grizzly Bears (which are all one species, namely *Ursus arctos*). The second enclosure possesses two species, the Himalayan and Black Canadian. This all seems straightforward, but a closer look can confuse.

For example, those Black Canadians (sometimes called the Black Americans – it depends where you are) are always black except when they are brown or a browny-black. Whatever colour they are that colour is all over unless they have some white on their chest. Conversely, the Himalayan, or Asiatic Black Bear, or Moon Bear (it's all the same bear) is genuinely black (and genuinely from the Himalayas and Asia, if not from the moon). It has the distinctive feature of a white V upon its chest, looking like the neck of a cricket sweater when the animal stands up (and possibly like a crescent moon to explain that other name) but the white V-moon can be invisible when the animal walks (which it often does). So, if you see just a flash of white on the chest of a black Bear, is it a Himalayan or a black Black Canadian with a touch of white? Unfortunately size does not help because the Black Canadian (or American) and the Himalayan (or Black Asiatic) are both smaller than the Brown Bears and quite a bit smaller than the Grizzlies. So, if it is fairly small and brown, what is it? A brown Black Canadian or a young Brown Bear? Perhaps, on reflection, you may find a second journey

51

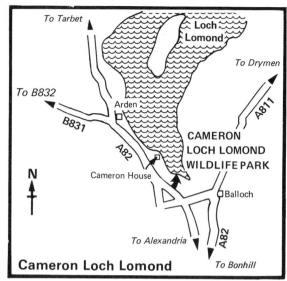

Cameron Loch Lomond

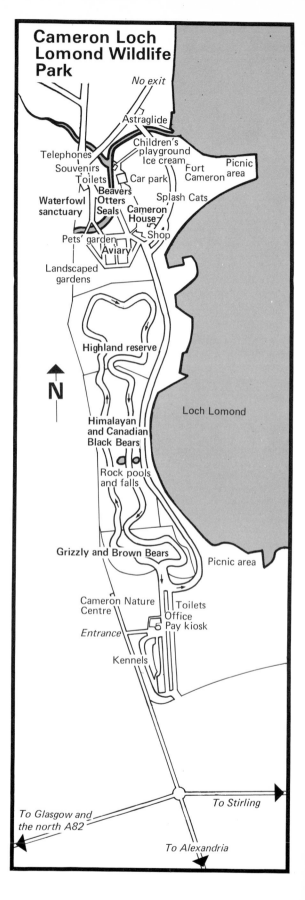

Cameron Loch Lomond Wildlife Park

through the Bear enclosures is necessary, to straighten things out – or confuse them irrevocably.

Bear identification ought to be easy, if only because there are no more than seven species in the world, with four of them being extremely distinctive, namely the Sloth Bear (shaggiest), the Polar Bear (whitest), the Sun Bear (smallest), the Spectacled Bear (which does have circles of light-coloured hair around each eye), and the three already mentioned, the Himalayan, the Black and the Brown. Only one species comes from the southern hemisphere, the Spectacled, and none from Africa.

The third Cameron Loch Lomond enclosure, called the Highland Reserve, is a pleasant mixture, although neither totally Highland nor high land. There are Highland Cattle and Red Deer, appropriately enough, and Yak, which certainly live at altitude, but there are also Bison, which do not. Thereafter the road twists back through the first two enclosures, giving excellent and further opportunity for elucidating which Bear is which sort of Bear.

All the remaining animals, plus the entertainments and Cameron House, are geographically just to the north of the third enclosure, but it is necessary to go right back almost to the pay-kiosk in the south to find the road that winds the visitor northwards once again. Just by this road are Geese, an excellent picnic site and good views across Loch Lomond. At the end of it is a huge parking area and everything else.

Patrick Telfer-Smollett, owner of the house and gardens, is not just another landowner who has had animals thrust upon him. He readily confesses a lifelong enthusiasm for wildlife and the new park has permitted many of his enthusiasms to run happily riot. There is neither apparent logic in his collection nor harsh commercial drive.

Bears (*above*) are the major species at the Cameron Loch Lomond Park, but there are many others. The Binturong (*right*), for example, a kind of Civet with a prehensile tail, is breeding well in this Scottish safari zoo.

It consists of the beasts that he has acquired, that he wanted and is now pleased to show to others. For instance, one of his greatest pleasures is the Binturong. Few of us know of such a creature but it has a breeding group. It is allied to the Civet and the Mongoose, looks like neither, has a prehensile tail (unique among Old World mammals) and, although it fails to resemble either a Bear or a Cat, is sometimes called a Bear-cat.

There are Roe Deer, Arctic Foxes, Chipmunks, Chinchillas, Badgers, Beavers, Malaysian Otters, Skunks, Seals, Wallabies, Guanaco, Sheep (Manx, Soay, Jacob and St Kilda), Raccoons, Rats, Hamsters and Mice (in their own cities). There are birds: Water Rails, Wood Rails, Peafowl, Guinea Fowl, Eagle Owls, Cranes and others. The grand total is about 550 animals. By no means is the Cameron Loch Lomond Wildlife and Leisure Park solely, as a rival establishment said, a 'few bears which can anyway be seen from the road'.

The house is extraordinarily packed with items. There are armour, guns, the world's biggest collection of different whiskies, a documents room, an oriental room, a nursery cluttered with ancient toys, a war room, a Tobias Smollett museum (the writer was one of the family) and a model aircraft room. There are 25 acres of gardens, arranged for the four seasons so that each area reaches a peak at one time of year. There is Scotland's biggest astraglide (six lanes and lots of bumps) and a commando course (for 14-year-olds and over). There is a helicopter and (if it comes on schedule) a tank. The astraglide and the house charge extra money, but not the pets' corner.

The policy is to have the minimum of charges and, if this practice proves commercially attractive, other places may have to change their current procedure for making visitors dig into their pockets, over and over again. Loch Lomond is not just a Bear park but, even if it were, there is a lot to be said for Bears and for knowing which is which. After all, there is only one species of Lion.

Lambton Pleasure Park (including Lambton Lion Park)

Address	Chester-le-Street, Co. Durham
Telephone	Fence Houses (038 579) 3311
Open	March–October 10.00–dusk
Acreage	200
Station	Durham (7 miles), Newcastle (7 miles)
Facilities	Guide book and information leaflet Lectures and guided tours Safari bus Bar; licensed restaurant and self-service cafeteria, both with children's menus Snack bar and kiosk Picnic area Gift and camera shop
Other	Pets' corner Donkey rides Playground Veteran aircraft museum Children's fairyland Garden centre

Opened as Lambton Lion Park in 1972, it became Lambton Pleasure Park in 1975. There used to be 57 Lions in three enclosures but there are now fewer Lions and one less enclosure. (It has been transferred back to the Lambton estate.) In other words, Lions are not the big draw they used to be and other animals, as elsewhere, are being brought in to keep attendance up. Similarly, the magic name of 'safari park' no longer has its former appeal. Both the Smart and Chipperfield families, so big in this line of business, resent the phrase today and long to see it go. However, they both helped to perpetrate it and it won't go away – just yet.

The Lambton park (Lord Lambton owns the land and is a partner) is excellently placed to catch people, being seven miles from Durham and seven from Newcastle-upon-Tyne. However, most of its visitors, staying with friends or relations in that part of the world or just wishing for a break from the A1, are not from nearby. What is very close at hand is considerable industry,

notably a coke works just over the road. When animals die (three Giraffes did so recently in six weeks with no apparent cause of death) it is inevitable that industrial pollution becomes suspected as the killer. There are advantages in being placed near urban areas but, as for humans, there are disadvantages to counter them.

The Lambton layout is not greatly dissimilar to other such parks (Jimmy Chipperfield used to be a partner) except that the enclosures area is a mile or so distant from the recreation area, and the connecting road runs through the private territory of the Lambton estate. The first animal enclosure, reached immediately after leaving the ticket office, is a vast paddock containing Zebras, Giraffes and Camels. Next comes the walkabout area where, among the humans, two Indian Elephants, Duchess and Millie, walk between the shop, restaurant, toilets and an artificial lake (dug originally for use in pit fires). This area is like a country zoo, with fenced paddocks on either side containing Rhea, Ponies, Llama and Guanaco. These last two are not easy to tell apart but there are behavioural differences sufficient to prevent the Guanaco, which is alive in the wild, from being confused with the woollier Llama, its descendant, which is extinct save in captivity. It is opportune to mention the two other similar but different South American camel-family species, namely the Alpaca, which looks like the Llama but is much, much shaggier, and the Vicuna, which looks like the Guanaco but is much smaller and has a relatively longer neck. These four animals and the two kinds of Camel make up the family *Camelidae*, about as confusing a group as any.

The next area contains the Lions. Of course the population numbers vary, as cubs are born

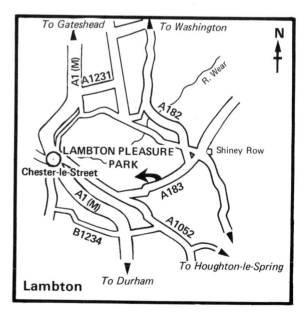

54

and others die or are sold, but the Lambton policy is to have very large groups. This can mean considerable in-fighting as the big males establish their dominance, and it demands vigilance from the wardens to prevent severe damage being done; but, once the power structure has been decided, the sight of a very large group, with cubs of various ages, can be most rewarding for the visitor.

It is disconcerting to see where the other Lion enclosure used to be, and there is a sense of missing out on something, but the road now takes a shorter cut back again to the walkabout area. From an observation platform, and having got out of the car, it is possible to look over a paddock with Wildebeest, Eland and other Antelopes, or to see Ostriches, Cranes and Audad (a kind of sheep), or to catch a miniature train.

The final part of the safari (a Swahili word, incidentally, meaning expedition) goes through a 'jungle' enclosure. This is a mixture of Donkeys, Ostriches, a Zebra (incompatible with the main herd), three White Rhino and some Crowned Cranes. It used to have Baboons but the County Durham breed of these Monkeys were even more destructive to cars and trees than their relations elsewhere and so, regrettably, they had to go.

(Their principal trick was to remove the rubber from windscreens, thus making stage two much easier, removing the windscreen itself.)

To reach the remainder of the Lambton Pleasure Park it is now necessary to take that road connecting the safari area with the entertainments section. There are notices on either side to ensure that visitors do not get out, do not make use of the woodland, do not even see the River Wear and do not disturb that gallinaceous bird so precious and then so vulnerable to the British estate owner, the Pheasant. It is a pity for visitors, who long to have access to the countryside, to realize that estates which have charged an entrance fee are still only partially open to them. Moreover, the entire Lambton Park is closed every winter, being open only from March to October, partly, one suspects, to leave clear the season when Pheasants are no longer determinedly preserved but determinedly destroyed.

The amusements area contains an adventure playground, a restaurant, a souvenir shop, astroglide (six-laned), overnight parking for caravans, a picnic area, a couple of dead aircraft, Lambton Castle (frustratingly closed, save for one room equipped with pin-ball machines) and a pets' corner. The great blessing of safari parks is the

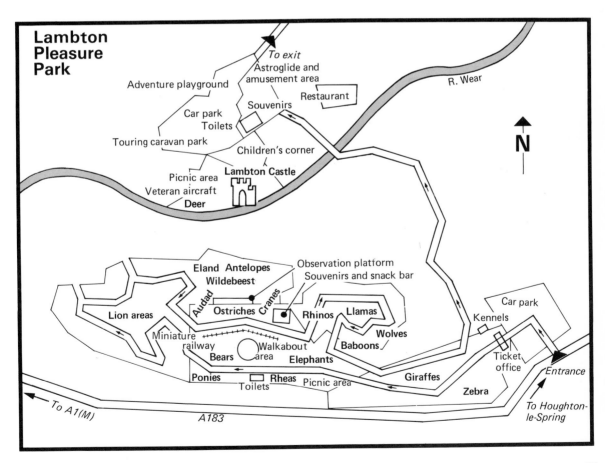

Only Indian Elephants have been bred in captivity, mainly because the mature African males are so 'difficult'. *Above* An African at Chester, and *below* an Indian at Lambton, about to open the author's car.

quantity of space accorded to each group of animals. This generalization does not necessarily continue to apply if there is a zoo of any kind as an extra to the large open spaces. Pets' corners, in particular, are often no more than a euphemism for nineteenth-century-type cages huddled together with little rhyme, reason or beauty. They seem, on occasion, to promote everything contradictory to the refreshing non-zoo atmosphere of the drive-through enclosures.

The pets' corner at Lambton possesses some Crab-eating Macaques in a former morgue, Vietnamese Pot-bellied Pigs, Macaws, Llamas, Spider and other Monkeys, Flamingos, Black-handed Gibbons, Barn and Tawny Owls, Goats, a Raven, a nice family of Porcupines and Wild Boars. There are pleasantly big trees of the stately home kind and the castellated house is in the background. The park receives over a quarter of a million visitors a year and is also host to special exhibitions, such as (for 1977) the Three Rivers Fish Show, a veteran car rally, the Durham County Agricultural Show, and a horse and pony show. The theme of the former Lambton Lion Park is now one of diversification and there are more different kinds of animals (38 mammals and 36 bird species) than in most of the rival safari parks.

West Midland Safari Park

Address	Spring Grove, Bewdley, Hereford and Worcester
Telephone	Bewdley (0299) 402 114
Open	April–October 10.00–17.00
Acreage	200
Station	Kidderminster (2 miles)
Facilities	Guide book and information leaflet Bar, snack bar and kiosk (summer); self-service cafeteria with children's menu Picnic area Gift and camera shop
Other	Animal nursery Dolphinarium Pets' corner Playground Amusement area Garden centre
Shows	Dolphins, hourly

At the start this West Midland Safari Park seemed to have everything going for it. The rolling parkland was bought by Jimmy Chipperfield. By then, having founded the safari side of Longleat and Woburn, he knew what he wanted

in terms of landscaping. He also knew how a road should wind in and out of the animals reserves, and what animals were best. With Birmingham just 20 miles away, and other cities in the area, he knew that this new park was within reach of millions of potential visitors. It was opened in 1973 with considerable optimism.

In 1974 there were 350,000 visitors. In the following year there were fewer, and in 1976 fewer still. Things were not as right as they should have been. An American company leased the land from Chipperfield. The new management built up the amusements side, with the park's name changing into the West Midland Safari Wonderland. There was a 'friendly animal forest', a bird garden and a lot for people to do apart from seeing animals. Dolphins were then brought in as extra entertainment, but they did not bring in the crowds that they should have done. There was also a certain amount of adverse publicity when animals escaped, notably the Houdini-like Baboons. The park took on a tired look, as Elephants and Giraffes killed off many of its trees. Something had to be done, both to get the people back again and make sure they had a better deal for their entrance fee.

At the end of 1976 some major decisions were made. Rather than have both an entrance fee and lesser payments for many of the other exhibits there would be one inclusive price for admission to everything, including the dolphinarium. The boat trips would go; so would the friendly animal forest, the bird garden, the Bears, and many fringe attractions. Instead this safari park would concentrate upon the safari side of things. The drive-through enclosures would be improved and quite reorganized.

As from 1977 there are four sections, namely African, Monkey, Eurasian and American. In the first there are Lions, White Rhino, Elephants, Eland, Wildebeest, Ostrich, Giraffe, Zebra, Camels and Ankole Cattle. Although the majority

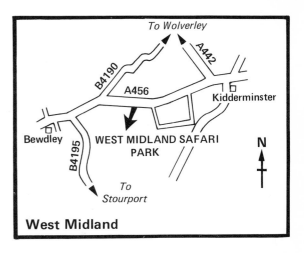

West Midland

of these animals are content with each other's company, they would be less ready to live with the Lions who are therefore within a separate enclosure. The Monkey section does not contain Baboons any more, but Rhesus Monkeys. The Baboons, though more arresting as animals, have earned themselves such a bad name as demolition experts, notably of vinyl roofing, that their gentler, kinder, smaller and more relaxing Rhesus cousins have had to take their place.

The third, and Eurasian, section contains Tigers, Highland Cattle (universal cohabitation is again not possible), Red Deer, Sika Deer, Fallow Deer, Père David's Deer, Blackbuck and Nilgai. In the fourth, and American, section there are Wolves, Rhea, Llamas and Bison. Completing the animals departments are a pets' corner and an animal nursery, both of which are part of the basic entrance fee.

With so many safari parks and other animal collections adding to their offerings with all sorts of swings and roundabouts it is interesting that this one, now renamed the West Midland Safari Park, should have decided that its future lies firmly with wild animals. Where fauna and funfairs have been mixed, as in one or two urban collections, it is easy to leave with the impression that animals do badly out of the joint deal. There is less likely to be the single-minded devotion to their cause that should exist. The change at West Midland therefore augurs well for the animals and may even, if careful replanting is carried out, be good for trees. It would be marvellous if the estate could be reimbursed with more of its original beauty.

The impending changes have also included amendment of the brochure for the basic reason that much of its (1976) information had become incorrect. Perhaps the opportunity will therefore be taken to include photographs in the new version that are only of the West Midland animals. The old brochure had some pictures taken in a

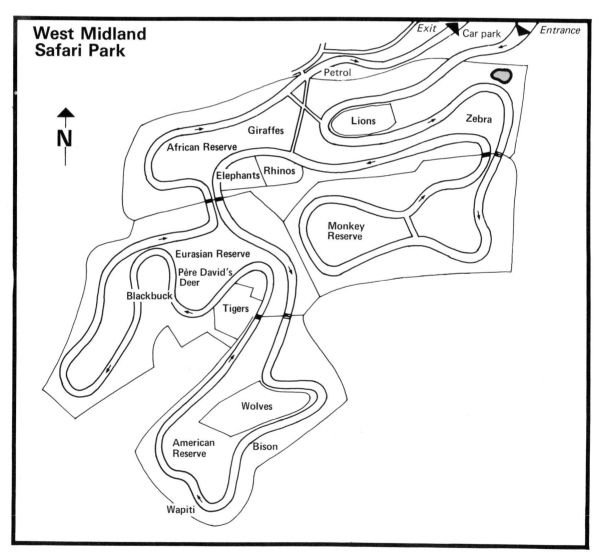

German park, therefore showing neither the right animals (although the right species) nor the right location. This, one feels, is a partial presentation of the truth rather than the whole.

At one time it seemed to many an outsider as if the West Midland Park might close. It is good that it has been able to carry on, and better still that it will concentrate more steadfastly upon its animals.

The Highland Wildlife Park

Address	Kincraig, Kingussie, Inverness-shire
Telephone	Kincraig (054 04) 270
Open	1 March–first Sunday in November 10.00–18.00 or 1½ hrs before dusk if earlier
Acreage	260
Station	Kingussie (7 miles)
Facilities	Guide book and information leaflet Lectures and guided tours Self-service cafeteria Picnic area Gift shop
Other	Pets' corner Pony rides Exhibition of the changing Highland wildlife through the centuries Audio-visual unit

The Highland Wildlife Park was not founded by any member of any well-known circus family and it has no Lions. It also has no Elephants, Tigers, Baboons, Giraffes, Leopards, Cheetahs, Hippos or Hamsters and it has no stately home. What it does have is a wide selection of the proper animals for the area, either those that used to live in it or those that still do and are not easily seen by the casual visitor. It is genuinely a highland wildlife park.

Nevertheless, it is also a safari park in the sense that some of the animals are seen by driving through their enclosure. Currently 200 acres are enclosed and stocked with Red and Roe Deer, European Bison (or Wisent), Soay Sheep, Highland Cattle and Ibex. It suddenly seems very right to see such animals in such a setting and, however pleasant a Giraffe may look among the beech and the oak, it is an exotic creature, a foreigner, and should be browsing among the thorned acacias of eastern Africa. Red Deer, resting among the bracken, heather and granite rocks, harmonize as they should. Indeed it is no surprise to hear that the Red Deer community within the park's enclosure was initiated by lowering the fence at the far end, putting down food within the area and then re-erecting the fence when sufficient animals from the wild had been enticed into captivity.

Roe Deer are more of a woodland species, European Bison were (and are in Poland where they survive in the wild) more forest dwellers than their American cousins, and Ibex still live upon the crags of the European Alps, but they all look well enough in a wild, rugged and natural piece of Scotland. The road itself leading through the park is also wild, rugged and somewhat natural, presumably without tarmac as an economy measure but more in keeping with the area than a smooth surface. It feels correct to have the tyres scrunching on the ground and not to be able to drive at speed.

The elementary idea of having the proper animals in their proper place is not new – many Scots have longed to see it come to pass – but Neil Macpherson, chartered surveyor and former factor, was the man who not only had the idea but made it work. He chose three sites and was lucky enough to end up with the one he favoured most. Over 11,000 acres were owned in the area by Sir Andrew Forbes-Leith, who was happy to lease 260 of them to the enterprise. The Highlands and Islands Development Board also welcomed the scheme by granting £40,000 to it and a further £10,000 to be repaid at 7 per cent interest after three years. Most English and Welsh zoo-type establishments receive no such support and look enviously at Scottish hand-outs. The Highland park was opened in 1972 and is just off the A9, the main road to Inverness and everything north-east. Therefore it is well placed to attract tourists who want to find 'something else other than scenery' (a common phrase) in Scotland, who want a break from that road and who would like to look at Scotland's past and present wildlife. Over 120,000 did so in 1976.

As there are 28 kinds of mammal to see, plus 30 kinds of bird, most of them are not in the large enclosure but in separate pens and cages of their own. Once again there can be the blessing of a right environment for the right animal. The Scottish Wild Cat is caged but sneaking about amid Scottish vegetation. The Wolves are in the kind of setting where wolves used (and ought) to be. Beavers, finally exterminated in Britain in the sixteenth century – they should not have had such excellent fur – are busy once again where they belong, having been imported from Russia. There are Lynxes, which were killed off in Britain even earlier, and Brown Bears which lasted until the tenth century or thereabouts. There used to be Reindeer wild in Scotland 800 years ago and there is now a group within this park, living largely off dehydrated lichen collected in Czechoslovakia. There are Wild Goats, Mountain

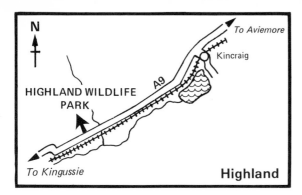

The Highland Wildlife Park possesses the most exciting collection of British animals, past and present. Some are in a drive-through area, but others, such as the Arctic Fox (*below*) and the Wild Cat (*bottom of page*), are in smaller areas that also contain vegetation entirely natural to this part of Britain.

Hares, Arctic and Red Foxes, Pine Martens, Badgers, Polecats, Red Squirrels (no Greys up here, even in the wild), European Otters (so rarely seen these days, and even more rarely seen in zoos), Saiga Antelope (bulbous-nosed and former natives here), and Przewalski's Wild Horse, hardly a Scottish animal as it is restricted (in the wild) to Mongolia, but there must have been wild horses in Britain in the past and Przewalski's, with its heavy head, stiff mane, small ears and low-slung tail, is the only wild one now available.

There are also all the birds, such as Capercaillie (extinct in Scotland by 1770, reintroduced from Sweden in 1837 and now thriving, save that it stays invisible for most visitors), Ptarmigan (even harder to find as it lives around the 3000-foot contour), Blackgame (easier to see, particularly the male, the so-called Blackcock), the Golden Eagle (whose outline, once seen in the sky, is never forgotten), the Eagle Owl and the White-tailed Eagle (neither of which now nest in Britain although they did and should), the Buzzard and Red Grouse (which both do), the Snowy Owl (which is making a come-back) and the Crane (which went extinct here some 500 years ago but still thrives in Europe). The British people in the past were scarcely conservationists, destroying much of the native fauna and replacing it with a wide variety of alien species, such as the Rabbit, Grey Squirrel, Coypu, Mink, Black and Brown Rats, the Muntjac and Sika Deer, and Fat (or Edible) Dormouse. In fact, 14 of our 56 resident mammals are relatively recent invaders. Therefore it is good to see in the Highland Wildlife Park what should be in Scotland but is not.

As so many visitors to Scotland are foreigners (and not just from England) the park provides lists of its main creatures translated into German, French, Italian, Dutch and Danish. Therefore Germans looking for a *Schottisches Moorschneehuhn* or Italians seeking a *Pernice Bianca di Scozia* can both be told to look out for a Grouse (which in Danish is *Grouse*). Besides, who could possibly know without such lists that *Hibou Grand-Duc*, *Uhu*, *Gufo Reale*, *Stor hornugle* and *Oehoe* are all the same bird, namely *Bubo bubo* (Latin) or *Comhachag Mhor* (Gaelic) or, as we also like to say, the Eagle Owl. The lists make fun reading for everyone on a wet day, but just think of going round a foreign zoo where you did not know a *Steinschmatzer* from a *Cinghiale* and how grateful you would be for the thoughtfulness (and work) behind such a list.

The creatures most asked for by the visitors at the gate are Highland Cattle. They could have been seen grazing in many an English field, and certainly in many an English animal collection, but visitors seem to reserve their curiosity for the

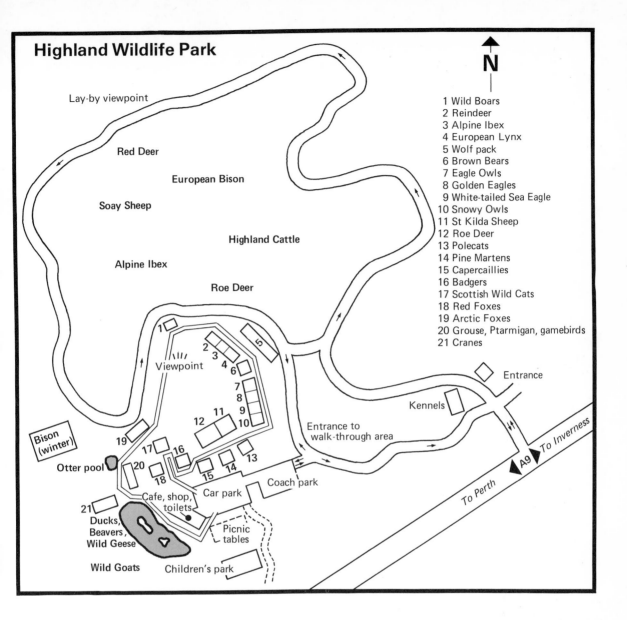

Highland Wildlife Park

N

Lay-by viewpoint

Red Deer

European Bison

Soay Sheep

Highland Cattle

Alpine Ibex

Roe Deer

1 Wild Boars
2 Reindeer
3 Alpine Ibex
4 European Lynx
5 Wolf pack
6 Brown Bears
7 Eagle Owls
8 Golden Eagles
9 White-tailed Sea Eagle
10 Snowy Owls
11 St Kilda Sheep
12 Roe Deer
13 Polecats
14 Pine Martens
15 Capercaillies
16 Badgers
17 Scottish Wild Cats
18 Red Foxes
19 Arctic Foxes
20 Grouse, Ptarmigan, gamebirds
21 Cranes

Viewpoint

Entrance

Kennels

Entrance to
walk-through area

To Inverness

A9

To Perth

Bison
(winter)

Otter pool

Coach park

Car park

Cafe, shop,
toilets

Picnic
tables

Ducks,
Beavers,
Wild Geese

Wild Goats

Children's park

animal until they reach its old kingdom. Contrarily the animal that visitors most resent seeing caged is the Golden Eagle. There may be a similarly sized and different Eagle in the next cage, but sentiment is not logical. It dictates that, of all places in the world, a Golden Eagle should be free to fly in wild Scotland. As antidote to this feeling is the knowledge that few such parks can attract as many birds to nest, like the Wheatear,

Oyster-catcher, Curlew and Snipe. Not far away are Buzzards, Kestrel, Raven, and even Osprey. Overhead, complementing the naturalness of this modern ancient piece of Scotland, are migrating Geese (in spring and autumn), Duck, Gulls, Grouse and, if your luck is in, a Capercaillie. Man, having killed it, brought it back. He is doing much the same in the Highland Wildlife Park, to make past wrongs right.

2 Estates

Abbotsbury Swannery

Address	Abbotsbury, Dorset
Open	May–September Monday–Saturday 10.00–16.30 and Sundays if fine
Station	Weymouth (9 miles)
Facilities	Guide book and information leaflet Lectures Picnic area
Other	Nature trail and woodland walk
Shows	Feeding at 09.00 and 16.30
Feeding	With own food, but not to cygnets

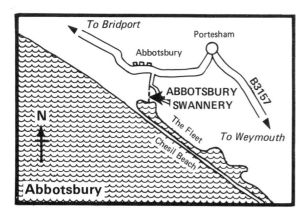

All places are unique but Abbotsbury, to twist the phrase a bit, is more unique than most. Firstly, it concentrates upon Mute Swans, for nowhere else in Britain do they breed colonially as here in Dorset. Secondly, there has been a continuity of interest, both by the Swans and their wardens, for an extraordinary length of time. A colony on the same spot was recorded in 1393 and the first count was made in 1591. Probably the colony had been in existence for much longer as the monastery nearby was built much earlier and the monks were partial to Swan as a regular supplement to their fare. The current owners have possessed the land since a Fox-Strangways ancestor (the family name of the Earls of Ilchester) bought it from Henry VIII after the monastery had been dissolved.

The parking area is a pleasant quarter-mile walk from the swannery, first across a field and then by the side of a stream. The whole area in this bowl of land has a most ancient feel to it and signs of modern things are minimal. The Swans nest on the northern side of the saline Fleet, a seven-and-a-quarter-mile stretch of water between the mainland and the Chesil Bank, itself a feature unique in the British Isles.

The principal peculiarity, even in a place so steeped in the unusual, is the colonial persistence of the Swans. Most of this species nest apart from others of their kind whereas those at Abbotsbury, nesting close to each other, then proceed to drown each other's cygnets as soon as they take to the water. In other words, there would normally be strong selective pressure to nest farther apart and prevent such internecine slaughter, but this is partially countered at the swannery by the interference of man. The procedure is to save a certain number of cygnets each year (about 100 – just as they did in 1591) and to keep them in seven pens until they are old enough and strong enough not to be drowned. They will then be further protected by the best pairs of Swans who will acquire most young.

This rearing is the only unnatural event in the Swans' lives. They are fed at this time (notably at 9 a.m. and 4.30 p.m.) but thereafter are free to feed on the zostera and sea lettuce. They are not pinioned and it is the good (natural) food that keeps them on the Fleet. In summer there are about 500, and in winter this number may double. Peak month is December (when the swannery is closed to visitors).

Take binoculars or a telescope, a bird book and food (if need be – there are picnic areas) to Abbotsbury. Many other species of water bird are with the Swans, and the luckiest visitors may see Osprey, Marsh Harrier, Snow Geese and even rarer individuals perhaps blown over in a gale. The place is also a nature reserve (for Roe Deer and Otter, for example); a reed bed (cut productively and burnt each year); and a duck-ringing centre (November–January). Fortunate visitors may also meet Fred Lexster, swanherd for 50 years, and the third generation of his family to have held the post. On a busy day there are 2000 visitors, and about 80,000 come a year. On any day each of them will have seen a sight quite unlike anywhere else.

Arundel

Address	Mill Road, Arundel, West Sussex
Telephone	Arundel (0903) 883 355
Open	09.30–17.30
Acreage	65
Station	Arundel (1 mile)
Facilities	Guide book and information leaflet Guided tours Picnic area
Shows	Birds fed 16.00–16.30
Feeding	With own food

The newest of the Wildfowl Trust establishments – although there may well be others in the future – opened in November 1976. Its speciality,

Previous pages Very few Cheetahs in captivity are breeding. This family is at Whipsnade, the first zoo in Britain to have success in this field.

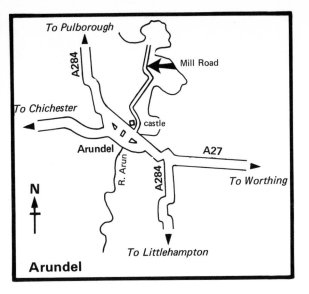

Arundel

able to do so. In the thirty years since its inception it must have fulfilled even the wildest dreams of Sir Peter Scott, its founder and current Honorary Director.

Banham Zoo and Woolly Monkey Sanctuary

Address	The Grove, Banham, Norwich, Norfolk
Telephone	Quidenham (095 387) 476
Open	All year 10.30–18.30
Acreage	20
Station	Attleborough (6 miles), Diss (7 miles)
Facilities	Guide book and information leaflet Self-service cafeteria with children's menu (summer); snack bar and kiosk Picnic area Gift shop
Other	Nature trail (school parties) Woodland walk International motor museum Putting green all adjacent Farm barn sales to zoo Garden centre
Shows	Sealions, Penguins, Pelicans fed 15.00–16.00, or as specified Lecture/talk about Woolly Monkeys on Sunday afternoons in summer, and other specified afternoons during summer

of course, is waterfowl, but the particular emphasis here is on sea duck and tropical species. By opening day, after three years of preparatory work, concreting ponds and planting trees, there was accommodation for about 1000 individuals of 80 species of bird. These animals include: Cuban Whistling Duck; Hawaiian (or Nene) Goose; Aleutian Goose; White-winged Wood Duck; Golden Eye; Long-tailed Duck, and Harlequins, Mergansers, Goosanders and Scoters. By the end of the year a total of 1900 people had come to see them.

The opening of Arundel means that it is now possible to take great strides all the way up Britain using the Wildfowl Trust locations as stepping stones. From Arundel to Slimbridge to Peakirk and Welney (both over by the Wash) to Martin Mere in Lancashire and up to Washington on the Wear and over to Caerlaverock on the Solway Firth there is never need to travel far before encountering another wildfowl reserve. Of course, each is different, but each has the same devotion to its collection and to the Trust's aims.

The Trust's Council undoubtedly wishes for more money to fulfil more of its aims, but there is a detectable sensation of solvency about its various establishments that is not encountered in all other animal collections, however similar and noble their aspirations may also be. Without doubt the Trust raises money well. For example, it received £276,568 in donations during 1975. Not every one of the Trust's places does equally well from the gate and ancillary sales; but some are definite honey-pots able to attract money while others do the kind of work more in keeping with the Trust's aims, such as research and conservation. It must be nice being able to play off Peter against Paul in this fashion, but the Wildfowl Trust now owns 3122 acres and is well

Banham is not particularly easy to reach but well worth the finding. Quite suddenly, and without anything much in the way of an entrance gate, there is one of the finest collections of Monkeys in Britain. More important still it is very new (starting in 1968, having been a Pheasant collection beforehand) and is obviously going places.

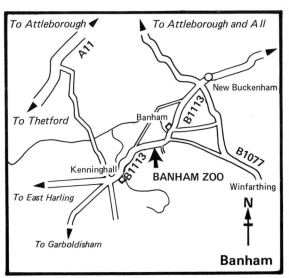

Banham

There is quite a difference to a captive Wolf that is a member of a pack. It shows an alertness and a vigour not observed in any solitary animal.

Someone someday ought to do a book about zoo-keepers and how they got into the business. Banham would be an interesting example. First there was a retired baker. He kept Pheasants, Parrots, and so forth. People wished to see them and he began to charge admission fees, as well as building up several companies quite independently. The zoo needed a full-time man. So a young hairdresser, originally from Germany but with a Welsh wife and a Welsh–German accent, took the lease. The zoo expanded, largely into Monkeys because the new man liked them, and there is now a partnership between the former baker's son and the former hairdresser. So, abracadabra, and there is a great zoo.

The twenty or so Woolly Monkeys have the most extensive cage system and, in return, have successfully reared half a dozen young. There is a big oak alongside, which is utilized, and also a lecture room where people and Monkeys intermingle. The zoo's loudest inhabitants are the Siamang Gibbons, with the Red Howlers coming a close second. At times they fill the Norfolk air with a remarkable chorus. Other Monkeys are the Black Howlers, White-faced Sakis, Diana, de Brazzas, Langurs such as the Silvered Leaf and Spectacled, the Abyssinian and Red Colobus, the Hoolock and Lar Gibbons, Spider and Squirrel Monkeys, Cotton-top Tamarins, and several Marmosets.

There are many other animals of a more general zoo type. The Malabar Squirrels are a favourite, and there are Wolves and Dingos in a small larch wood. There are plans for a Lion house (which seems a shame, as Lions are common enough) and considerable intent to use some of the large fields bordering the current cages as well as the five-acre wood for a series of aviaries. Here and there already are Patagonian Sealions, Small-clawed Otters, Chimpanzees, Porcupines, a Deer paddock, and a large assortment of birds, such as Sulphur-breasted Toucan, Hornbills, Eagle, Scops, Barn and Snowy Owls, Egrets, Heron, Peafowl, Kestrels, Waxbills, Finches and Flamingos. In all (at the end of 1976, although it is easy to suspect new inhabitants are steadily arriving) there were 37 species of mammal, over half being Monkeys, and 64 of bird, adding up to a total of 302 individuals.

It is a small zoo but will get bigger. It so far attracts 65,000 visitors a year but needs double that number to make itself pay. If visitors are content to see a predominantly Monkey exhibit, with some individuals not seen anywhere else in Europe, they will thoroughly enjoy themselves at Banham. Just, in fact, as the Monkeys seem to do.

Bentley Wildfowl Collection

Address	Bentley Farm, Halland, nr Lewes, East Sussex
Telephone	Halland (082 584) 260
Open	Easter–end of September
Acreage	25
Station	Uckfield (4 miles), Lewes (6 miles)
Facilities	Guide book and information leaflet Guided tours (if booked) Tea and biscuits available afternoons Picnic area
Shows	Feeding 16.00
Feeding	With own food

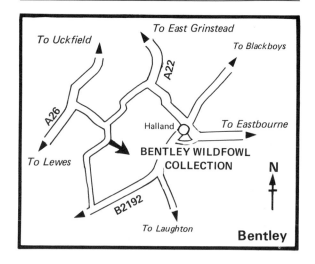

Think of wildfowl and you will be excused if you think simultaneously of Sir Peter Scott, but you should also think of the Bentley Wildfowl Collection. In numbers of species, if not in numbers of individuals, it rivals Slimbridge because the collection currently contains 124 kinds of bird.

Its theme is rare wildfowl and the majority of the world's waterfowl species are on show here in 25 acres of a delightful part of Sussex. Ponds and lakes have been created, and trees have been planted both to act as windbreaks and to improve the natural setting. Among the birds on show are Red-breasted Geese (one of the most handsome of them all), Hawaiian (or Nene) Geese, Bewick's Swans, Cereopsis Geese (from Australia), Trumpeter Swans (which so nearly went extinct), Greater Snow Geese, Black Swans (descendants of those originally acquired for Sir Winston Churchill) and many more, large numbers of which have been bred successfully.

For the enthusiastic ornithologist, Bentley has much to be said for it over similar collections because its attentions are so concentrated upon the birds. There are no cafés, restaurants, kiosks or shops but tea and biscuits are available in the Pump House (which also possesses a superb exhibition of colour photographs of wildfowl, a must for identification). It is open just in sum-

mertime, but is never overwhelmingly crowded as only 36,000 visit it during the year. The collection was started in 1962 by the late Gerald Askew but he did not open it until 1966. Mrs Askew now carries on the work.

Caerlaverock Wildfowl Refuge

Address	Eastpark Farm, Dumfriesshire
Telephone	Glencaple (038 777) 200
Open	1 September–15 May
Acreage	1400
Station	Dumfries (7 miles)
Facilities	Information leaflet

The Caerlaverock refuge is, like the Wildfowl Trust's place at Welney in Cambridgeshire, purely a good spot for seeing wild birds. The natural exhibits here are thousands of Barnacle and Pink-footed Geese and several thousand Golden Plover during the winter months. Other regular visitors range from Peregrine Falcons, Hen Harriers and Merlins to Bewick's and Whooper

The Black-winged Stilt, a common sight in Africa and, happily, one that is becoming commoner in British collections.

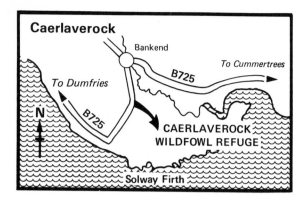

Swans. But, as there is no captive collection, either of local or exotic bird life, the refuge is only included here to distinguish it from other Wildfowl Trust centres with both penned and wild birds for us to see.

Child-Beale Wildlife Trust

Address	Church Farm, Lower Basildon, Reading, Berks
Telephone	Upper Basildon (049 162) 325 and 593
Open	Easter–September: Wednesday, Thursday, Sunday and Bank Holidays 11.30–18.30; Saturdays 14.00–18.30
Acreage	15
Station	Pangbourne (2 miles)
Facilities	Information leaflet Kiosk Picnic area
Other	Playground

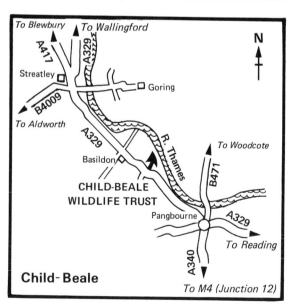

As a Peacock is this collection's emblem, a row of Peafowl cages is appropriately set in the grassy car-parking area outside the Trust grounds. There are many more in spacious enclosures within, among them White and Black-winged which have bred. The feeling of quantity (as well as elegance and quality) is continued throughout cage after cage of (generally) pairs of Pheasants (the rare ones, including Brown-eared, Mikado, Elliot's and Swinhoe's). The Child-Beale Wildlife Trust, a member of the Pheasant Trust, has bred Himalayan Monal, Cheer, Pallas's or Blue-eared, and Japanese or Green Pheasants, as well as Sonnerat's or Grey Jungle Fowl. The various species are not all grouped together but are intermingled down a long line, which much encourages the visitor to study the first example, learn its distinguishing features and recognize it later on. There are over 15 varieties of Pheasant, but even the beauty and attraction of, for example, Golden, Lady Amherst's and Reeves's Pheasants cannot overshadow this natural setting beside the Thames.

This is a place in which to relax, to wander, sit and watch (and read – with nearly 90 species listed on the information leaflet, a bird identification book is almost a must). The waterfowl enclosures are well populated (the ground under-

Good aviaries are places where birds not yet seen suddenly appear from the vegetation and then pause before vanishing once again. The Red-headed Gouldian Finch, pausing.

foot can also be at times) and there are ten species of Goose, five of Teal, three of Pintail, three of Wigeon, both New Zealand and Common Shoveller, and Shelduck, as well as other types. On a moat (around a pavilion of hand-cut Wiltshire stone) there are Whooper Swans, and elsewhere are many statues, Flamingos (Chilean and Cuban), Budgerigars, Finches, Demoiselle Cranes, Ring-necked Doves, Curlews and Oyster-catchers.

There are minor concessions to keeping children entertained and refreshed but the aim of this charitable Trust, which was founded in 1956, 'is to preserve this beautiful part of the Thames Valley and create a place where the opportunity for enjoyment and relaxation can be appreciated by the public'. You drive away, past Highland Cattle and Soay Sheep, full of remembered appreciation of the tree-shaded Pheasant walk, the open spaces and wide paths, the stately-home feeling (though no stately home), and for the fact that all this happiness can be enjoyed for no cost at all (if you go on a Wednesday or Thursday) or for a 50p car-parking fee (at weekends and Bank Holidays).

Cotswold Farm Park

Address	Guiting Power, Cheltenham, Glos
Telephone	Guiting Power (045 15) 307
Open	15 May–3 October 10.30–18.00
Acreage	30
Station	Moreton-in-Marsh (9 miles)
Facilities	Guide book and information leaflet Lectures and guided tours Self-service cafeteria Picnic area Gift and camera shop
Other	Pets' corner Playground Pony and float drives
Shows	Occasional demonstrations of Sheep-rearing, Sheepdog handling and seasonal farming activities
Feeding	With purchased food

Neither a zoo nor in any way a collection of wild animals, the Cotswold Farm Park receives attention here because its animal collection is both worth a visit and worthy of support. We know about the extinction of the Great Auk and the Passenger Pigeon, but do we know of the Lincolnshire Curly Coat Pig or Alderney Cattle? They too are as dead as the Dodo, and it is believed that 20 breeds of our domestic livestock have gone since the Second World War ended.

The diminution, coupled with a growing feeling of concern, led to the formation in 1973 of

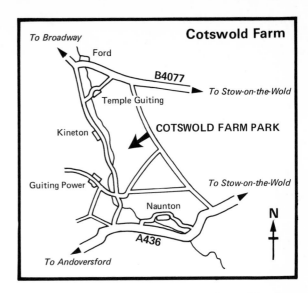

the Rare Breeds Survival Trust. One of its first concerns was to understand the current status of all breeds, to discover whether Gloucester Cattle and Portland Sheep do exist only in dangerously low numbers (as proved to be the case). A second priority was the establishment of a suitable shop window for the cause whereby the rest of us could learn about the history of British livestock breeding, see some of the rare breeds in danger and understand what this Trust was trying to do. Plainly there was interest in the subject as 110,000 of us visited that window, the Cotswold Farm Park, in 1976.

It forms a small part of Bemborough Farm, a 1000-acre piece of Cotswold land right in the middle of an officially-declared Area of Outstanding Natural Beauty. The Trust's park is currently the home of 8 breeds of Cattle, 14 of Sheep, 5 of Horses, 3 of Pigs, 6 of Goats and 20 of Poultry. Most of these breeds are on the danger list, as defined by the Rare Breeds Survival Trust, but here in the Cotswold Farm Park every one of the groups is breeding annually. There are also working Shire Horses, of interest both to those who remember when such a sight was commonplace and to those who presume that tractors have always been part of the agricultural scene. The only British team of six working Oxen operate here in the Cotswolds, of particular interest as we may have forgotten just how important this beast of burden was to our ancestors. For children there is a special corner containing the hand-reared baby animals being bred on the farm.

Breeds on view include Warwickshire Longhorn, thought to be the nearest direct descendant of the wild cattle domesticated by Neolithic Man; Soay Sheep, last survivor of Europe's prehistoric domestic sheep; St Kilda Sheep, the last remnant of the extinct Hebridean breed that may have been brought over by the Vikings; Manx Loghtan

Sheep, the native breed of the Isle of Man; Jacob Sheep; West Highland Cattle; Cotswold Sheep, once the pride of the country, accounting for half its production, but there are only a few Cotswold flocks alive today; Dexter Cattle, which are very small; and many others. Surprisingly, for admirers both of Highland Cattle and Brigitte Bardot, there is a cow here called after her and no other name, even at first glance, could be more apt.

There is a magazine, *The Ark*, that helps to keep those interested in the Trust's work in touch with its activities.

Cotswold Wildlife Park

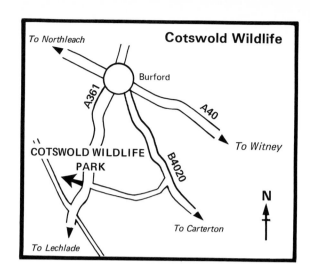

Address	Burford, Oxon
Telephone	Burford (099 382) 3006
Open	All year except 25 December 10.00–18.00 or dusk if earlier
Acreage	120
Station	Charlbury (11 miles)
Facilities	Guide book and information leaflet Lectures and guided tours (by arrangement) Train within park Bar; self-service cafeteria; snack bar and kiosk Picnic area Gift shop Pushchairs on loan
Other	Manor House (ground floor open) Aquarium Invertebrate and Butterfly exhibition Pets' corner Pony and Donkey rides Pony and Donkey traps Playground Garden centre Brass rubbing centre Nature trail and woodland walk
Feeding	Penguins 16.00 (except Friday)

The safari parks undoubtedly gave a great boost to the idea of keeping animals in the countryside, whether or not their successors followed the general drive-through safari park idea. In fact, there are now more country places without a drive-through area than with one, even though there may be an ancient homestead, rolling parkland and plenty of wild animals where only cedars of Lebanon and copper beeches used to stand before. Many an estate has moved into the animal business, but without adopting the 'safari' idea.

Such a one is the Cotswold Wildlife Park. About 120 acres at the centre of the 3300-acre Bradwell Grove estate (what a shame that we cannot roam everywhere), it now contains a magnificent collection of animals, beautifully displayed, that has done wonders since opening day in 1970. The house was built only in 1804 but this neo-Gothic structure was erected where a Jacobean house had stood. In other words, the estate itself is much older. At every opportunity the current management has taken advantage of the inherited beauty, the grounds themselves, the superb walled garden, the old conservatory, even an ancient tree (with 460 rings) that fell down in a gale of 1976. It suddenly seems as if the earlier inheritors had animals firmly in mind as they landscaped, built upon and created their world about them.

Top animals at the Cotswold park are the Red Pandas (the only other representatives of the subfamily containing the Giant Pandas, and symbol of the park), White Rhinos (whose sleeping quarters are garlanded internally with flowers), Meerkats (they have bred here, and are rarely seen in Britain), Coatis (which have also bred), Spider and Squirrel Monkeys, Leopards and Pumas, Humboldt's and Rockhopper Penguins (looking very well with Pelicans in the walled garden), Red-billed Hornbills (which have bred in that extraordinary hornbill fashion of imprisoning the female by walling up the nest entrance with mud), Red Squirrels (a rarity for southern England, whether in zoos or the wild), Brazilian Tapirs, Wallabies, Emus (which have bred), Grévy Zebra (the largest and, many say, the most handsome, with the narrowest of stripes), Thomson's Gazelle or 'Tommies', and Waterbuck (with that distinctive white ring around their buttocks). In total there are 35 mammal species and a remarkable 140 bird species.

But what makes this country zoo yet more distinctive is its possession of so many other kinds of creature. There are 20 invertebrate species (and plans to increase this number considerably), 50 kinds of fish (in an aquarium fashioned from

Can a White Rhino ever have had it so good? A bed of straw, sleeping quarters garlanded with flowers, and a vast paddock of the Cotswold Wildlife Park for grazing on.

old stables), 10 of amphibia and 55 of reptile. This last figure makes the Cotswold reptile collection the fifth largest in Britain and the largest anywhere in the countryside (as opposed to the urban collections). The reptile house itself is well maintained and also built off the old stable yard. The Pythons have bred and the Puff Adder is an exceptionally fine specimen, that is for all those people who can see as much beauty in the snake kingdom as in other kinds of animal.

There are plenty of facilities, such as an excellent adventure playground (near the restaurant, permitting parents to be taking in energy while children lose it), Pony and Donkey rides, shops, a pets' corner (which actually contains pet-type animals) and a narrow-gauge railway (which can even be useful in getting about the park, as well as fun). Although visitors leave about £1 behind on average apart from the entrance fee, the general Cotswold intent is *not* to charge wherever possible. Train and Donkey rides are, of course, extra, but the basic entrance ticket provides access to practically every exhibit, a principle not applying in many other estates.

Fences are also kept to a minimum here, with ha-has used wherever possible so that the animals do seem to be grazing right in front of the house. The place is poorly signposed in nearby country lanes, but 230,000 people found their way to it in 1976. If the honey-pot of Burford, just three miles away, appears crowded and expensive, there can be few more refreshing places to go for a change than Cotswold Wildlife Park.

Curraghs Wildlife Park

Address	Ballaugh, Isle of Man
Telephone	Sulby (062 489) 323
Open	Easter–September 10.00–18.00
Acreage	26
Facilities	Guide book Restaurant and snack bar
Other	Pony trap Nature trail
Shows	Penguins and Pelicans fed 11.00 and 15.00; Sealions fed 11.30 and 15.30

71

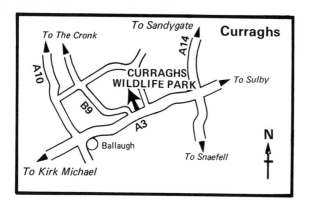

In 1964 the Manx Parliament acquired 211 acres of the Ballaugh Curraghs as a nature reserve, of which 26 acres were developed as the Curraghs Wildlife Park. Consequently, it is easy to expect a feeling of space in this collection and such is actually the case, even though it receives 57,000 visitors during the summer season.

The collection is very general, with 20 kinds of mammal, 96 of bird, 1 of reptile and 2 of

There are four kinds of Tapir: all have striped young but only the Malayan Tapir ends up half-black and half-white.

amphibia. The newest buildings include an Otter exhibit (the animals can be seen swimming underwater, which is where they make most sense) and a Sealion pool. The most striking enclosure is the Noah's Ark which has been constructed traditionally (it is very easy to wonder where this tradition of a house situated within the middle of a boat sprang from). The mammals on view include Père David's Deer (which breed), White-fronted and Brown Capuchin Monkeys (which also breed), Brazilian (or American) Tapirs (which have bred a remarkable 50 offspring), Llamas, Diana Monkeys, Pumas and Four-horned Sheep (which have every right to be in the zoo as they are a Manx variety).

The birds include Humboldt's and Jackass Penguins (normally found in South America and South Africa respectively), White Pelicans (which fly free, making a very rare and beautiful sight since they, like the Otters in their water, only really make sense when in their element), Flamingos, Great Indian Hornbill, Red and Green Macaws, Pheasants and Owls. There are two main aviaries but there are also birds along with various small mammals within the Ark. In all there are almost 1000 animals on show.

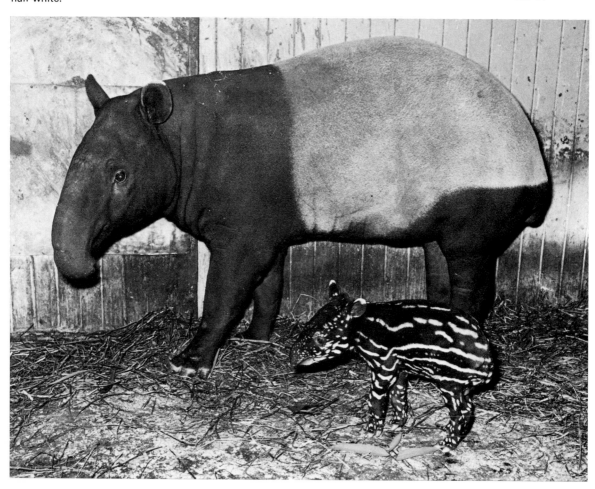

Dartmoor Wildlife Park

Address	Sparkwell, Plymouth, Devon
Telephone	Cornwood (075 537) 209
Open	All year 10.00–dusk
Acreage	25
Station	Plymouth North Road (6 miles)
Facilities	Guide book and information leaflet Guided tours Tearoom; kiosk (summer and winter weekends) Picnic area Gift shop Pushchairs for hire
Other	Pets' corner Playground Donkey rides
Feeding	With purchased food

Practically every animal in the Dartmoor Wildlife Park collection is European. The more one sees of zoos specializing in either British or European creatures, the more one sympathizes with this idea. Before we get to know about Tigers, Giraffes and so on, we should certainly learn about our own fauna; either that which is still resident in Britain, or used to be, or lives on the mainland of Europe.

The park was started in 1968 and Mr E. B. Daw is still in charge. There are about 320 animals in residence, namely 26 species of mammal, 44 of bird, 6 of reptile, 2 of amphibia and 1 of fish. The most exciting exhibit is a two-acre walk-in enclosure. The most bizarre item is an animal graveyard begun in 1820.

The animals include the Badger, Fox, Polecat, Wild Cat, several kinds of Deer, Grey Seal, Wolf and Coypu, all of which are British in the sense that they either have lived here or do so now. The main breeding successes have been with Owls, notably the Eagle, Tawny and Barn. Other birds on show include many waterfowl, Ravens, Buzzards, Pheasants and Herons. Exotic creatures here are the Palm Civet, Malaysian Otter (British Otters are much harder to come by), Black Swan, various Monkeys and Peafowl. It is also good to be able to see the Adder, Britain's only (moderately) poisonous snake.

There is an observation tower, permitting the visitor to get an overall view of a zoo which is changing rapidly. Many of its houses and enclosures have been completed in the last five years and its arrival on the scene is to be welcomed. It is quite possible to spend time in the Dartmoor area, particularly in the summer, without seeing too many of its indigenous creatures. The Dartmoor Wildlife Park can therefore help redress that lack.

Drayton Manor Park and Zoo

Address	Nr Tamworth, Staffs
Telephone	Tamworth (0827) 68481/2/3
Open	Easter–October 10.30–18.00 (for all amenities); October–March 11.00–17.00 (zoo)
Acreage	15
Station	Tamworth (3 miles)
Facilities	Guide book and information leaflet Guided tours Bar Licensed restaurant; self-service cafeteria; snack bar; kiosk; party tea-rooms, all with children's menu (summer) Picnic area Gift shop
Other	Pets' corner Pony and Donkey rides Playground Train, chairlift, jungle cruise boats, boating, garden centre, etc, all in entertainment park Nature trail and woodland walk
Shows	Animal feeding

Calling itself 'The Pleasure Centre of the Midlands' Drayton Manor Park and Zoo is, as the name implies, both an entertainment park and a collection of animals. In all there are 160 acres of wooded parkland that include the 15-acre zoo (entrance to which is covered by the park admission charge). The park itself is full of various and colourful amenities whereas the zoo, reasonably enough, is relatively free from them.

The animal collection is very mixed, containing 46 species of mammal, 37 of bird and 26 of reptile. The Reptile house is particularly striking, containing Mississippi Alligator and Spectacled

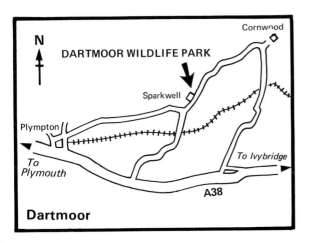

Dartmoor

Above The haughty profile of a Llama. *Right* The Arabian Camel is designed for deserts, with two rows of eyelashes for protection against sand and sun.

Very few of the 248 kinds of marsupial find their way to Britain. Wallabies (*left*) are common, but seen much less frequently are Tree Kangaroos (*above*).

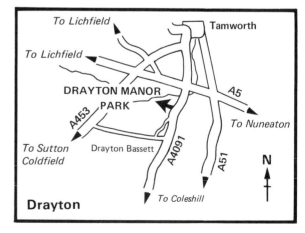

To Lichfield

To Lichfield

Tamworth

DRAYTON MANOR
PARK

A5

A453

To Nuneaton

To Sutton
Coldfield

Drayton Bassett

A4091

A51

N

To Coleshill

Drayton

Cayman (both of which are officially endangered species), Giant Zonures, Western Diamond-backed Rattlesnakes (which have bred), Geckos and many Snakes and Lizard species. Among the mammals there are Chimpanzees, many Monkeys, Bears, Pumas, Leopards, Lions, Sealions, Wallabies, Llamas, Deer, Sheep, Ponies and Highland Cattle. As might be expected in a park atmosphere, the Sealions and Chimpanzees are star entertainers. Among the birds are Flamingos, birds of prey, Pelicans, Cranes, Storks, Ducks, Geese, Peafowl and very many tropical varieties.

The nearest thing to a zoo in the amusements area is a jungle cruise in the lower lake which navigates past islands occupied by simulated animals, such as Crocodiles. The total number of real animals at Drayton is about 300.

Drusilla's Zoo Park

Address	Alfriston, East Sussex
Telephone	Alfriston (0323) 870 234
Open	Daily 11.00–18.00 (winter 17.00)
Acreage	10
Station	Berwick (1¼ miles)
Facilities	Information leaflet Lectures Licensed restaurant with children's menu; self-service cafeteria and kiosk (summer) Picnic area Gift shop
Other	Aquarium Donkey rides Shire Horse wagon rides Playground Garden centre Working pottery Cottage bakery Antique shop

Compared with most animal collections in the countryside Drusilla's has been going a long time. It started in 1923, eight years before Whipsnade, but it is zoo-sized. Most of the animals are in small cages and therefore cannot compare with the vastness of the Whipsnade conception. It calls itself a zoo park, which can imply considerable size, but the whole business of nomenclature is somewhat awry. Whether somewhere calls itself a park zoo, a zoo park, a safari park, a leisure park, a sanctuary, a wildlife park, a zoological park, a game reserve, a zoological garden or a pleasure park must be important to the owners, in that they have chosen the name, but the disparity can be misleading (at worst) or unhelpful (at best) to the rest of us. Anyway, for the record Whipsnade Park Zoo is 500 acres and Drusilla's Zoo Park is 10.

Nevertheless Drusilla's, despite its size (and whatever its name), does contain a lot of animals. Its location is pretty enough, being just north of the bastion of the South Downs, and the Drusilla's feeling is of a farm plus farmhouse that has switched to exotic creatures rather than maintain the old domestic kind. The fact that it possesses a good selection of British Cattle, Rabbits, Goats and Chickens merely emphasizes the feeling of a farm that has taken a different turning.

The animals distinctly foreign to Sussex include Cuis (a kind of Guinea Pig rarely seen), Malabar Squirrels (also rare in captivity), Gerbils, Macaques and other Monkeys, Penguins, Coatis, Porcupine and Kinkajou. There is also an albino Grey Squirrel, which may or may not be considered foreign according to your point of view but which is certainly odd. One Wallaby is also albino, which is foreign (unless you count the ones running wild in, for example, the Peak District) and no less odd. The zoo spreads out at its far end where birds, in particular, have large areas. There is a Flamingo lagoon, a model Hippo (sufficiently good to fool most of us quite happily), Cranes, Guinea Fowl, Black Swans, Pheasants and lots of Ducks.

Someone has gone fairly wild with a paintbrush here and there around the zoo. And there are all sorts of other extras, such as a gift shop, tea house, cottage bakery, restaurant, train, pottery, garden centre, art gallery, antique shop, Butterfly exhibit (dead ones) and 'wagon walk' – making use of the fact that farm equipment of a very short time ago has suddenly become of historical interest. The place began with teas and a pets' corner. Even though it has grown since then, both in the range on offer and the numbers of animals, it still retains that flavour, whatever its name.

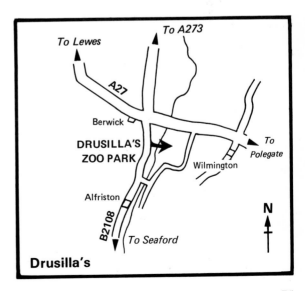

Drusilla's

Flamingo Land

Address	Kirby Misperton, Malton, North Yorks
Telephone	Kirby Misperton (065 386) 287
Open	All year except 25 December 10.00–dusk
Acreage	320
Station	Malton (6 miles)
Facilities	Guide book and information leaflet Lectures Bar; licensed restaurant and self-service cafeteria with children's menu; snack bar and kiosk (summer) Picnic area Gift and camera shop Pushchairs for hire Petrol station
Other	Aquarium Children's farm Dolphinarium Playground and fairground Train, tractor train Jungle cruise Crazy golf Model railway Children's show Haunted Castle, Gnomeland Zoo trail Garden centre
Shows	Big Cats fed 15.30; Penguins fed 15.45; Sealions fed 16.00; Dolphins hourly
Feeding	Some animals, with own food

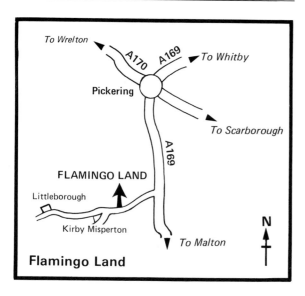

Flamingo Land

Set right in the middle of North Yorkshire, and quite a way from any large community, Flamingo Land has been a considerable initiator. Started five years before Longleat, the Flamingo Land venture was the first British establishment to import Dolphins and is now, so they also say, 'Britain's largest Pleasure Park and Zoo'. All those who assert that animals and entertainments do not mix, or mix to the detriment of both these features, should certainly head for Kirby Misperton, near Malton, and put their views to the test. Flamingo Land is, without doubt, a place that believes in mixing everything possible, such as jungle cruises 'through untamed, crocodile-infested country', a model railway show, garden centre, crazy golf, Gnomeland, Haunted Castle (with varied menus and macabre cabaret: coffins are used as tables in the Dungeon Bar), 'Yorkshire's biggest permanent inland fairground', adventure playground, miniature railway, children's farm – and a zoo. Not, so they say on the brochure, 'a fun-filled moment is wasted'. No opportunities have apparently been neglected for giving people things to do once they have found their way through the Wolds to Kirby Misperton. And to the 300 acres of Flamingo Land.

Where to start? Perhaps with Ocean World, the dolphinarium, if only for the good reason that Flamingo Land pioneered this kind of entertainment (and used to have a Whale). It gives hourly Dolphin shows, possesses the largest indoor pool in Britain and also a large external pool. Certainly the Flamingo 'school' give one of the best performances in Britain.

Despite the plethora of entertainments the zoo side of things is quite distinct; there are no merry-go-rounds among the animals. As the collection contains 65 species of mammal, 95 of bird, 6 of amphibia, 44 of reptile, 35 of fish and even 2 invertebrates, totalling 1100 individuals, it is again difficult to know where to begin. But there are all the ABC animals, such as Antelope, Bear, Camel, Deer, Elephants, Flamingo (naturally), Giraffe and so on down to Zebra. Particularly good breeders have been the Flamingos, Tigers, Lions, Leopards, Eagle Owls, Black Swans, White Storks, Giraffes, Zebras and Orang-utans. The most endangered species (from the point of view of their survival in the wild state) are the Arabian Gazelle, Père David's Deer (this man was also the first westerner to send Europe a Giant Panda skin), Giant Anteater, Giant Tortoise (already 100 years old), and Tiger. As Tigers breed well in zoos, and as zoos like them, there are probably more of this species living safely in captivity than in their former kingdom of the Indian sub-continent.

Many zoos try to keep every manifestation of 'show business' away from their animals. Flamingo Land is different once again. The Sea-lions, who never seem averse to putting on entertainment, blow trumpets and put on a show, and there are odd people/animals at the gate to welcome visitors. Feeding animals with ordinary food is also permitted in certain cases, as for the Elephant Suzy. She, say the organizers, 'likes men, dancing and fast buns'.

Animals not often seen at other zoos include

the Lechwe, an Antelope that lives on swampy land; the Spotted Hyena, which certainly does not deserve the feeling of disgust maintained for it by so many humans; and the Douroucouli, the only nocturnal Monkey in the world (which can make it a poor, however intriguing, exhibit if all that is presented to visitors is a gently heaving ball of fur). This last animal lives in the tropical house which possesses good pools for Turtles and Terrapins, Alligators and Crocodiles.

So, if it is animals that the visitor is after, there will be more to see at Flamingo Land than almost everywhere, save for a few of the city zoos. If other interests are sought (that Haunted Castle, for instance, offers as its star cabaret 'an authentic re-enactment of an eighteenth-century hanging') there are plenty to choose from. Consequently, it is reasonable for the Flamingo literature to suggest that 'getting round all the sights and entertainments' can take more than a day. It comes as no surprise to discover that the place also contains a caravan village for those who wish to spend a night. Or two, or more. So what is Flamingo Land? A zoo, or a pleasure park, or a novel mixture of the two? Well, they even have the answer to that one. They say that 'itsazoopaspookycruisin jumpingnomypuffinwhirlin sidesasplittinflamingoland'. So that's what it is, and half a million people go to it every year.

More slender than the Spotted Hyena (and also without spots), the Striped Hyena is less able to kill prey for itself. Both kinds are rare in British zoos.

Heathfield Wildlife Park

Address	Hailsham Road, Heathfield, East Sussex
Telephone	Heathfield (043 52) 4656, 4748 and 4919
Open	All year except 25 and 26 December 10.00–18.00 or dusk if earlier
Acreage	200
Facilities	Guide book and information leaflet Self-service cafeteria with children's menu; kiosk (summer) Train within park Picnic area Gift shop
Other	Pets' corner Car and agricultural museums Gibraltar tower Royal box Wheeler statues Tanks Nature trail and woodland walk Craft and garden centre
Shows	Sealions fed
Feeding	With purchased food

The 200-acre Heathfield Park estate has been in existence for a long time but it was only opened up to visitors in 1973. It is a confusion of inter-

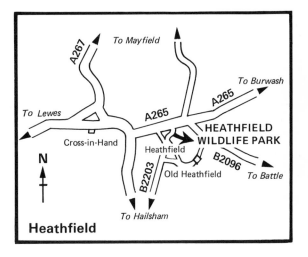

Heathfield

ests without too much apparent logic behind the various attractions on show, and animals only form a part of the curious collection.

As might therefore be expected these are of a general nature without any particular theme to them. There are 20 kinds of mammal and 50 of bird, adding up to about 250 individuals. Prominent among them are the Californian Sealions, the African Elephants (whose house was completed in 1976), American Bison (which have bred here), Vultures and Deer. There are also Zebras, Llamas, Monkeys and Coatis.

The so-called Bird City contains, among others, Ibis, Hornbills, Owls, Penguins and Pelicans. If current plans go ahead more species will be added to the collection in the next few years. For many visitors the statues, museums, entertainments and so forth may provide a more exciting part of their Heathfield day than do the animals. Virtually all the items of interest, both animal and mineral, are ranged on either side of a roadway one-and-a-half-miles-long leading from the park's entrance to the lake at its centre. Visitors' cars are parked at this entrance but, for those for whom such a long road would be an ordeal, there are free 'fun trains' which run from one end of it to the other.

Howletts Zoo Park

Address	Bekesbourne, Kent
Telephone	Littlebourne (022 778) 440
Open	All year 10.00–18.00 or dusk if earlier
Acreage	55
Station	Bekesbourne (1 mile)
Facilities	Guide book and information leaflet Self-service cafeteria Picnic area Gift shop
Other	Nature trail/woodland walk
Shows	John Aspinall plays with Tigers 14.30 and with Gorillas 15.15 on Sundays

It is difficult to dissociate many zoos from the men who run them. It is impossible at Howletts. The place *is* John Aspinall. It is also a very large quantity of his money (can gambling ever have been put to a better use?) and a firm expression of the views he holds about animals. There is, for example, no cage into which that particular animal's keeper does not go every day. Aspinall believes that the gulf between animals and man is man-made; therefore it is up to us to repair it.

Howletts did not so much open as gradually get permission from the local authorities to be open for more and more days in a year. (There was extraordinary outcry from nearby residents at the idea of wild animals sharing this part of Kent with them, but all the stories of British reaction to novelty, as at Longleat, as at Marwell, are equally disturbing.) The zoo park's founding stems from 1957 but not until 1975 did Canterbury City Council give permission for Howletts to stay open for eight months, and only in 1976 were the final four months added. It is now open, at last, every day of the year.

Aspinall bought his first animal, a Tiger, shortly after he had 'made money', aged 29. He played with the Tiger and continued to do so. Since then he has maintained this policy, getting all his animals used to him, his keepers and his family. Playing with a Gorilla is not easy, particularly when the same games are pursued with equal zest by an animal two or three hundred pounds heavier than when that play began. Nevertheless, the human–animal relationships are preserved. Aspinall has many hates. One of them is to see meat poked into, say, a Lion's cage without affection being expressed or interest being shown. He also dislikes the traditional zoo practice of feeding big cats with daily food (or possibly missing one day a week). His Tigers, for example, receive haunches of meat once about every ten days. The food cannot be eaten at one go but, once it has gone, there is a week-long period of hunger – as in the wild.

Without doubt the Howletts Lowland Gorillas are the outstanding feature of the collection.

The 55 acres of Howletts Zoo Park have a quality and style of quite a different class from most countryside collections. The large herds of exotic Deer are among the prized exhibits.

There are nine males and eight females, making not just the largest number of these magnificent creatures on exhibition anywhere in Europe, but also the most prolific. Four babies were born and reared just in 1976, and no animal has died for nine years. Almost all of them live as a great group in a cage 180 feet long, 60 feet wide and 30 feet high (save for a small bite taken out of this area to house Chimpanzees). It cost £20,000, which is expensive by many zoo standards but extremely modest when compared with some of the prestige animal enclosures, costing thirty times that amount, that have been erected elsewhere. Its most exciting feature is a deep bed of straw litter, which provides a springy surface and is changed twice a year. Some argued that it would also provide a ready supply of infections but, if so, the animals seem immune to them. The roof is also a play area with the main structural supports a few feet below the actual roof

netting; this enables the Gorillas to walk up there, hang from there and even fall from there onto the straw. There are many furnishings within the cage but Aspinall wants more, such as a large trampoline and a mirror.

If Tigers and Gorillas are the superstars of Howletts there are many other species of star rank, such as the Roan Antelope (the Howletts group of this magnificent animal is the only one in Britain), the largest Axis Deer herd in Europe, the only Sambar Deer herd in Britain, a group of Calamianes (Hog) Deer from the Philippines, the largest Wolf pack in Britain, the Honey Badger (or Ratel), another rare British sight, four African Elephants (shouldered, of course, with the responsibility that they provide the first successful African Elephant birth in Britain), Clouded Leopard, Amur Leopard and Snow Leopard. A beautiful cage around a tree had been built for this last species, it being a well-known fact that

John Aspinall playing with Tigers. He also plays not only with adult Tigers, but with adult Tigers plus young – a much more hazardous proposition.

Howletts contains some fine specimens of creatures very rarely found elsewhere, such as this beautiful Clouded Leopard.

Leopards often climb trees. An equally solid fact, albeit little known, was discovered after their transference: Snow Leopards never climb trees. Of course they have little need or possibility for so doing high up in the Himalayas, and failed to change their attitude in Kent.

The Cheetahs are what Aspinall calls his 'outstanding failure'. They are sufficiently mature, but have not bred. In 1976 Aspinall wrote: 'It is the policy of the zoo to breed from all the species in its care, regardless of the cost in human or financial terms. So far, of the 30 kinds that are old enough to reproduce, 29 have bred successfully.' The Cheetah is the exception but, one suspects, not for long. (There are, inevitably, plans to rectify the shaming failure, a sense of loss that few other zoos feel quite so acutely.)

The Howletts mansion, set in the middle of 55 acres, is lived in by the Aspinalls. Therefore they are surrounded by all their animals (at the last

Opposite Spiders are hardly ever found in zoos, but deserve a place in them. *Above* A Crab Spider, and *below* The Spider *Argiope argentata*.

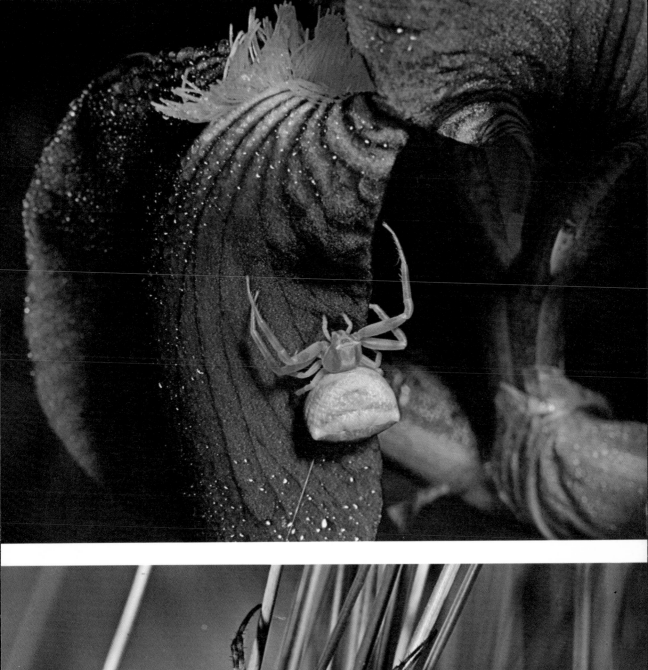

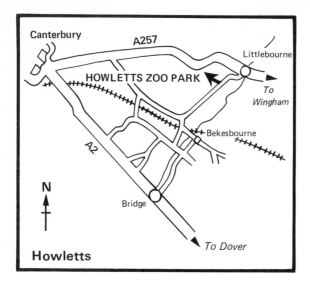

Howletts

count 38 species of mammals and 7 of birds), a lifestyle that does not apply to every director of a zoo. However, even Aspinall has to break this rule and absent himself because he keeps another large collection of animals over at Port Lympne. The two collections are complementary to each other, in that animals are moved from here to there, or back again, for every kind of reason, for a better cage, a better mate, more space. It is as if one were Regent's Park and the other were Whipsnade, and both must be seen in order to examine each more clearly.

In 1976, the first proper year, 140,000 visited Howletts. At £1.50 for adults and 75p for children it is expensive but the place is run expensively. The animals get a better deal and therefore the visitors get a better deal in seeing them. In some zoos it is difficult to decide where all one's money goes. In Howletts it is easy to know; it goes straight to the animals.

Kilverstone Wildlife Park

Address	Kilverstone, Thetford, Norfolk
Open	Summer 10.00–18.30; winter 10.00–17.00
Acreage	50
Station	Thetford (2 miles)
Facilities	Guide book and information leaflet Lectures and guided tours Self-service cafeteria (summer); teas on Sunday (winter) Picnic area Gift and camera shop Invalid chairs for hire
Other	Playground
Shows	Penguins fed 15.30 (except Wednesday)

It was a good idea to specialize in New World fauna as has been done at the Kilverstone Wildlife Park. Having a Tiger next to a Lion next to a Kangaroo, as they tend to do in other places, may be all very well for variety, but it does little for a greater understanding of the reasons why certain animals live together.

Not too far away in Norfolk is Philip Wayre's Wildlife Park concentrating on European animals. Therefore it is just as well that the new place (Kilverstone only opened in 1973) has a different range of goods on show. These include the Guanaco, Alpaca, Llama (possibly the Llama group says 'South America' at us quicker than any other animal), the Collared Peccary, Capybara (an excellent rodent swimmer that should have ample clear water for showing off its underwater capabilities), Viscacha, Margay, Tayra (the South American equivalent of the Marten, but much bigger), the Brazilian Tapir (three Tapirs come from the New World and only one from the Old), the Prairie Dog (or Marmot), the Coati (sometimes called Coatimundi but this name refers to the solitary adult males who only meet up with the Coati groups during the breeding season), American Bison, Grey Squirrel, Raccoon (Kilverstone sometimes calls itself a Latin American collection, but many of its animals come predominantly from farther north, such as the last three), Penguins (of a South American kind), and many Deer.

The birds at Kilverstone are a particular delight, although a few are not from the New World. They are none the worse for that but, as there are so many fantastic American birds to choose from, it is easy to wonder why these outsiders were included: such as the Barnacle Geese (from northern Europe), the Golden Pheasant (from eastern Asia), the Occipital Blue Pie and White-cheeked Touraco (also Asians). However, there are excellent New World specimens, such as Parrots, Macaws, Conures, Oropendolas, Tanagers, Flamingos and the Crested Curassow.

In the walled garden, such an important feature of stately homes, there are Monkeys along with many birds. These include the Spider Monkey (appealing face, a prehensile tail seemingly more useful than any limb), the Woolly Monkeys (thick coat, a worldly-wise look about them, and a well developed thumb), and Capuchin Monkeys (whose four species are the commonest of all in South America). There is also Allen's Olingo, certainly not a Monkey but a sort of primitive Kinkajou without the Kinkajou's prehensile tail. It is well worth a look, whatever it is; that is if it is not just a ball of fur.

Other creatures are the Mara (a rodent that looks like a Hare), the Maned Wolf (a most elegant animal that is, unfortunately, becoming rarer

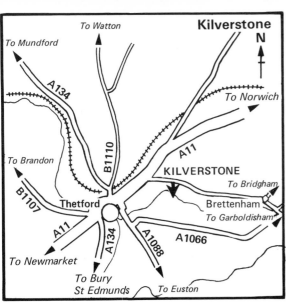

Two ways of carving up an old estate. *Above* 15 acres for a Sable Antelope at Port Lympne, or *below* Many smaller enclosures for more species at Kilverstone.

every year), the Sooty Agouti (much less common than the Orange-rumped kind), Otters, Marmosets, Tamarins and Falabella Miniature Horses. In one of the greenhouses, as well as many free-flying birds, there are plants from South America. There could be many more of exceptional interest to everyone (and not just the gardeners among us), such as the New World plants that have so enriched our diet since their world was discovered, like the pineapple (though there are some bromeliads), the peanut, Brazil nut, cashew, quinine, cocaine (or, on reflection, perhaps not), tomatoes, paw-paw, cocoa, cassava, maize and vanilla. But there need not be a coffee tree as that, however well it grows in South America, came from Arabia.

Kilverstone is owned by Lord Fisher (of the naval family) and he has now amassed the largest collection of Latin American fauna in Europe. Hopefully it will become larger still – there are all the splendid South American reptiles and fish, for instance. But already it has 48 species of mammal, and 125 of bird, making a total of 650 animals which were seen by 90,000 people in 1976. A school of Piranha, for example, should make them flock in faster still. After all, they are probably the most famous South American species living on that continent.

The best place in Britain for observing lepidoptera in captivity is Worldwide Butterflies in Dorset. *Above* The Indian Moon Moth, and *opposite* The English Swallowtail.

Lowther Wildlife Country Park

Address	Lowther, Penrith, Cumbria
Telephone	Hackthorpe (093 12) 392
Open	April–September: April, May, June, September 10.00–17.00; July, August 10.00–18.00
Acreage	130
Station	Penrith (5 miles)
Facilities	Guide book and information leaflet
	Lectures and guided tours
	Licensed restaurant; self-service cafeteria and snack bar
	Picnic area
	Gift and camera shop
	Pushchairs (free loan)
Other	Pets' corner
	Pony rides
	Pony-carriage drives
	Playground
	Garden centre
Feeding	Ducks, with own food

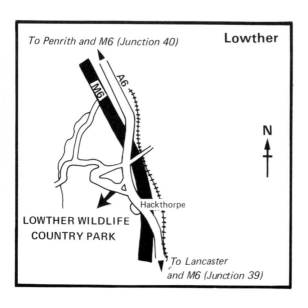

Lowther Park could make a claim, even though it would be warmly contested by other veterans, to being the oldest safari park of all. Nearly 700 years ago Sir Hugh de Louther received permission from Edward I to make a deer park. The Red Deer now living at Lowther are the descendants of those enclosed in the thirteenth century. They are therefore accustomed to this form of wild captivity. However, for the first 666 years of their confinement, they were protected from the public. Only in 1969 was this part of the vast Lowther estates opened up to visitors.

Lowther Wildlife Country Park, conveniently placed just off the A6 and the M6, is another mixture of a place, being neither a true safari park with potentially dangerous animals just a windscreen away, nor a zoo with all its creatures comfortably caged for us. It does have a touch of the safari to it because the main parking area is one mile by single-track tarred road from the entrance gate, and this road winds its way past many animals, such as herds of Deer and ancient forms of Cattle. It also has a touch of zoo to it because, somewhat randomly, there are pens and cages for those animals that could not be trusted to roam, like the Deer, within the park and still stay loyal to Lowther.

What is most un-safari about this park is that, having driven for a while past the Deer, Cattle and other species, the visitors can stop their cars within the same area and walk instead. The Red, Fallow, Formosan, Sika, Japanese Sika and Chinese Water Deer can be inspected, both with caution and more closely. They are not wild, of course, but they are not entirely tame. As with all animals it is often better to let them inspect, approach and sniff you rather than make too hasty an approach yourself. Children, who are not the best of our kind at giving the necessary confidence to any animal, can learn much in Lowther. They can realize that sudden jerky movements, so much part and parcel of all their energy, are not entirely appreciated by anxious animals. Not every Lowther animal is equally approachable (some being as tame as pets, while others maintain a flight distance – in other words, the animals keep sufficient distance between them and the human onlookers to make a speedy getaway, if necessary). Not every animal behaves similarly throughout the year (there is the autumnal rut, for instance, when the males are particularly unpredictable). But the tame/wild mixture is a most attractive phenomenon. The Deer are neither so wild as to be virtually invisible (think of the Deer in Scotland used to being shot at) nor so tame as not to be themselves, like those normally wild animals that live *en famille* in people's sitting-rooms.

The sycamore, beech, chestnut and oak trees are well scattered and grouped throughout the area. The Deer trim branches from beneath but the trees have not suffered the kind of damage meted out by Baboons, Elephants and Giraffes in other parks. The Lowther Cattle, of course, are even less of a problem and look equally right chewing the cud in this very English setting. There are Old English Longhorns, once common but now quite rare, and Highland Cattle, the traditional breed of the Western Highlands, now commoner on English estates, or so they say, than in Scotland.

Red Deer have been enclosed at Lowther for almost 700 years, and the park was opened up for all to see in 1969.

Also under the trees, and near to the general parking area, is equipment for children, climbing things and swinging things. There are Peacocks and Cranes, and down by the lake on the other side of the restaurant and shop are Flamingos, Geese, Swans and Ducks. It is a pleasantly informal atmosphere, with the birds taking their cue from the Deer, just wild enough to resent excessive curiosity and yet tame enough to be very close at hand. The free-flying Macaws are probably the most free-flying of all in Britain as they hurtle themselves magnificently around the trees. There are good notices, with pictures, to help identification, notably of the waterfowl.

Here and there are the various enclosures for animals that cannot be allowed to wander at will throughout the 130 acres of park accessible to people. There are Otters (but they could do with, say, a waterfall), Foxes, Wild Cats, Beech Martens, Polecats, Badgers and even Rabbits. The collection's general theme, despite its Macaw and Flamingo exceptions, is to show species native to Europe. The bigger animals, namely the Wolves, Wild Boar and Mouflon, have their unimaginative but spacious enclosures within a portion of the forest. They are reached via a pleasant path which goes through the trees past a few bird cages. It is easy to wonder, on looking at the three large pens and noticing how the vegetation has been treated by their different occupants, whether the prodigious earth-moving energy of the European Wild Boar could not be put to effective use. No blade of grass is left unturned, no stone, no clod of earth. They do better than mechanical excavators, only relaxing when all the green has gone and is replaced everywhere by an earthy, muddy brown.

Sadly the Lowther park is only open for the six summer months. The fact that 135,000 visitors turned up in 1976 shows that quite a few winter visitors could also be expected to arrive. After all, the 21 kinds of mammal and 58 of bird, totalling almost 700 individuals, must be still in residence, and the wintry scenes of Deer among the trees must be almost as magical as in leafy summertime. Presumably there are reasons for winter closing, and also for shutting the gates so early even on summer evenings, but many visitors

87

There are millions of insect species, but no one would think so from the attention they receive in zoos. *Above* Javanese stick insects to be found at Worldwide Butterflies.
There are conversely only two species of Elephant. *Right* The African kind at Longleat.

most appreciate communing with nature, however tamed, when the big crowds have gone home. And where better for this kind of natural communication than within a beautiful and ancient piece of land like the Lowther park?

Martin Mere

Address	Burscough, nr Ormskirk, Lancs
Telephone	Burscough (0704) 895 181
Open	All year except 25 December 09.30–18.30 or dusk if earlier; last admissions 17.30
Acreage	363
Station	Burscough Bridge (1½ miles), New Lane (1 mile)
Facilities	Guide book and information leaflet Lectures (occasional) and films Guided tours (educational, by arrangement) Kiosk Picnic areas Gift shop
Other	Nature trail
Feeding	With own food

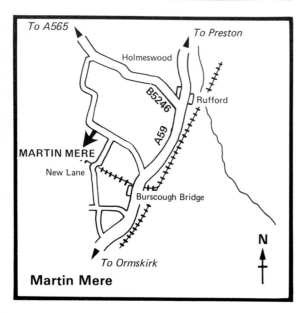

Martin Mere

Unlike most zoos all the Wildfowl Trust establishments have been created in places either highly satisfactory for or already used by Ducks and Geese. Near Ormskirk in Lancashire there used to be the largest stretch of inland water in England. Consequently, it is no surprise that part of the ancient marsh land, mid-way between Southport and Wigan, is yet another of the Trust's refuges. Martin Mere was opened to visitors in 1975, received 70,000 in the remaining ten months of that year and 100,000 in 1976.

It also received, as was more customary, its fly-ing flocks of wild visitors, the 5000 or more Pink-footed Geese who arrive each winter, the thousands of Pintail and of Teal, the hundreds of Wigeon. There is an 18-acre lake and, of course, large hides from which to watch the birds.

There is also a collection of about 1500 waterfowl representing 80 species that, as with other Trust establishments, are part and parcel of the exhibit. The captive animals complement the natural scene. Rare animals here are the Hawaiian Goose (surely there are still more of this species in Britain than on the Hawaiian Islands, despite successful reintroduction there of British-reared birds), Trumpeter Swan (recognizable by its all-black bill), Ruddy-headed Goose (also breeding well here, as with the first two species), White-winged Wood Duck, Aleutian Canada Goose, Cereopsis (or Cape Barren) Goose, New Zealand Brown Teal, Mexican Duck, Laysan Duck and Hawaiian Duck.

One trouble with plans for reintroducing Hawaiian birds, like the Nene and the last two species, is that the original habitat has been dramatically changed, partly in a direct manner by man and less directly by the introduction to the islands of, for example, rats. Thanks to the Wildfowl Trust the Hawaiian animals can fare better in the heart of Lancashire than on their native islands. But human interference is still a problem here. The two Trust establishments nearest to industrial centres, namely Martin Mere and Washington (just down the road from Sunderland), have both been plagued by vandalism. Hopefully such destruction is only temporary. The more people who visit the Wildfowl Trust, the more converts there must be to its cause. And 100,000 to Martin Mere in its first full year is highly promising for the future. After all, there are no Lions and Tigers here, just Ducks and Swans and Geese.

Marwell Zoological Park

Address	Colden Common, nr Winchester, Hants
Telephone	Owslebury (096 274) 206
Open	All year 10.00–17.30 or dusk if earlier
Acreage	180
Station	Winchester (8 miles)
Facilities	Guide book and information leaflet Bar and self-service cafeteria with children's menus (in winter, weekends only); snack bar and kiosk (summer) Picnic area Gift and camera shop
Other	Children's zoo Pony and Camel rides Playground

Hardly ever seen in a British zoo is the beautiful Springbok, the national emblem of South Africa.

Marwell Zoological Park claims in its literature that it is neither a safari park nor a conventional zoo. Despite that truth, it is possible to drive round in a car, as with the safari parks, and it does house a considerable number of different animals, 50 sorts of mammal and 50 kinds of bird, which is much more like a zoo. The Marwell difference is that those in cars have to leave them to see the exhibits well and the animal collection is as much like a normal zoo as a palace is to a prison.

Marwell is a tonic. It can restore faith in those who, having had some bad experiences, are wondering whether animals should ever be captive for our satisfaction. It shows that conservation need not be just a platitude, mouthed when occasion demands it, but a guideline for policy and endeavour. It also exhibits many species of animals we had forgotten about, or did not know about. There is considerable uniformity about most zoo inhabitants and we, the visitors, have to make do over and over again with yet another

Vietnamese Pot-bellied Pig, another Puma, another Porcupine. There are 4237 different kinds of mammal and it is easy, even after visiting many zoos, to be astonished at this fact. A child can think of 37, but can we adults think of 237 different kinds? As for 4237 . . . !

Hoofed animals are the speciality at Marwell. Some places manage to make their Deer and their Antelope a dull lot, not half as exciting as the carnivorous creatures next door that traditionally live off them but, if this is your opinion too, a Marwell day will do its best to change it. Look at the herd of Scimitar-horned Oryx, brown-necked, white-bodied, magnificent. Look at the Sable Antelope, also beautifully horned, whose males are the blackest of them all. See how Nyala should look, and Blackbuck and Waterbuck, Addax and Impala, Onager and Kulan, Nilgai and Goral. And certainly do not forget the biggest of all the Oryxes, the Gemsbok, straight-horned (up to four feet long) and wonderfully marked in black, brown and white.

Overleaf Among the oddest animal relationships are those of the Cleaner Fish and their hosts. The Cleaner *Labroides* with the Flag-tailed Surgeon-fish (*left*). *Right* The amazingly marked Angel Fish.

The largest herd of Przewalski's Horse in Britain is at the Marwell Zoological Park, a supreme form of zoo.

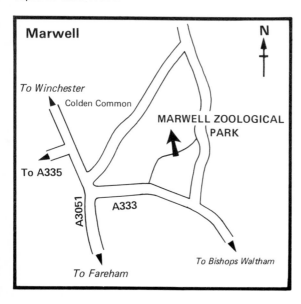

There are plenty of other animals, such as European Bison and Wild Boar, Sumatran and Siberian Tigers, Brazilian Tapir, the Northern Lynx, Hunting Dogs, Grévy, Chapman and Hartmann Zebras, Wildebeest, Capybara, Przewalski's Horses (the largest herd in Britain), and Deer – Formosan Sika, Hog, Axis, Père David's, Swamp and Fallow. Among the birds there are Emu, Rhea, Cassowary, Black Swans, Kori Bustard, European Stork and various Cranes – Demoiselle, Sarus and Crowned.

Almost more important at Marwell is the list of animals not present. There are no Lions, no Giraffes, no Elephants, no Sealions, no Chimpanzees, no reptiles, no Dolphins, no Rhinos, and many people would say that such a wealth of lack adds up to no zoo. Whoever heard of a zoo without a Lion? The Marwell counter-argument is that all such animals can be seen easily elsewhere (such as Lions), that it resents the idea of keeping any animals that cannot be bred (such as Elephants), that the important task is to breed rare and endangered species, and that every 'ordinary' animal uses up space, time and money. The ideal is laudable but it is easy to wonder if it will continue to survive intact. Ordinary people, the hordes of us who are the financiers of every zoo, expect to see, say, Elephants in any place that calls itself a zoological park. We repeatedly ask to see the Elephants and express a sense of loss on learning the truth, on being told there is no room for Elephants among the finest collection of ungulates in Britain today. 'Mum, what's a hungalat, and where's the Elephants?' Should the heavy, silent tread of the world's largest land mammal ever be heard at Marwell the rest of us will know that public pressure has won, and that

94

the desire of 'the gate' has had to be respected. 'Look, Mum, there they are!'

Marwell is as new as or even newer than some safari parks. It was started in 1972 by John Knowles, a successful chicken breeder who suddenly found himself, aged 39, with a large lump sum. In the United States he had been inspired by the Catskill Game Farm and, impulsively buying two Siberian Tigers, wished to have somewhere to house them and also to start breeding hoofed animals (as at Catskill). He bought Marwell because it fulfilled almost all his criteria. Its major omission was still or running water. However, it is large – 488 acres – and therefore can supply him with the bulk of his feeding needs (certainly the straw, oats and, usually, hay, but not the meat). Its size also acts as a buffer between his collection and farm animals, making it difficult for disease to pass in either direction. There is no domestic livestock within a one-mile radius. Knowles sees himself as a 'dictator with consultation' and therefore is consistent with a well-known generalization that the best zoos are run by dictators whose authority and initiative is not sapped by committees.

'Have any new animal houses been completed in the past five years?' is a question answered by most zoos with a proud 'Yes', as details are given of Monkey houses, Seal ponds and the like. The Marwell answer is: 'Everything.' In the main they are simple houses, resembling agricultural sheds and looking much as if they have arrived by parachute, dotted here and there over the 180 acres of the actual zoo. There is a kind of pattern to the layout, with visitors following a clockwise circuit through the Australian, African, Eurasian and American zones, but there is a more fundamental feeling that it could all be changed overnight. This hut could be shifted here; those animals could be moved into these paddocks; a few more huts, ponds and fences could be built and, hey presto, quite a different grouping could have been achieved. City zoos, as they know to their cost, are constructed with too many bricks and too much mortar for similar mobility of thought or action to be feasible.

No outstandingly large conurbations are nearby, but Marwell receives 240,000 visitors a year. Only about 20 per cent of these bring in their cars (at extra cost) and the proportion of return and off-season visits is high. There is an active Marwell Zoological Society, which runs lectures and provides unlimited access to the zoo for its members. There are some concessions to commercialism, such as a gift shop and other happenings, like the Pony and Camel rides, but without doubt it is the Marwell animals that are the main attraction and the dominant concern of the organizers. It is a *zoological* park, and not a pleasure park with animals.

Mole Hall Wildlife Park

Address	Widdington, nr Saffron Walden, Essex
Telephone	Saffron Walden (0799) 40400
Open	All year 10.30–18.00
Acreage	25
Station	Newport (2 miles)
Facilities	Information leaflet Guided tours Ice creams and soft drinks Picnic area Gift shop
Other	Nature trail
Shows	Feeding 15.30–16.00 (summer)

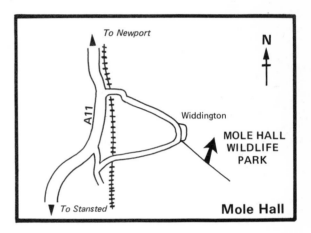

Many animal collections now on general show to visitors started privately. Then, either because they grew too large, or because of local wishes to see the animals or merely because the gate could help to pay the food bill, they opened to the rest of us. The Mole Hall collection was started in 1948 and opened in 1964. One of its principal assets is Mole Hall itself. It has a complete medieval moat crossed by four bridges and the actual dwelling was first mentioned in 1286. Most of the current building is Elizabethan and it sits within the 25 acres that are now largely dedicated to the animals.

It is a general assortment containing what could be called middle-sized mammals, as well as a larger number of birds. There are five primate species, namely Chimpanzees, Woolly Monkeys, Talapoin Monkeys and two kinds of Capuchin. Among the hoofed animals are five sorts of Deer, the Pot-bellied Pig and various other domestic forms. (Some believe the Vietnamese Pig was the first wild pig to be domesticated.) The carnivores include Foxes, Servals, Jungle and Wild Cats, Raccoons, Coatis and Dingos. The only other Australian species are Red-necked Wallabies.

Among the birds are 2 kinds of Swan, 2 of

Varieties of Goldfish. Such Carp have been considerably altered by mankind's enthusiasm for selective breeding.

Flamingo, 19 of Geese, many Ducks and Cranes, Owls, Macaws, Peafowl and Currasow. Particular breeding successes include Canadian Otters, Servals, Black Swans and Black-necked Swans. According to the brochure: 'To enjoy animals and see them at their best – be quiet and slow in every way.' In 1976 over 40,000 people came to see the Mole Hall collection, hopefully just as quietly and slowly as the owner would wish.

Norfolk Wildlife Park

Address	Great Witchingham, Norwich, Norfolk
Telephone	Great Witchingham (060 544) 274
Open	All year 10.30–18.00 or sunset if earlier
Acreage	40
Station	Norwich (12 miles)
Facilities	Guide book and information leaflet Self-service cafeteria with table licence and children's menu; kiosk (summer) Picnic area Gift shop

Philip Wayre has been with animals a long time – his passport says he is a zoologist – but only in 1961 did he open up his collection of animals to general visitors. Since then a pleasant 40 acres of Norfolk with a stream flowing through it has become the largest collection of European animals in the world. Almost 120,000 people found their way to it in 1976.

There are very few common factors in the way our wildlife collections have been amassed, but Philip Wayre's tale is odder than most. After leaving the Navy he first farmed, but then turned to pedigree Turkeys and Pullets. Fowl pest hit him for three consecutive years, which meant that he ended up with a fat cheque as compensation. Simultaneously, he 'fronted' an Anglia TV series which required, in its 36 programmes a year, a steady succession of tractable wild animals. Thus

Philip Wayre, with one of his Asian Small-clawed Otters.

he gathered a considerable population of creatures who, their turn over, had to go somewhere. What better idea, therefore, than to house them where the Turkeys and Pullets had roamed, where space and some money awaited them? The Norfolk Wildlife Park was born.

It is also the home of the Pheasant Trust. While the Turkeys were still alive Philip Wayre learned there were more endangered Pheasants than any other kind of bird, and a friend said, 'If somebody doesn't do something they'll all be dead.' At the Norfolk turkey farm Wayre did something, and started breeding all manner of Pheasants. When fowl pest struck at the Turkeys and Chickens, neither did the Pheasants die nor did they have to be slaughtered by law. Therefore, assisted by some of that compensation money, the Pheasants boomed. The Trust was started in 1960. Its aims are to help prevent extinction and to display a large variety of the 150 forms of Pheasant in the world. They all come from Asia, save for the Congo Peacock. Already some Pheasants have been sent back to their native lands, such as Swinhoe's Pheasant to Taiwan, and the Cheer Pheasant to Simla.

The Pheasant work is laudable but could never be expected to make turnstiles click loudly. That has to be achieved by the very considerable display of European animals, large numbers of which breed at the Norfolk park. Particular successes include many believed firsts, such as the Green Acouchi (first in Europe), British Brown Hare (first in Britain), Canadian Otter (first in Britain), European Lynx (first in Britain for 30 years), Common Otter (another first in captivity, remarkably, for over 90 years), European Wild Cat (first in Britain for 86 years), Alpine Ibex (first in Britain) and so on. Of course it is marvellous that such achievements have been made

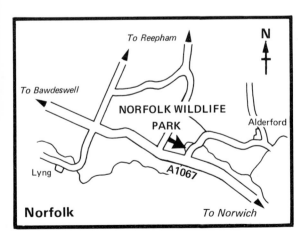

Rarely seen in zoos today, but once wild in Britain, is the Wolverine or Glutton, sufficiently powerful – it is said – to overcome a Reindeer.

led with trees and of enclosures (certainly cages is too harsh a word) here and there but not everywhere. It is not an estate with vast estate-type trees, but an ancient piece of farmland, lavish with willows down by the stream, that has been fashioned into an obstetric unit for (in the main) Europe's traditional wildlife. The entrance area (despite parking for 1000 cars) is most unprepossessing and, although there is a self-service cafeteria and a shop, commercialism is kept to this bare minimum. For example, rather than a price list of various foods or an advertisement for some delicacy, one conspicuous notice in the café area is of animals that have bred at Norfolk during the current year. It surely sums up the place.

The Otter Trust

Address	Earsham, nr Bungay, Suffolk
Telephone	Bungay (0986) 3470
Open	1 March–30 November 10.30–18.00 or sunset if earlier
Acreage	27
Station	Diss (13 miles)
Facilities	Guide book Self-service cafeteria Gift shop
Other	Woodland walk

but it is also somewhat shaming, for animal collections as a whole, that Cats, Otters, Lynxes and others in captivity have not been persuaded to breed either before or for a long time. Wayre has also done well with birds, such as the Stone Curlew, Spur-winged Plover, Alpine Chough and Wheatear. All of them were 'firsts' of one sort or another.

At the Norfolk Park there are 48 mammal species, 130 bird species and 4 kinds of reptile, adding up to 1350 individuals. They include Brown Bear, Wolverine (rarely seen in captivity), Lynx (which, like many of the species, have a vast area to themselves), Suslik (which are like Marmots, and burrow), Polecat, Coypu (not everyone's friend, particularly in East Anglia), Sun Bear, Mouflon, Badger (which can be seen in their sett should they be asleep), many kinds of Deer, Wolf, Raccoon Dog, Bison, Red and Arctic Foxes, Wild Boar, Beaver, two kinds of Seal (Common and Atlantic), Barbary Apes (Europe's only Monkey although somewhat artificially on Gibraltar) and Caribou. It is easy to think that other parts of the world have a far more exciting fauna than Europe has (or had) but a visit to the Norfolk Park will show just how rich the European assortment is (or should be).

The feeling in the park is of large lawns sprink-

On 9 September 1976 the Otter Trust's location at Earsham was formally opened. Its 27 acres are almost entirely dedicated to the objectives of the Trust. These are to promote Otter conservation; to maintain a representative collection; to carry out breeding research; and to promote field studies.

Although the idea of such a Trust started in the early 1960s it was not actually initiated until 1971. Sixty acres near Hadleigh in Suffolk were bought where, or so it was hoped, the headquarters of the Trust would be situated. However, as stated in the Norfolk Wildlife Park's annual report for 1974, 'it became increasingly apparent that the Minister [for the Environment] would be unlikely to find in favour of the application, in view of the strenuous opposition of the Dedham Vale Society.' Philip Wayre, who had bought the property for the Trust, had to sell and find somewhere else. The story is important in showing that opposition groups, if sufficiently strident, can cause the stoppage not just of impending airports or nuclear plants but of charities dedicated to the peaceful pursuit of conserving Otters.

The Trust's current home is on the site of an old marsh farm near Bungay. It is bounded by the River Waveney, includes a lake of over three acres, a small stream (which conveniently flows

The European Otter – here a four-month-old cub with its mother – has only been bred in captivity in Britain seven times in the past 90 years, and every time by Philip Wayre in his Norfolk Wildlife Park. Now he and the Otter Trust have set up a separate establishment dedicated to Otter conservation.

through all the enclosures) and 15 acres of marsh. At present it is also home to 31 Otters – European, Eurasian, Indian Smooth-coated, Asian Small-clawed and North American. A public appeal for £66,000 raised £36,000 within six months, enough to allow the essentials – the paths, the chain link fencing with sheet steel overhang, the raised walkway for visitors, lavatories, shop, tea-room, gatehouse, heating for breeding dens and a parking area (for 400 cars).

Without doubt Earsham will be the major British establishment for the breeding of Otters, a feat very rarely achieved. In the Norfolk Wildlife Park, the other Wayre collection, the so-called Common Otter 'has been bred only seven times in captivity in Britain in the last 90 years, each time in the Park'. This success, and similar success with other Otter species at the Norfolk Park, occurred even though the area was not planned, as at Earsham, specifically for the subfamily *Lutrinae*. There are 18 distinct kinds of Otter in the world, and the Trust has no plans for restricting

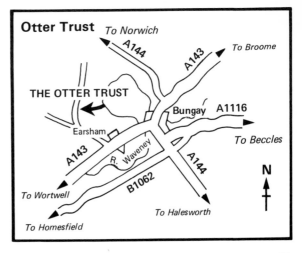

99

itself to the local or easily accessible varieties.

Otters, unlike Monkeys, great carnivores, or even fish, are not particularly good animals for viewing. Their most striking antics are below the water-line. To breed they like to retreat into their holt and do not welcome disturbance. The young do not leave this retreat until they are eight weeks old. They do not swim until they are ten weeks, and so people do not see much of them in those important, box-office, early days. However, one Earsham Otter, Kate, brought out her cubs and even suckled them in view of batteries of photographers, a very rare (and laudable) event.

Nevertheless, despite the fundamental Otter drawbacks, and being just one kind of animal, the auguries are that Earsham will be successful. On opening Sunday there were over 900 visitors. Three Sundays later the figure was 997. Such figures are most encouraging when all that is on view is five species of one kind of animal and 20 species of bird to keep them company. Perhaps people relish the conservation ideal behind the Trust. Perhaps they are growing weary of the normal zoo image, with rows of pens and rows of different animals. Or perhaps the Otter, as Gavin Maxwell and Henry Williamson discovered so capably, does have a very special appeal all of its very own.

Peakirk

Address	Peterborough, Northants
Telephone	Peterborough (0733) 252 271
Open	All year except 24 and 25 December 09.30–18.30 or 15 minutes after sunset if earlier. Grounds may close 1 hour earlier in spring and autumn on weekdays. Admission up to 1 hour before closing
Acreage	16
Station	Peterborough (8 miles)
Facilities	Guide book and information leaflet Guided tours (schools) Self-service cafeteria (summer) Picnic area Gift shop
Feeding	With wholemeal bread

Whereas Slimbridge is large, being the headquarters of the Wildfowl Trust, the collection at Peakirk is more intimate and can be equally rewarding in its own relaxed manner. Just as the Severn Estuary, broad and brown, is a bit of Britain that should be seen, so is the Fen district, with dykes flowing through a flatness quite unlike anywhere else. The Waterfowl Gardens at Peakirk were fashioned from an osier bed that lay right across the old Car Dyke, a principal water-

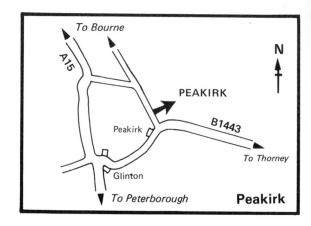

way of Roman Britain. Therefore, as a home for waterfowl, it has not so much been manufactured as amended from the past.

There are 85 species of bird and 650 individuals in this branch of the Wildfowl Trust. Most of them are Swans, Geese and Ducks, but there is also a good flock of Chilean Flamingos. Particular breeding successes here have been with Trumpeter Swans, who do bugle most excellently for fortunate visitors. Officially endangered species at Peakirk are the Hawaiian Goose (a bird whose name is now more synonymous with Slimbridge than Hawaii, owing to the rescue and breeding operation carried out in Gloucestershire), Cape Barren Goose, Laysan Teal (another from the Hawaiian group of islands), and White-winged Wood Duck. Other rarities include the Red-breasted Goose (which is becoming a kind of painted symbol of the Wildfowl Trust) and the Marbled Teal.

Peakirk receives about 50,000 visitors a year, as against four times that number at Slimbridge. It is neither a refuge, like the Trust's other establishments, nor a spot for scientific research. Instead it is primarily a place for breeding wildfowl and for human recreation, a honey-pot, an area where we can be drawn agreeably into assisting the Trust's aims, either immediately through our pockets or more indirectly through enthusiasm acquired during a Peakirk afternoon. Certainly, it is very pleasant to stroll through this place. There are lots of unassuming pools and fences beneath well-established ash and much new willow. The collection has scope, one suspects, for boring children, in that there are no concessions to their normal passions, but this is another way of saying that adults can find it to be gentle, sympathetic and most restful. Perhaps the children will be satisfied with feeding the birds – with wholemeal bread only.

Opposite The Trumpeter Swan is the rarest (7000 individuals), heaviest (up to 27 lb) and the blackest billed of all the Swans, as the colour leads all the way up to the eye. Two Trumpeters at Peakirk.

Penscynor Wildlife Park

Address	Cilfrew, nr Neath, West Glamorgan
Telephone	Neath (0639) 2189
Open	All year 10.00–18.00 or dusk if earlier
Acreage	16
Station	Neath (2 miles)
Facilities	Guide book and information leaflet Lectures Restaurant (summer); snack bar and kiosk Picnic area Gift shop
Other	Aquarium Pets' corner Playground Woodland walk
Shows	Sealions fed 12.00 and 16.15; Penguins fed 15.30; Pelicans fed 16.00; paddock animals fed 16.15
Feeding	Trout, Llamas, Donkeys only, with purchased food

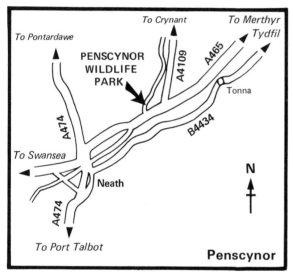

Penscynor

Having travelled the world filming animals Mr Idris Hall knew precisely what he wanted. He wished for a beautiful piece of Britain where exotic animals could be as free as possible and where people would be refreshed by seeing both the creatures and their situation. Therefore in 1966 he bought Penscynor on the slopes of a wooded valley at the opening of the Vale of Neath. He began filling its 11 acres (5 more were added later) with animals and in 1971 opened it to the rest of us. It now possesses 23 kinds of mammal, 165 of bird, 3 of reptile, 1 of amphibia, 28 of fish and 4 invertebrates, all of which add up to 605 individuals (and therefore an average of two to three per species).

If anything the birds are even more resplendent than the other animals and certainly they have some excellent opportunities (tropical house, walk-through aviary, glass-sided Penguin pool) for showing off their merits. Rare ones include Rothschild's Amazon Parrot, Hyacinthine Macaw (the most brilliant of all the Macaws), Duyvenbode's Lory, Sonnerat's Jungle Fowl, Turquoisine and Splendid Grass Parrakeet (Parrakeets are a speciality of Mr Hale's) and Rothschild's Mynah. Particularly splendid is the Great Indian Hornbill which virtually has the run of the place.

The major group animals are Sika Deer, De Brazza Monkeys, Woolly Monkeys, Mayotte Brown Lemurs, Humboldt's Penguins and Chilean Flamingos. There are also some particular characters about the place, apart from Joey the Hornbill, such as Cosmo the Gibbon, Jacko the Cockatoo, Happy the Penguin and Percy the Pelican.

The park is blessed not only with excellent scenery but a superb stream running through it which spills, at one point, over a 40-foot waterfall. Its water is used lavishly within the zoo and the Trout in one of the many pools are allowed to be fed by visitors (as are Llamas and Donkeys in their areas). There are none too many good animal collections in Wales. It is therefore doubly delightful that, when one exists, it is as excellent as the one at Penscynor.

Port Lympne Wildlife Sanctuary and Gardens

Address	Hythe, Kent
Telephone	Hythe (0303) 60618/9
Open	All year 10.00–18.00 or dusk
Acreage	280
Station	Westernhangar (3 miles) or Sandling (4 miles)
Facilities	Guide book and information leaflet Self-service cafeteria Picnic area Gift shop
Others	Port Lympne House and grounds Nature trail and woodland walk

The Port Lympne Wildlife Sanctuary and Gardens is complementary to Howletts Zoo Park. Both are the property of John Aspinall and both, in their different fashions, have permitted a few of his dreams to become reality. Each has features not possessed by the other and, as a pair, they make a partnership of outstanding merit in the zoo-keeping world.

The crucial distinctions at Port Lympne are that it has more space (280 acres as against 55 at

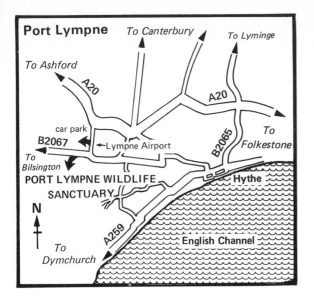

Port Lympne

To Canterbury
To Lyminge
To Ashford
A20
A20
car park
B2067
To
Folkestone
←Lympne Airport
B2065
To
Bilsington
PORT LYMPNE WILDLIFE
SANCTUARY
Hythe
N
To
Dymchurch
A259
English Channel

Howletts), that it possesses a house of considerable interest to visit and that its gardens match the house in quality. It is not a traditional stately home, with an estate cared for over the centuries (as with some of the safari parks), but a creation of this century. Nevertheless, its location is superb, the area has been magnificently exploited and includes a wonderful amphitheatre of land. There are views over the flat countryside lying to the south, over Dungeness and the Channel to France. The setting, as with Whipsnade, is half the excitement of being in such a place.

Port Lympne's theme is the presentation of rare animals in spacious surroundings. To this end there are African Honey Badgers, Siberian and Indian Tigers, Barasingha Deer (a rare form from southern Asia), Indian Buffalo (with a vast paddock to run and frisk about in), Sable and Roan Antelope, Black Rhino, Przewalski's Horse, Cheetah, Black (or Melanistic) Leopard, Wapiti, Hunting Dog, American Bison, Brazilian Tapir and Eland. Some are rare, others less so, but the surroundings are as spacious as those found anywhere in Britain. The Sables, for example, have 15 acres in which to graze, gallop and look quite excellent.

However nice a place may be at the beginning, many a wildlife park has destroyed much of that excellence in catering for its animals. There seem to be fences everywhere, notice-boards, hunks of concrete, pipes, electric wiring, kiosks, car parks, huts, and all the other nuts and bolts involved in keeping animals apart from people. At Port Lympne there has not been such savagery. The fences tend to follow the lie of the land. They are often of handsome wood rather than wire (even though it is more expensive, less practical and often less effective). Many of the animal sleeping quarters manage to look extremely ancient ('But

you are so lucky to have gotten these old sheds,' said an American, admiring a structure erected 12 months beforehand) and their roofs are often covered with turf, good for insulation (cool in summer, warm in winter) and certainly pleasing to the eye. Even the concrete, that practical, inexpensive and foul material, has been dyed brown on a stairway, a cheap but thoughtful improvement for those places where concrete has to be.

Inevitably, with such a big area, there is a lot of walking to do, and the recommended route round the estate is two-and-a-half-miles long. Cars are not allowed and wheel- or pushchairs will encounter difficulty in certain sections. As most of the visitors to this very new establishment are local, who are expected to come again and again, they will spread the word about the exceptional and scattered merits of Port Lympne. However, all locals will know about that view to the Channel and how it will refresh those for whom two-and-a-half miles may be a long walk.

There is also the house and garden. There are 12 acres of garden, and the plan is to make it the finest in Kent within five years. This will be a major feat in itself as the place had been allowed to decay for 40 years, but considerable planting has been carried out (many trees, plus 4500 plants in borders 18 feet wide, assisted by a few tons of Elephant dung). There is one mile of hedges, the only terraced vineyard in England, a clock garden, a grotto (which is to be a 'very smart' tea area), a superb display of Catalpa trees, and a magnificent flight of steps.

The house was described by *Country Life* as the 'most historic country house built this century'. Finished in 1920, it was the home of Sir Philip Sassoon and a great place for the famous to spend weekends between the wars. Built in the Cape Dutch style, its outside gives little hint of the variety within – a Rex Whistler room, a Moorish colonnaded section, a flight of marble steps, and a 'Clemenceau library', which is a miniature of Oxford's Radcliffe Camera.

Both the house and garden will stay virtually free of animals and will therefore be separate attractions, but it is expected that 35 per cent of visitors will come because of the gardens, 7 per cent for the house, and the rest for the animals. Certainly all those weekenders of the 1920s and 1930s would be amazed at the turn of events. Sassoon died in middle age in the gloomy days at the start of the Second World War (he always did have an impeccable sense of timing, said Winston Churchill). The fun stopped most abruptly but has now started again after that lapse of four decades. May the Port Lympne Wildlife Sanctuary and Gardens be as magnificent as the estate used to be, now that it has been reborn in a superbly different guise!

Riber Castle Wildlife Park

Address	Matlock, Derbys
Telephone	Matlock (0629) 2073
Open	All year: summer 10.00–18.00; winter 10.00–16.00
Acreage	30
Station	Matlock (1 mile)
Facilities	Guide book and information leaflet Bar (summer); self-service cafeteria (closed winter weekdays); snack bar Picnic area Gift shop
Other	Riber Castle Pets' corner Playground Model railway MG car and motorbike collections Full-sized models of prehistoric animals Farm carts

It is easy to wonder when the trend began for animal collections to specialize in animals normally nearer at hand than, say, the traditional Lions and Tigers; but quite a few places in Britain now specialize in European fauna and have no truck with those whose normal homes are farther away. The Riber Castle Wildlife Park is one of these and, although there has been an occasional foreigner from time to time, the collection's theme since it opened in 1963 has been European Wildlife.

Currently there are about 40 species of mammal and 20 of bird. The mammals include European Lynx, four species of Deer, Otter, Wild Boar, Wild Cats, Polecats and Pine Martens. There are also Cattle, Horses, Sheep, Pigs and

Poultry as Riber Castle has been recognized by the Rare Breeds Trust as a Survival Centre.

The aviaries contain Owls, birds of prey, Pheasants, seabirds and waterfowl. It is always a pleasure when an animal collection bothers to include any invertebrates and Riber Castle possesses a Butterfly house where these insects are bred. The views from the picnic area and other parts of the park are particularly outstanding.

Slimbridge

Address	Slimbridge, Glos
Telephone	Cambridge (Glos) (045 389) 333
Open	09.30–17.30 or 15 mins after sunset in winter
Acreage	100 enclosed; refuge covers 443
Station	Stroud (12 miles)
Facilities	Guide book and information leaflet Lectures Guided tours (by appointment for educational parties) Licensed restaurant and self-service cafeteria, with children's menu Kiosk Picnic area Gift shop
Shows	Birds fed 16.30
Feeding	With own food

It was a pair of Lesser White-fronted Geese that did it. Peter Scott had visited Slimbridge before the Second World War and, in 1945, went back to see the place again. He wanted to find a suitable wildfowl area that might serve as a refuge and therefore satisfy his longings for such a place. He drove through Slimbridge village, over the canal on its far side and down towards the invisible Severn river. On and over the flat fields he counted seven kinds of Geese but it was the sudden arrival of the two Lesser White-fronts that equally abruptly made up his mind. This was the spot he had been looking for.

It is now the spot that hundreds of thousands of us have sought out in the past 30 years since its opening (in 1946). Estuarine locations, with flat fields and water never far below the surface, do not have the honey-pot appeal of, say, rolling hills or stately estates; but they do for wildfowl, and therefore we follow suit. About 175,000 of us go each year to the 443 acres of the Slimbridge refuge. One hundred of these acres are enclosed and have enabled Slimbridge to possess the world's largest and most varied collection of wildfowl.

Not every inhabitant is a Duck or a Goose. There are others, such as the 60–70 species in a tropical aviary who bear little relation to the family *Anatidae* honking and quacking outside, but the grand total of bird species amassed at Slimbridge is 189 with an even grander total of about 2500 individuals. Some stars among this collection include: Mrs Noah, the first Bewick's Swan to lay in captivity and still doing so aged 30; some Trumpeter Swans (presented to the Queen by the Canadian government) and their descendants; the largest flock of Hawaiian Geese in captivity; the winter flock of about 400 Bewick's Swans that come every year from Russia; and the breeding Flamingos. The somewhat contrary theme of the Slimbridge collection is wildfowl *and* Flamingos, although some authorities include the Flamingos in the same order, *Anseriformes*, that includes the Swans, Geese, Ducks and Screamers. Be that as it may, Slimbridge is the only place in the world where four Flamingo species breed (and no Flamingos were bred in Britain before 1965).

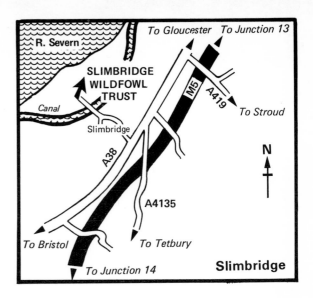

Its endangered species (as defined by the *Red Book*) are Cuban Whistling Duck, Hawaiian Geese, Aleutian Canada Geese, Cereopsis Geese, Mexican Duck, Hawaiian Duck, New Zealand Brown Teal and White-winged Wood Duck. Other rare species (as distinct from endangered) are the Spotted Whistling Duck, the Pink-eared Duck, the Musk Duck, and the Black-headed Duck (which behaves cuckoo-like, using the nests of others). On breeding wildfowl Slimbridge has an extraordinary record because over 100 different kinds have been reared including 15 for the first time anywhere in the world.

Slimbridge started with a 6d entrance fee (it is now £1) and with most of the attraction being the chance to see wild Geese with reasonable ease. That is still a major draw, notably in winter when the wild arrivals (probably) exceed the captive collection. In a severe season 8000 birds may fly in. This natural side of things is still being improved, both for the human visitors and the birds. In 1975 and 1976, for instance, the sea wall was raised by 18 inches. The necessary soil for this work was scraped from nearby areas which, when they fill with water, should attract more Ducks. There are large hides (all of them donated) from which people can watch the birds, and there are battleship-type binoculars to assist them.

Sir Peter Scott sees the Slimbridge function as being split between conservation, research, education and recreation (not necessarily in that or any other order). In a year 700 busloads of schoolchildren are brought to this remote spot in Gloucestershire. Considerable research is done; it is not just a mouthed platitude as so frequently

Peter Scott, founder of Slimbridge.

elsewhere. There is more of a feeling of reverence for the place, not detectable in every animal collection. There is also, no less crucial than every other attribute, a tremendous feeling of cash. Of course the gate collects quite a sum, and so does the restaurant, and the smart shop, but Slimbridge also gains handsomely from its many members and from legacies. Naturally it does not find any difficulty in spending the money – food alone costs £20,000 a year – but there is a prestige atmosphere to Slimbridge not encountered to

Midwinter at Slimbridge when large numbers of Swans, Geese and Ducks congregate, particularly if other areas are frozen.

the same degree in other animal places. It cannot be irrelevant either to the Wildfowl Trust (whose headquarters are at Slimbridge) or to many of its visitors that its patron is the Queen and its president is Prince Philip. Few conservation trusts up and down the country are so lavishly endowed.

Slimbridge is unique but has done its best to replicate itself. Since the Trust was founded in 1946 it has established other wildfowl conservation centres, notably Peakirk in Northamptonshire, Martin Mere in Lancashire, Washington in Tyne and Wear, and Arundel in West Sussex, and two important refuges (also open to general visitors), Welney in the Fens and Caerlaverock on the Solway Firth. At all of them (but read the respective pages) there is the same sense of privilege at seeing the sights they have to show. Perhaps this is caused by the most important patronage of all, namely that the birds themselves choose to fly in to them. To see great skeins of Geese circling over the River Severn after their journey south from farther north, and then to see them land in the Slimbridge fields, is to make each visitor intensely aware that he too has chosen wisely. It is a refuge both for the birds and for the people who have, for a day, got away

from the cities that are such a different kind of home.

Suffolk Wildlife and Country Park

Address	Grove Farm, Kessingland, Suffolk
Telephone	Lowestoft (0502) 740 291
Open	10.00–18.00 or 1 hr before dusk if earlier
Acreage	50
Station	Lowestoft (5 miles)
Facilities	Guide book and information leaflet Self-service cafeteria (Easter–October) Picnic area Gift shop Pushchairs and wheelchairs for hire
Other	Aquarium Pets' corner Playground Nature trail River walk
Feeding	Some animals, with bread only

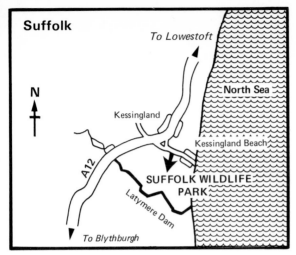

Suffolk

To Lowestoft

N

North Sea

Kessingland

Kessingland Beach

A12

SUFFOLK WILDLIFE PARK

Latymere Dam

To Blythburgh

In the flat low-lying country of eastern Suffolk, just to one side of the River Hundred and not too far from the sea at Kessingland, lies the Suffolk Wildlife and Country Park. This particular area, officially classified as one of outstanding natural beauty, is well suited for being the home of a mixed collection of wild animals. Its size means that there is plenty of good walking space, particularly down by the river.

The animals are tame, wild, small, large, home and foreign creatures. Among the birds are Peafowl, Flamingos, Crowned and Sarus Cranes, Rhea and Sacred Ibis. Among the waterfowl (and lakes for them are not difficult to excavate in such a landscape) are Swans, several kinds of

The Puma, or Mountain Lion, or Cougar, has a colossal range for a single species, as it lives all the way from Canada down to Tierra del Fuego.

Geese and many kinds of Duck. Many of the creatures wander at will within the park, such as Goats and Sheep. Other animals include Deer, several kinds of Monkey, Wallaby, Lion, Tiger, Puma, Wolf, Dingo, Squirrel (of three kinds), Raccoon and Civet Cat. There are also Parrots, Macaws, Budgerigars, Lovebirds, Cockatiels, Conures, Mynahs, Toucan, Penguins, Vultures, Owls and Hornbills.

Among the enclosures are a very small aquarium, a pets' corner, a Deer paddock and a walk-through aviary. Visitors are allowed to fish in the river (in season) and there is no difficulty in finding nice picnic sites within the park. It was opened in 1969.

Tropical Bird Gardens

Address	Rode, Bath, Avon
Telephone	Beckington (037 383) 326
Open	Summer 10.30–17.00 (last admission 18.30); winter 10.30–sunset
Acreage	17½
Station	Trowbridge (5 miles), Frome (5 miles)
Facilities	Guide book and information leaflet Self-service cafeteria, snack bar, kiosk (summer) Picnic area Gift shop Wheelchairs for hire
Other	Pets' corner Donkey rides Woodland walk Butterfly exhibition (summer)
Shows	Penguins fed 15.30

From Cranes to Waxbills, and from talking Hill Mynahs to all the relatively silent species, this is a collection emphatically dedicated to the birds. There are 1000 individuals here of some 185 species. The place was opened in 1962 as an all-bird zoo because, or so it was felt, the avian departments of many large zoos are generally overshadowed by the big mammals also in their possession. The gardens at Rode, in concentrating upon the birds, permit people really to look at them and not be distracted by louder, bigger, fiercer, stronger and funnier animals next door.

It is just six miles, as any crow would fly it, from these birds to the Longleat Lions, but just one such Lion caged here would have many of us rushing over to look, yet again, at this king of the box office. We would then be disregarding Long-tailed Glossy Starlings (a gorgeous blue), Virginian Cardinals (bright red), Napoleon Weavers (yellow and black), and Hunting Cissas (a strident green) all for the sake of one dun-coloured beast, being as energetic on a hot day as

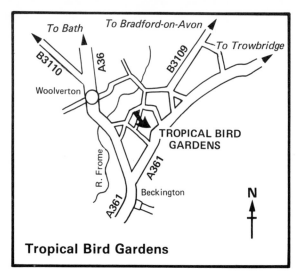

Tropical Bird Gardens

The grounds are extremely handsome, and thick with conifers, ornamental trees and shrubs. The place is what it says it is (a rare enough event) for its inhabitants are frequently tropical, they are birds almost entirely, and the gardens are undeniable.

Washington Wildfowl Refuge

Address	Middle Barmston Farm, District 15, Washington, Tyne and Wear
Telephone	Washington (0632) 465 454
Open	All year except 25 December: main winter months 09.30–16.30; rest of year 09.30–18.30, except June and August 09.30–21.00
Acreage	100
Station	Newcastle (7 miles), Durham (11 miles)
Facilities	Guide book and information leaflet Lectures (on request) and guided tours Refreshment room Vending machines Picnic areas Gift shop Pushchairs for hire
Other	Playground Woodland walk Nature trail
Shows	Main feed at 16.00 (15.00 winter)
Feeding	With purchased food

a moist rag. The only non-birds allowed into Rode are some pets' corner species – Guinea Pigs, Goats, Donkeys and Rabbits – and, for an exhibition of their own, Butterflies.

Birds fly here in amazing fashion. Wherever possible they are flying completely free, able to leave should they so wish, such as the Macaws (Blue and Yellow, Red and Yellow, and Green-winged). Many of the actual aviaries are huge, so that the birds within are flying as freely as possible. Birds – most of them – do fly, and this bird place is a flying place rather than a spot for hopping from perch to concrete to perch again. It is also a breeding place, claiming that it produces as many birds as it loses. Not every zoo is a net-producer of its stock, for more living animals usually enter their gates than leave them. The bird collections are generally worse, with many more living specimens entering than leaving, because they are cheaper to acquire than mammals, easier to import and harder to breed in zoo conditions. Therefore, it is all the more admirable if a place is self-supporting in its bird community. Not every species breeds but, if there are sufficient groups that do, the numbers overall will be satisfactory. At Rode the Penguins (Black-footed, or Cape, or Jackass), Ibis (Scarlet, Sacred), Macaws, Pheasants, Cockatoos, Parrots and Parakeets are particularly productive.

Species not mentioned so far include: Secretary Bird (a most striking bird of prey that eats even snakes); Flamingo (Chilean, Rosy); European Stork (breeding at Rode, but how wonderful if it would use our rooftops as well); Jay (Lanceol-ated, Lidith's, Pileated); Hornbill (Black-and-white Casqued, Pied, Giant, Cock Wreathed); Crane (Crowned, Demoiselle, Sarus); Spoonbill; Wild Turkey; Whydah (Paradise, Pintail); and many Ducks (Mandarin, Carolina, White-faced Tree, Pintail, Red-crested Pochard, Eider) and Geese (Barnacle, Emperor, Bar-headed).

From a Goose's point of view Washington is undoubtedly a refuge, but the birds have to make certain where and how they land. The neighbourhood is rich in industry, laced with roads and strung about electrically in a most stri-dent manner. A bird must aim carefully to reach the haven's one-sixth of a square mile on the north bank of the River Wear just three miles up from Sunderland. Nevertheless, many wild birds either on migration or looking for a winter's rest-ing place do make use of the refuge. People are then able to make use of them, watching at the feeder stations or by the 400-yard-long 'wader lake'. As at Slimbridge, the headquarters of the Wildfowl Trust which operates Washington, suitable hides have been built at appropriate spots.

There is also a captive population of 1200 Ducks, Geese and Swans representing 105 species. Some of these, however accustomed to the place, are not truly captive as they are full-winged and provide the additional spectacle of free-flight. Such groups include the flocks of Pin-tail Duck, and Greylag and Barnacle Geese. Among the captives – as is virtually obligatory for any Wildfowl Trust establishment – are some Hawaiian and Red-breasted Geese. Other prominent individuals include Snow Geese, Trumpeter Swans, Coscoroba Swans, Eider Ducks, Goosanders, and Hooded Mergansers.

This last bird is an American species. Various other North American wildfowl, such as Emperor Geese, have been gathered here to draw attention to the link between this part of the world and the first president of the United States. There are many Washington connections in the area and the wildfowl refuge has added to them in its distinctive fashion. The place was opened in 1975 and the 85 acres currently in use will soon be supplemented by a further 15. There were 19,000 visitors in the seven remaining months of its opening year, and 34,000 in 1976. Breeding at Washington has not been up to the Slimbridge standards but a new propagation house should improve the ratio of eggs laid to young birds successfully reared. Enteritis (probably carried by rodents), chilling and aspergillosis (a respiratory disease) provided the principal setbacks in the early days, but all three should be much reduced by the new house.

In one sense it is odd having a wildlife establishment surrounded by so much wire and industry. In another sense, particularly if it is seen on a day when skeins of birds are circling down to land there, the place appears as a most perfect form of refuge. So many nearby areas have been consumed, but this sanctuary is now assured.

Welney Refuge

Address	Pintail House, Hundred Foot Bank, Welney, Wisbech, Cambs
Telephone	Ely (0353) 860 711
Open	All year except 25 December
Acreage	679
Station	Littleport (8 miles)
Facilities	Guide book and information leaflet Guided tours Guided walk (summer) Pushchairs and wheelchairs for hire
Shows	Birds fed 16.00 (winter)

As only wild birds may be seen here it does not really merit inclusion in this book. But it is situated on 700 acres of the Ouse Washes, a vitally important area for wildfowl, and is just 24 miles and 45 minutes' drive from Peakirk, another wildfowl centre. Over 1000 Bewick's Swans winter at Welney, as well as tens of thousands of Duck. Summertime is good for flowers and for quite a different assortment of birds. There are several hides and an observatory from which to see the wildlife that also comes to Welney.

Birds flying in to the Washington Refuge must take care. It is the Wildfowl Trust establishment most surrounded by industry and most worthy of that name of refuge.

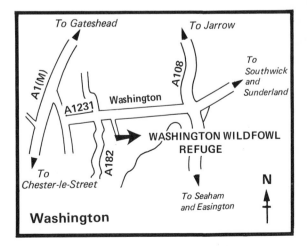

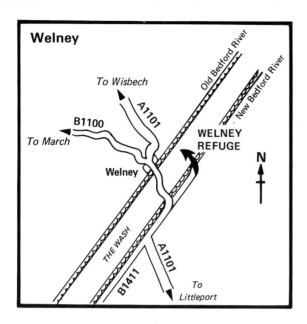

Welney

To Wisbech
B1100
To March
Welney
Old Bedford River
New Bedford River
A1101
WELNEY REFUGE
N
THE WASH
B1411
A1101
To Littleport

West Country Wildlife Park

Address	Cricket St Thomas, Chard, Somerset
Telephone	Winsham (046 030) 396
Open	All year 10.00–18.00
Acreage	40
Station	Crewkerne (5 miles)
Facilities	Guide book and information leaflet Guided tours (of farm) Restaurant with children's menu; self-service cafeteria; snack bar; kiosk (summer) Picnic area Gift and camera shops Pushchairs for hire
Other	Aquarium Pets' corner Playground Pony rides
Feeding	With purchased food

The West Country Wildlife Park, also known as Cricket St Thomas and more affectionately referred to as Cricket (it has nothing to do with the game, but means 'little hill'), is among the most fortunate of all the wildlife country parks in its setting. The inevitable house (built in 1804 by Sir John Soane) is modest, handsome and with all sorts of naval affiliations – the Hoods lived here – but its supreme splendour is the land that it overlooks. The gardens are excellent, the trees magnificent and the view down to the valley is without its parallel in any animal country park. In all of this the wildlife has been amassed to increase and not detract from the original splendour.

In a book about Cricket it is written that: 'Most wild-life parks or animal collections have one of three head-start advantages: either they have some stately patronage – a name like Bedford, or a "home" like Woburn or Longleat; or they have associations with a famous zoological name like Durrell or Scott or Chipperfield; or they have some firm financial footing. "Cricket – the West Country Wild Life Park" started out with none of these.' Be that as it may, the place shows no sign of having missed out. Without a big name, or a big house or (apparently) big money, it is undeniably a big success and a big attraction.

That view across the valley is remarkable. At the bottom is a stream, dammed with weirs to make nine lakes and waterfalls. On both sides of it, and in the water, are animals that look entirely appropriate, Llamas, Deer, Wapiti, Flamingos, Ducks, Geese and Sealions. Needless to say, there are plenty of spots from which to watch the tranquillity of this scene. There are, for example, the Magnolia Walk, the Lavender Walk and the Long Walk to stroll along, all designed generations ago to look over the scene, however much the exotic creatures had not by then arrived.

Once again a walled garden is a high spot of a stately home. Originally designed for vegetables and fruit it is now no less rich with strange fauna as against the more prosaic flora there used to be. Creatures to be found at Cricket (some of them within those walls) include Leopards and Pumas, Civet Cats, Lynxes and Caracals, Raccoons and Coatis, many kinds of Monkey, Otters and Marmots, Fish Eagles and Vultures, Owls and Pheasants, dozens of smaller birds in a Tropical House, Peccary and Wallaby, Porcupines and Penguins, and various Deer, such as Sika, Wapiti and Red. The Indian Elephants, Twiggy and Chiki, do not have a very satisfactory enclosure (as compared with those of many other inmates) but do go down to a lake from time to time to bathe. The Elephant yard is reached through a grotto-type tunnel allegedly possessing Bats as well as small aquaria let into the wall. On a recent visit the fish tanks were clearly visible but, sadly, not a Bat.

There is no point in a car at Cricket, save for reaching the place. However, as it is near nowhere in particular, being between Chard and Crewkerne, and roughly equidistant from Bristol, Bournemouth and Torquay, there is a large parking area to accommodate visitors who arrive via the estate drive at the rear end of the house and gardens. The owners' expressed aim is 'to provide a comprehensive collection of animals and birds which will live in relative harmony together in this picturesque valley using the natural resources of the lakes, and sheltered woodland, and to pro-

Above and *right* The West Country Wildlife Park, also known as Cricket St Thomas, has made excellent use of a beautiful estate. It almost seems as if such places had animals in mind when they were originally designed.

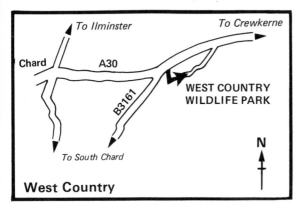

COLLARED PECCARY
Tayassu Tajacu
THE WILD BOAR OF THE NEW WORLD,
LIVING IN LARGE HERDS & FEEDING
ON FRUIT, ROOTS, SEEDS,
LIZARDS ETC.

vide an enjoyable and peaceful day out for our visitors. . . .' Not every intention elsewhere is vindicated by events, but the Cricket aim has been most faithfully followed. To sit looking at that string of lakes, with a Buzzard flying overhead (they are common in the area) and a happy mixture of home and foreign animals in, under and above the trees, is to feel that aimed-for peace with gratitude.

There is a tale, in the book (by Peter Spence) already quoted, most worthy of a second telling. The local stationmaster, impressed by a parcel of maggots labelled 'Urgent', asked the reason for their urgency. 'We're starting a wildlife park,' came the reply. There was silence as the information was absorbed. Eventually the stationmaster spoke again. 'Starting a bit small, aren't you, sir?' Maybe Cricket did start small, but it has grown most excellently since it began one summer's day in 1967.

Weyhill European Wildlife Park

Address	Weyhill, nr Andover, Hants
Telephone	Weyhill (026 477) 2252
Open	Summer 10.30–18.00; winter 10.30–16.00
Acreage	15
Station	Andover Junction (5 miles)
Facilities	Information leaflet Lectures (schools) Snack bar (summer) Picnic area Gift shop
Other	Pets' corner Donkey rides Countryside museum
Shows	Seals fed 16.00 Birds of Prey demonstrations on fine Sunday afternoons only

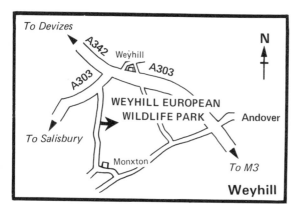

Lying on the gentle slope of a hill this collection is largely of European mammals and birds. The enclosures are mostly extremely simple, permitting a degree of access and of familiarity not possible in more formal establishments. The largest animals are Brown Bears, Seals, and Red, Fallow, Sika and Muntjac Deer. Other mammals are Otters, Badgers, Monkeys, Foxes, Lynx, Wild Cat, and a few of the cosier kinds, such as Rabbit, Guinea Pig and Goat.

Birds of prey are a speciality here. Not only are they being bred quite successfully, but the flying displays of several kinds of bird have considerable appeal. Afterwards, for those photographers who may have missed the bird in action, a closer (and easier) shot may be obtained of the same bird resting on the falconer's arm. There is a vagueness to this zoo that can attract, a lack of jostling making it most suitable for a day with a sketchpad. The place resembles a hobby that has spread to a neighbouring field rather than anything more severe and better planned.

With equal casualness are old agricultural carts, the snack bar, a museum, other animals, a traction engine, some birds, and perhaps a Heron dropping in from a nearby stream to keep them company. The rigid kind of zoo forbids all feeding of animals, and also discourages contact between visitors and visited; but at Weyhill, with proper produce for sale at the entrance kiosk, it is perfectly easy to distribute food correctly. Young people may find this place more to their liking than bigger establishments, and 40,000 of all kinds visited it in 1976.

Whipsnade Park

Address	Dunstable, Beds
Telephone	Whipsnade (0582) 872 171
Open	All year except 25 December 10.00–19.00 or sunset if earlier
Acreage	500
Station	Luton (7 miles)
Facilities	Guide book and information leaflet Lectures (for schools, through Regent's Park) Bar and snack bar (summer); self-service cafeteria with children's menu and kiosk Picnic area Gift and camera shops Pushchairs for hire
Other	Children's zoo Dolphinarium Pony, Camel and Llama rides Pony traps Playground Steam train through some exhibits (all summer and most winter weekends)
Shows	Sealions, Lions, Tigers, Penguins, fed during afternoon Dolphin shows in summer, training sessions during winter, at intervals throughout day

The idea and then the fulfilment of the Whipsnade idea were both magnificent. The man to push them through was Sir Peter Chalmers Mitchell, Secretary of the Zoological Society of London from 1905 to 1935. He had increased the annual attendance at Regent's Park from 700,000 to two million but had always been in favour of more fresh air and open space for animals, particularly since he had seen the earlier pioneering efforts of Carl Hagenbeck at Hamburg. Before his time the general feeling was that exotic animals should be kept in hot (and therefore poorly ventilated) conditions. It was revolutionary to

Opposite The sense of space at Whipsnade was revolutionary when it opened in 1931. Current animals on view include Thomson's Gazelle (*above*) and Jaguar (*below*).

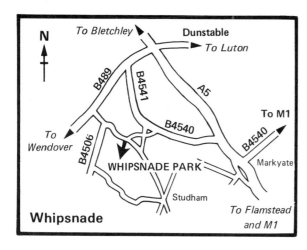

Whipsnade

Whipsnade was the first British zoo to breed
White Rhino

wish to put them out-of-doors and Whipsnade,
when it came about, was a revolution in animal
management.

The site chosen (in 1927) for this important
turn-about was a run-down, 500-acre farm high
up in the Chilterns 35 miles north-west of London. There were supreme views over the countryside, considerable landscaping possibilities (by
burrowing into the chalk) and an area over 20
times larger than the confines of Regent's Park.
Opening day was planned for 1931 and in the
zoo's annual report for the depression year of
1930 it was written:

The scheme under which the Ministry of Labour sup-
plied 150 men from distressed areas has worked to the
satisfaction of the Ministry and to the advantage of the
Society. The Ministry paid three-quarters of the
cost. . . . The men were changed at intervals of two

months; with a very few exceptions they improved very rapidly in health. . . . During the year over three miles of internal roads have been made and footpaths got ready. Four chalk-pits have been excavated, the material being used for road-making . . . every effort is being made to preserve and improve the natural amenities of a very beautiful district. . . . It is hoped that it will attract not only those interested in animals but the even greater numbers of the public who take pleasure in the beauties of rural England.

Came the day, 23 May 1931. Perhaps the zoo authorities, even though they had been in the business then for over a century, had underestimated the numbers of people who wanted to see the animals. Or perhaps everyone really did flock to see a bit of rural England. At all events they flocked. On 26 May the *Morning Post* declared: 'Whipsnade Besieged. Overwhelming rush of people to the new open-air zoo. Traffic facilities break down. Railway bookings from London to Luton cancelled. For the first time for many years, railway bookings from London were suspended by order of the police authorities. . . .' Whipsnade had indeed got off to a dramatic start. There was not to be similar traffic trouble caused by animals for another 35 years, not until the car queues formed on the roads leading to Longleat and its Lions.

Whipsnade is now approaching its fiftieth anniversary. So how has it fared, particularly in view of the competition from all the other open-air country zoos now in being? On visitors it still does fairly well, with 450,000 a year – or about half the number achieved by the Woburn Wild Animal Kingdom just down the road. On layout, landscaping, paddocks and cages it is pretty much as it was all those years ago. There have been changes but, like many a city zoo, it is showing some signs of age. Similarly, as with any pioneer, the open-air ideas have been overtaken in more recent years by those other country establishments that have arisen since that crowded opening day. The Lion and Tiger cages must have been magnificent then, but they now look like large cages. Better views of Lions can be had in every safari park. On the other hand the Bear pits must have been less appealing even in their heyday. The views, of course, are still superb, with gliders swooping overhead from the nearby club and with that 161-yard-long lion cut from the turf as noble as ever.

Walking round Whipsnade can become wearisome, and the winds can blow sharply over those Downs, but the prime purpose of the place was to make a better place for animals. In that it has succeeded triumphantly. It is easy not to admire the iron-work surrounding the big enclosures of the larger carnivores, but in 1931 there was considerable iron-work surrounding the small enclosures of virtually every inhabitant of Regent's Park. Space, air, healthier circumstances and better breeding possibilities were the original and novel keynotes to Whipsnade. They still are, and have brought a rich return. Eighty per cent of the mammals now resident at Whipsnade were born there, an excellent record.

Particularly excellent have been the Cheetah and White Rhino successes. There is an anomaly with Cheetahs: they are about the easiest of all cats to tame and the most difficult to breed. Although kept in captivity for centuries they were generally reckoned to be non-breeders in zoos until 1956 when three were born in Philadelphia. Unfortunately they died, and not until 1966 did any captive Cheetah offspring survive. One year later the Whipsnade Cheetah Juanita produced three cubs successfully and followed this litter with others. By 1976, a mere ten years after the first Cheetah breeding, 37 had been born and litters have even been born to Whipsnade-born parents. No news, one feels, would have given Sir Peter Chalmers Mitchell greater pleasure.

White Rhinos are the second success story. In the 1920s only 30 of these remained in South Africa and not many more elsewhere on the continent. The Natal National Park did sterling work building up their numbers, then sending them as re-stocking units to others parts of Africa and finally deciding that zoos could help with this work. Whipsnade was selected as the first conservation centre outside Africa for the White Rhino (not white in colour, but grey, and probably a corruption of the Dutch word for wide (*weit*) which certainly applies to the broad, grazing type of mouth possessed by this species). In 1970 the Chilterns suddenly became home to 20 such Rhinos, and the first calf was born only a few months later. As the gestation period is 18 months it had been conceived in Africa, but the herd has been breeding well ever since.

The world's first captive breeding of a Warthog was achieved in 1957 at Whipsnade, which has also been the first British zoo to breed White-tailed Deer, Snow Leopards and Moose (as well as those Cheetahs and White Rhinos). No less satisfactory is the fact that in 1957 and again in 1973 four Père David's Deer calves were sent to China, their original home and the place where they became extinct at the turn of the century. Whipsnade keeps the Père David's register of the 600 individuals now in existence throughout the world.

A safari park may possess only 20 mammal species. Regent's Park's total is nearer 200. Whipsnade is intermediate between park and zoo, possessing 72 kinds of mammal, 133 of bird, and 4 of reptile. Its endangered species, as defined by the *Red Book* of endangered wildlife, are Polar

A pair of baby Alligators.

Bear, Tiger, Przewalski's Horse, White Rhino, Black Rhino, Pygmy Hippo, Père David's Deer, European Bison and Scimitar-horned Oryx. Its other rare animals are the Rosy (three were bred for the first time in 1971) and Chilean Flamingos, Cereopsis Geese and Manchurian Cranes. There is a dolphinarium, built in 1972, and a steam train (called the Umfolozi Railway after the place the Rhinos came from) that in particular goes past the White Rhino herd. A notable feature of Whipsnade, ever since the beginning, has been the free roaming of some of its inmates among the visitors. These animals now include Peafowl, Muntjac Deer (originally from India but also wild in Britain), Turkeys (the name first applied to Guinea Fowl which were wrongly thought to have come from Turkey, but today's Turkeys are from North America), Wallabies, Chinese Water Deer and Indian Jungle Fowl.

The children's zoo is a genuine small people's zoo, and is not a pets' corner into which a miscellaneous bunch of creatures, tame and fierce, has been deposited for convenience. At Whipsnade are Ponies, small Donkeys, Fawns, Bushbabies, Chicks, Terrapins, Guinea Pigs, Goats, Mice and Rabbits. Most of the creatures are strokable but the population changes all the time. Coaches are not allowed in the park, but cars are at extra cost. Unless the day is cold or wet, or there is repeated need of things, it is just as well to leave the car outside the entrance in the large car park.

When Whipsnade was first built they made the overhang on the periphery fence face inwards to help keep the animals in. They then had to re-do that fence, putting the overhang facing outwards,

to keep out the Bedfordshire wild animals which had learned how to climb into the new zoo park. It must have been expensive but the idea of creatures climbing into a zoo has a pleasing ring to it. So does much of the Whipsnade story, the idea itself, its fulfilment, its wide open spaces, its breeding record, and its current success – despite all the competition sprung up on every side.

Zoo Park (Twycross) Ltd

Address	Twycross, nr Atherstone, Warwicks
Telephone	Twycross (0827) 880 250
Open	Summer 10.00–18.00; winter 10.00–dusk
Acreage	80 in all; 30 zoo development
Station	Nuneaton (11 miles), Tamworth (9 miles)
Facilities	Guide book and information leaflet Educational guided tours, lectures and trail Bar (winter); self-service cafeterias, snack bar and kiosks (summer) Picnic area Gift shop
Other	Pets' corner Donkey rides
Shows	Feeding times announced over loudspeaker system

A deaf visitor would miss much of his or her day out at Twycross for here is a whooping and a honking that is virtually continuous. There is also considerable movement. The Gibbons leap, from swing to swing to swing. The Monkeys climb, up, down, round, and back again. Not every zoo is either a loud or an active place; but Twycross is not like every zoo.

There are many differences. For one thing it is run by two women. For another it is not near anywhere in particular, and looks a little like an urban zoo set in the countryside. It specializes determinedly in primates and, although there are Lions and Tigers, Elephants and Giraffes, it is the Monkeys and Apes that dominate the place. They live, in the main, on grass, another distinctive and most attractive feature. Twycross may be near nowhere in particular, save for Market Bosworth, Measham and Ashby de la Zouch, but people know a good thing when they see or hear of one, and about 430,000 find their way to this zoo every single year.

As befits a primate collection the three Great Apes are all here, the Chimpanzees, Orange-utans (both species have bred here) and Gorillas, which have yet to do so, even though they are mature. The Ape enclosures are large, and there are trees to climb, but the adults do not seem to attract

Above A family of Proboscis Monkeys, which live wild only in Borneo.

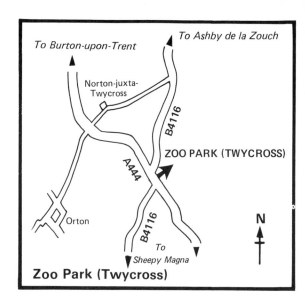

The Twycross primate collection is the best in Britain. *Above* Molly Badham, who wanted to keep Monkeys properly, and has succeeded admirably.

A small Squirrel Monkey from Amazonia (and Twycross): 'If you see me out of my pen – please do not report me.'

A Spider Monkey, also from South America.

the crowds as do the Gibbons and Monkeys over the way. Perhaps the noises attract, or the activ-ity, or the fact that so many Monkeys in so many other places look dismal and the Twycross lot do not. Certainly, there are many primates to choose from. There are Squirrel Monkeys, with the young squeezing through the wire mesh to climb about externally. There are Uakaris, shaggily dressed, short-tailed, red-faced, and not the most handsome of beasts, but none the less appealing. The Proboscis Monkeys would also win few conventional prizes, for a pendulous nose that only straightens when its possessor shouts is a feature of the oddest kind, but the Twycross group of these Monkeys is the only one in Britain.

There are also Woolly Monkeys, Spider Monkeys, Ring-tailed Lemurs, Silvery Marmosets, Howler Monkeys (aptly named as, so it is said

and so it is readily believed, they can be heard a mile away), Douc Langurs (another rarity in zoos), Silvered Leaf Monkeys, Spectacled Langurs (Twycross had the first British birth of this species), De Brazza Monkeys (looking like patriarchs with their white beards), Colobus Monkeys (whose excellent coats have often singled them out for destruction), Pileated Gibbons, Siamang Gibbons (another splendidly noisy group), Cotton Top Tamarins (or Cotton-headed, so some say) and Diana Monkeys. Whichever and whatever you remember longest, whether that proboscis, the red face or the gymnastics of the Gibbons, it will be impossible to forget the Twycross primates. Their grass is particularly important. This zoo was the first to keep Monkeys on it, against advice from die-hard sages who warned of the disease it would harbour, but the animals

here have thrived on it. Parasites have not been a problem and grass is of far greater interest to captive Monkeys than that tedious alternative, a concrete slab.

Other animals here include Cheetah, Leopard, Cuscus (in the spotted version of this Australian Opossum only the male possesses spots), Tree Hyrax (whose extraordinary call is one of the most hysterical of night cries), Camel, Llama, Alpaca, Brazilian and Malayan Tapir (similar to each other in outline but not in colouring), Otter, Capybara, Giant Anteater (also rarely seen in zoos, but enormously worth the seeing), birds of prey (including some excellent Vultures), and many flightless birds. The Twycross total is 50 species of mammal (and 240 individuals), 66 species of bird (236 individuals), 33 species of reptile (82 individuals), and 3 species of amphibian (with 9 individuals).

There was no long-range planning in the creation of this zoo. Its two principal partners owned rival pet-shops in Sutton Coldfield and they met at dog shows. They acquired one or two primates in the early 1950s, and then rather more as time went on. Advertising films helped to bring in necessary money, and in 1963 there was sufficient to buy one house and 22 acres, the central nucleus of the Twycross Zoo. In the first season 140,000 came to see the animals on show, and the collection has steadily grown along with the numbers of visitors. It was never anybody's

There is a whooping and a shouting at Twycross that is a joy to see and hear. It is the Gibbons who dominate this collection.

intention that the zoo should be as big as it is today. It just grew. However, whatever its humble beginnings and whatever its primary intent, it is now one of the best zoos in the country and houses the finest collection of primates. The major urban zoos have been going for a century or more but they could learn a lot from the youngster that has suddenly sprung up just because two women found themselves looking after Monkeys and wished to do so properly.

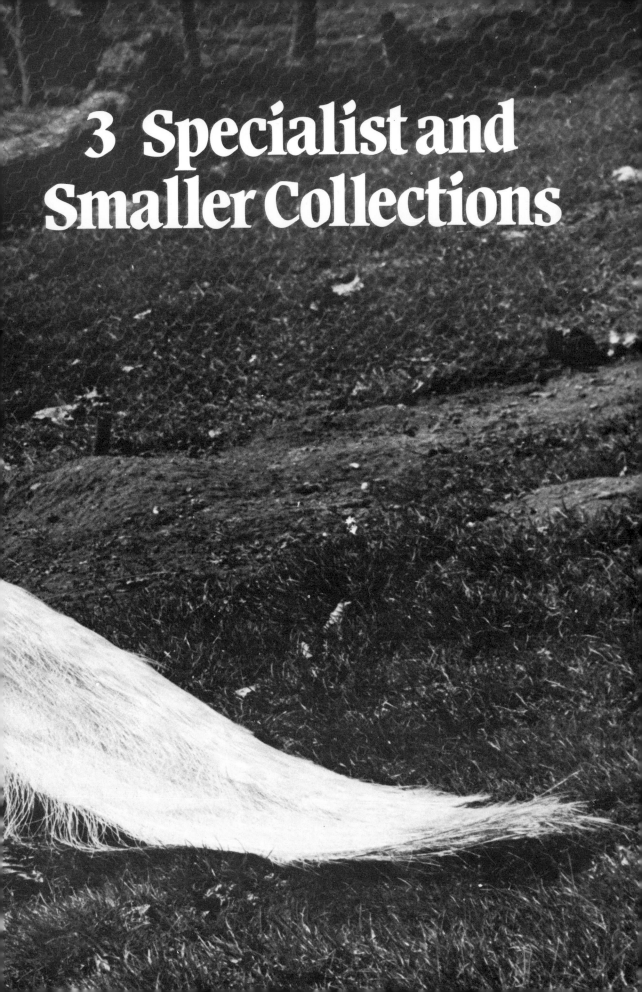

3 Specialist and Smaller Collections

Ambleside Water Gardens and Aviaries

Address	Lower Weare, Axbridge, Somerset
Telephone	Axbridge (0934) 732 362
Open	Summer: Tuesday–Saturday 10.30–18.30; Sunday 14.00–18.30
Acreage	1½
Access	On N side of A38 at W end of village of Lower Weare, 1½ miles from Axbridge
Station	Weston-super-Mare (8 miles)
Facilities	Kiosk; (café immediately outside)

A lake covers much of the acreage here, and a quantity of waterfowl cover the lake. In the gardens is a walk-through aviary. Birds here include Touracos, Glossy Starlings, Rosellas and Parakeets; and there are a few small mammals.

Animal Land

Address	Stapleford Park, nr Melton Mowbray, Leics
Telephone	Wymondham (057 284) 245
Open	Early April–September 10.00–18.30
Acreage	1
Access	Turn S off B676 Melton Mowbray (5 miles W) to Saxby (1 mile NE) road
Station	Melton Mowbray (5 miles)
Facilities	Guide book and information leaflet Licensed restaurant; self-service cafeteria; snack bar and kiosk Picnic area Gift shop including African curios
Other	Stapleford House Passenger-carrying miniature railway 12.00–18.00 Miniature liners on lake Children's amusements Crazy golf

In 1976 the Lions were withdrawn from the Stapleford Lion and Game Reserve. They had been installed when the drive-through reserve was opened in 1968, just two years after Longleat's safari opening. Now, perhaps as an indication that the species is not what it used to be, they have gone. What is left is Animal Land and, initially at least, an awful lot of fencing.

A small zoo was started in 1974 to supplement the drive-through Lion and Monkey areas. It was designed to attract children, and possesses modest enclosures for a fairly standard set of animals. There are Rhesus Monkeys (which are breeding well), Bears, Wolves, Pumas, Dingoes, a Chimpanzee named Joe, Macaques, Tortoises, Guinea Pigs, Budgerigars, Cassowary, Porcupines, Fantailed Pigeons, Goats (which are not living on concrete), Conures, Parakeets and many other birds. There are plans for expanding the zoo, but at present there are 27 resident mammal species and 32 kinds of bird.

Animal Land is just one of several sources of entertainment grouped round a large car park area. For many the principal attraction of Stapleford lies in its magnificent 10¼-inch gauge railway, which takes passengers on a round trip of two-and-a-half miles into stations, through a tunnel, over proper points and down to the lakeside where there are two passenger-carrying model liners. For others the 800-acre estate may be the main attraction or the Stapleford mansion (started in 1500 and beautifully added to in later years). On the other hand, if Lions still attract and must be seen, there are two or three inside Animal Land as remnants of the pride that, for eight years, brought in the crowds to Stapleford.

Appleby Castle

Address	Appleby, Cumbria
Telephone	Appleby (0930) 51402
Open	May–September every weekday except Monday
Acreage	25
Access	To W of A66 Penrith to Brough road, and W of River Eden, on SW side of town
Station	Appleby (1½ miles)
Facilities	Guide book and information leaflet Guided tours (by arrangement) Kiosk Picnic area Gift shop
Other	Appleby keep (Norman) Pets' corner Nature trail Woodland walk Kitchen garden

Appleby Castle collection is another whose theme is the conservation of rare domestic breeds. Its mammals include Donkey, Vietnamese Pig, Soay, St Kilda and Manx Loghtan Sheep, Bagot Goats, White Park Cattle and Shetland Ponies. Its birds, of which there are 50 species, include Pheasants (such as the rare Swinhoe's, Mikado and Cheer), Bantams and Owls, but the speciality of the place is waterfowl. Among the endangered species are Hawaiian Geese (which have bred) and Laysan Teal, but there are many other Ducks, Geese and Swans.

All the animal houses have been built in the

Previous pages The Spring Hill bird collection was started as a constructive method of dealing with poorly drained land. White Peacocks are a feature of the place.

A common sight in Britain these days is the Vietnamese Pot-bellied Pig, said — by some
— to have been the ancestor of the domestic Pig.

last five years and 5000 people visited Appleby in
1976. The land is too undulating to be suitable
for disabled visitors.

Arlington Court

Address	Barnstaple, Devon
Telephone	Shirwell (027 182) 296
Open	Park all year during daylight hours; house April–October inclusive 11.00–13.00 and 14.00–18.00
Acreage	Over 3400 but not all open
Access	On E side of A39 Barnstaple (9 miles) to Kentisbury Ford (2 miles) road, minor road to Arlington (1¼ miles)
Station	Barnstaple (9 miles)
Facilities	Refreshments (at house)
Other	House (in season) Nature trail

The park of this National Trust property has
been a wildlife sanctuary for over 30 years and,
while there are many wildfowl to be seen on and
by the lake, the heronry is perhaps of most interest. There are Shetland Ponies, Jacob Sheep

and Peafowl in the grounds, as well as a one-
and-a-half-mile nature trail, but the major
attraction is the house with its varied collections.

Basildon Wildlife Park/Vange Zoo

Address	London Road, Vange, Essex
Telephone	Basildon (0268) 553 985
Open	Summer 10.00–19.00; winter 11.00–½ hr before dusk
Acreage	5
Access	London Road is old A13 running parallel with and just N of railway line
Station	Pitsea (2 miles)
Facilities	Guide book Guided tours by arrangement Self-service cafeteria
Feeding	Some animals, with own food

The new zoo, confusingly calling itself a wildlife
park as well, was opened in 1973. Its modest

acreage puts it into the zoo class more than that of a park, and it contains 18 species of mammal as well as 25 of bird.

Beautiful Butterflies

Address	Bourton-on-the-Water, Glos
Telephone	Bourton-on-the-Water (0451) 20712
Open	All week 10.00–17.00
Access	In centre of town on S side of High Street linking A429 (½ mile W) with Little Rissington (3 miles E)
Station	Moreton-in-Marsh (8 miles)

The exhibition is part sales room and part exhibit with the sales side being just as interesting, if not more so. In theory visitors are charged for entering the exhibition section. This, despite the Butterfly name, contains Gecko, Chameleon, Spiders, Stick Insects and Mantis, as well as living Butterflies. Naturally the population changes from time to time. Breeding of Butterflies is carried out in this exhibition/shop and, although the style is

Countless insects are well worth a second stare, particularly in the case of the Praying Mantis who tends to stare back.

somewhat vague, it has appeal much like a man's 'den' where, untidily, he pursues his hobby. The place is commercial in that there are things for sale but is more casual about business than other places in this tourist honey-pot.

Berkeley Castle Deer Park

Address	Berkeley, Glos
Telephone	Berkeley (045 381) 332
Open	April–September except Monday; October Sunday only
Access	From B4066 leading from A38 (1½ miles E) to Berkeley village
Station	Stroud (13 miles)
Facilities	Guide book (to castle) Refreshments (at castle) Picnic area (at castle)
Other	Berkeley Castle Kennels of Berkeley Hounds

The deer park is one mile from the castle but, unlike the castle, can be visited at any time. The herd includes Red and Fallow Deer.

Bird Paradise

Address	Hayle, Cornwall
Telephone	Hayle (0736) 753 365
Open	All year 10.00–dusk
Acreage	14
Access	½ mile from Hayle on B3302 to Leedstown
Station	Hayle (½ mile)
Facilities	Guide book Audio-visual programme on endangered species of birds Self-service cafeteria and snack bar (summer) Gift shop Picnic areas
Other	Children's zoo Donkey rides Miniature railway
Feeding	Mammals only, with purchased food

Hayle itself is set back from the sea and St Ives Bay, and the Hayle Bird Paradise is inland from the town. Its speciality is a good collection of rare and endangered species of bird, many of which have been bred here. In all there are about 350 animals representing 100 bird and 10 mammal species.

The most striking birds are the free-flying

Macaws and Parakeets, the St Vincent Amazon Parrots (only ones of their kind in Britain), White-eared Pheasants (first to breed in Britain), Thick-billed Parrots and Rothschild's Grackles (which both breed here). There are many other rare Parrots and there is also a walk-through aviary. Although the mammals can be fed with food bought on the premises, this does not apply to the birds.

Hayle is on one of the main tourist routes through Cornwall and 100,000 people diverted from it in 1976 to look at the Bird Paradise.

Birdland Zoo Gardens

Address	Bourton-on-the-Water, Glos
Telephone	Bourton-on-the-Water (0451) 20689
Open	10.00–dusk
Acreage	3
Access	From Riverside Walk on S side of River Windrush crossed by footbridge from High Street linking A429 (½ mile W) to Little Rissington (3 miles E)
Station	Moreton-in-Marsh (8 miles)
Facilities	Guide book Lectures Gift shops
Other	Art gallery (wildlife)

Len Hill, owner of Birdland at Bourton-on-the-Water, with two of his Macaws.

Once upon a time there was a local builder doing well out of restoring and erecting Cotswold-type houses in the picturesque village of Bourton-on-the-Water. As a boy he had been more interested in birds. So, when he prospered from all the building, he bought Chardwar, a large house with almost three acres of garden, and set about stocking it with birds. In those days he was known just as a good local builder. Now he is famous, far and wide, as the curator of an exceptionally beautiful bird garden. Started in 1957, it pioneered new techniques in aviculture and, although many of these have been sensibly exploited elsewhere, Birdland has managed to maintain much of its old supremacy. It would be unthinkable for anyone to start a bird world of their own without first paying a visit to the Bourton birds.

The entrance, just by the River Windrush, is modest for such a famous place and quite difficult to find. But, once inside, the visitor is in a land of birds. Macaws fly overhead. Penguins swim. Cranes and Pelicans strut. Touracos run up and down. Hornbills clatter their bills. Hummingbirds hover. Stilts paddle. The talkers talk. Sun Bitterns slink. And down from somewhere comes a shape, which grabs a mealworm, and hurtles back again whence it came, all long before

the visitor has time to focus, let alone identify. Birds do live here, fly here, breed here, and generally rule the roost.

The main tropical house, with its separate entrance fee, is a particular delight. Unlike a cage where an animal, once seen, has shown all there is to see, this hot-house aviary has a seemingly inexhaustible supply of occupants. Stay for 15 minutes, think you have seen the lot, and another bird will pop up from nowhere. Stay for an hour and the same thing will happen.

The birds here include Jackass, Humboldt's, Macaroni and King Penguins, Lear's and Hyacinthine Macaws as well as commoner kinds, Great Palm and Sulphur-crested Cockatoos, Red-breasted Geese, Toucans, Crowned Pigeons, Birds of Paradise, Lorikeets, as well as dozens and dozens of small varieties. One might have thought the assortment would assuage any desire for collecting birds, but the curator had money left over to buy a couple of Falkland Islands whose resident population is around a million, largely of Penguins, Flightless Ducks, and Black-browed Albatross.

For the Cotswold visitor, even though money must be spent and there is a gift shop (run by the curator's wife), the feeling is of wandering through a private garden. A large lawn leads up to the big house and this is about the only space not occupied by birds. Therefore, however private the garden may seem to be, others have invaded it before you. In fact they, the birds, have taken it over, and what a brilliant show they have made in doing so.

125

The shapes of bills and beaks. *Left* Marabou Stork, *above* Ostrich, *below left* Griffon Vulture, and *below* White Pelican.

Birdworld

Address	Holt Pound, nr Farnham, Surrey
Telephone	Bentley (042 04) 2140
Open	All year 09.30–18.00 (or 1 hr before dusk)
Acreage	4½
Access	On W side of A325 Farnham to Petersfield road, just S of Holt Pound
Station	Farnham (2½ miles)
Facilities	Guide book and information leaflet Self-service cafeteria Picnic area Gift shop Wheelchairs for hire
Other	Aquarium
Shows	Penguins fed 11.15
Feeding	With purchased food

The Crowned Pigeon, a remarkable blue, here sunning itself with wings outstretched.

On arriving at Birdworld the first thing visitors may notice, curiously, is the new aquarium, opened alongside the car park in the spring of 1977. Hitherto, the first striking feature of the place has been the happy noise of the birds, singing, squawking, quacking – and talking. Within minutes of a visitor entering the gardens one of the Macaws may call out a greeting. They are free-flying and can disappear (temporarily) into the adjacent forest from which Birdworld has been cleared. About half the site is beautifully landscaped and stocked with gardens. The other half is shady, being dominated by spruce and other fir trees. There are free-roaming Peafowl beside the Pheasant aviaries, rare inmates here being Mikado and Swinhoe's; most colourful being Lady Amherst's and the Himalayan Monal, and most fertile being Reeves's and Yellow Golden.

In this area also are waterfowl enclosures and another pool from which Ducks and Geese can mingle with the visitors who may, nevertheless, turn their backs to look into a log-cabin of a glass-fronted aviary containing, among others, Crowned Pigeons and Spur-winged Plovers. In more traditional enclosures are Secretary Birds, American King and Lappet-faced Vultures, Bataleur and Tawny Eagles, several species of Owls, Kestrels (that produced four young in 1976), Toucans and Touracos.

The woodland joins the gardens beside the Penguin pool, where Humboldt's, Jackass and Rockhoppers can be seen to advantage swimming underwater. Crested Seriemas run free over the lawns, but the most prized exhibits are caged behind notices announcing their breeding achievements (if young are visible, so is their date of birth). Birdworld is proud of its seven species of Hornbill, but supremely proud of the Black-and-white Casqued Hornbills which recorded the first-ever captive birth in 1972, breeding again subsequently. The Dusty Lorikeets provided another first, and further sources of pride are the Maximilian Parrots and the Macaws.

Other birds in this area include a pair of Kori Bustards, a cloud of yellow, blue and green Budgerigars, and Cockatoos, some of whom are as vociferous as the welcoming Macaws. It is a hard place to leave, but there is always the comfort of something new next time.

Birmingham Botanical Gardens

Address	Westbourne Road, Edgbaston, Birmingham B15 3TR
Telephone	Birmingham (021) 454 1860
Open	09.00–dusk or 20.00 in summer; Sunday from 10.30
Acreage	12
Access	1½ miles SW of city centre, leading E off Harborne Road
Station	Birmingham New Street (1½ miles)
Facilities	Guide book and information leaflet Lectures Guided tours (for fee) Self-service cafeteria (summer) Gift shop
Other	Playground Nature trail and woodland walk

The Birmingham Botanical Gardens concentrate, as is only to be expected, on plants, and there are 5000 living specimens here from all over the world, making it the widest botanical exhibition

The Little Ringed Plover (*above*) and the Crowned Plover (*right*). Resentment is sometimes expressed at any British bird (such as the Little Ringed Plover) being kept in captivity, but the feeling is very rarely extended to similar birds of foreign origin.

in the Midlands. But there is also an animal side, which consists of a tropical bird house, a water-fowl enclosure and a few small pets such as Rabbits and Guinea Pigs. The number of bird species is approximately 50.

Birmingham Nature Centre (Cannon Hill)

Address	Pershore Road, Birmingham 29
Telephone	Birmingham (021) 472 7775
Open	Daily except Tuesday: winter 10.00–16.00; spring and autumn 10.00–18.00; summer 10.00–20.00
Acreage	5½
Access	Opposite Pebble Mill Road, on E side of A441 to Pershore, 2 miles S of city centre
Station	Birmingham New Street (2 miles)
Facilities	Guide book and information leaflet Lectures and guided tours (occasional)
Other	Aquarium

The Centre's aim is to show the flora and fauna of Britain and North Europe, and the fauna comprises some 13 species of mammal, 6 of amphibia and 15 of fish, with an increasing number of invertebrates. The larger mammals are European Lynx, Wild Cats, Badgers, Weasels, Alpine Marmots and Soay Sheep; the smaller ones include several other species of rodent, most of whom are breeding. There is a Butterfly garden, a Hymenoptera house and an aquarium, as well as many static displays on natural history subjects in the main hall.

Bognor Regis: Hotham Park Children's Zoo

Address	Bognor Regis, West Sussex
Open	March–November 10.00–dusk; December–February weekends only 10.00–16.00
Acreage	5
Access	At E end of town on S side of A259 to Felpham (½ mile E)
Station	Bognor Regis (½ mile)
Other	Aquarium Playground, trains, etc. in park adjacent to zoo

Set in a shady corner of the park, the zoo allows no opportunity to relax on the seats, for the children will need you to help with identification as any notices are five or six feet from the ground. The exhibits (except the aquarium) are more accessible, through bars and netting. There is a small tropical bird aviary, and outdoor cages contain Toucans, Parrots, Cockatoos, Mynahs and Cranes, with a pool for Penguins and a castle for the Pelican. Other animals have Wendy-type houses, in which they can sleep invisibly, but there are Wallaby, Capuchin Monkeys, Llama, Deer, Raccoon, Coati and Porcupine to be seen, as well as a number of more familiar creatures such as Bantams, Rabbits, Hamsters, Ducks, Chickens, Sheep, Tortoises and Ponies.

Opposite One of the sights of the ornithological world is a flock of Scarlet Ibis at roosting time. At least visitors to aviaries occasionally have a chance to see this beautiful bird.

Breamore Countryside Museum

Address	Breamore, nr Fordingbridge, Hants
Open	April–September Tuesday, Wednesday, Thursday, Saturday, Sunday and all holidays 14.00–17.30
Acreage	22
Access	1 mile NW of village of Breamore off A338 Salisbury (9 miles N) to Fordingbridge (2 miles S) road
Station	Salisbury (9 miles)
Facilities	Guide book Lectures and guided tours (by arrangement) Home-made teas and kiosk Gift shop
Other	House and carriage museum to visit Woodland walk

A collection of 21 animals covering four species of rare British domestic livestock – St Kilda, Soay and Jacob Sheep, and Longhorn Cattle.

Bridgemere Wildlife Park

Address	Bridgemere, nr Nantwich, Cheshire
Telephone	Bridgemere (093 65) 223
Open	Easter–October 10.30–18.30
Acreage	35
Access	On S side of minor road linking A529 (2 miles W) Audlem to Nantwich road and A51 (½ mile E) Nantwich to Woore road
Station	Crewe (8 miles)
Facilities	Guide book Snacks and teas Picnic area Gift shop
Other	Pets' corner
Feeding	Some animals

There is considerable variety of animals here, ranging from Penguins and Otters to Deer and other mammals, but the most impressive feature is the waterfowl. There are excellent ponds for them, and many birds have bred successfully, such as the Red-breasted Geese (now becoming a commoner sight in Britain) and Brent Geese (whose presence at Foulness helped to prevent the airport being built there). Bridgemere is one of the few places (Norfolk Wildlife Park is another) to have bred the Stone Curlew.

Although comparatively new (opening in 1973), Bridgemere is quite large and has parking for 1500 cars. Plainly it will expand its number of species and will become more famous than at present. Commercial facilities are modest but there is a self-service cafeteria selling home-made cakes, sandwiches, teas and so on.

Brixham Marine Aquarium

Address	12 The Quay, Brixham, Devon
Telephone	Brixham (080 45) 2204
Open	May–mid-October
Access	On N side of inner harbour
Station	Paignton (4 miles)
Facilities	Guide book

Just opposite the crowded Brixham Harbour lies the fairly crowded Brixham Aquarium. All of its exhibits were caught within 40 miles of the harbour. There are some 11 tanks, including a huge one thought to be the longest in Britain. The 18,000 gallons of water are pumped from the outer harbour. Therefore the exhibits are both easy to see and look in good shape. The population varies but there are generally Sharks, Rays, Octopus, Conger Eels, File Fish, Cod, Whiting, Pollack, Bass and Mullet. At any one time there are about 100 animals here, representing 30 fish species and 10 invertebrates, such as Lobsters, Prawns, Shrimps, Crabs, Molluscs, Starfishes and Sea Urchins. There is also a pleasing and useful exhibition about Brixham trawlers.

Broadway Tower Country Park

Address	Broadway, Hereford and Worcester
Telephone	Broadway (038 681) 2390
Open	April–October 11.00–18.00; rest of year Sundays only 11.00–15.00; Natural History Centre open in summer only
Acreage	35
Access	On W side of B408, leading S from A44 just E of Fish Hill
Station	Moreton-in-Marsh (7 miles)
Facilities	Information leaflet Refreshments Information centre for area
Other	Natural History Centre Nature trails Observation tower with exhibition and gift shop

This is not an animal collection of the kind normally encountered in this book, but the Natural History Centre does contain living material (in the form of local animals such as Squirrels, Voles, Hedgehogs, Newts, Frogs and Snakes) as well as museum-type displays. From the park there are two nature walks (30 minutes and 1 hour), with excellent views over the Cotswolds.

Brontë Zoo

Address	Station Road, Oakworth, Keighley, West Yorks
Open	11.00–dusk
Acreage	1½
Access	Turn SE off B6143 in centre of Oakworth (3 miles SW of Keighley) towards station
Station	Oakworth (immediate)
Facilities	Restaurant, kiosk Gift shop

A small zoo, opened in 1972, which possesses some exotic mammals (Puma, Coyote, Dingo, Raccoon), birds (Parrots, Cockatoos, Parakeets, Ducks, Geese) and a few domestic animals.

Broxbourne Zoological Gardens

Address	White Stubbs Lane, Broxbourne, Herts
Telephone	Hoddesdon (099 24) 62852
Open	Summer 10.00–18.00; winter 10.00–16.00
Acreage	24
Access	Leave A117 at Broxbourne or Wormley, cross A10 and White Stubbs Lane runs W towards Epping Green
Station	Broxbourne (2 miles)
Facilities	Guide book Snack bar; kiosk (summer) Picnic area Gift shop
Other	Children's zoo Pony and Donkey rides Pony traps Playground Train Woodland walk and adventure playground
Shows	Lion and Tiger training sessions twice daily
Feeding	Some animals, with zoo food

The theme of this open-air collection is a children's zoo in a natural setting. There are 38 species of mammal, and 25 of bird, adding up to 200 animals in all. These include Chimpanzees (within a new enclosure), Tigers, Leopards, Llamas, Lions, Baboons, Wallabies and Emus, most of these species having bred recently. A new Monkey house was opened at Easter 1977.

Burton Constable Hall

Address	Nr Hull, Humberside
Telephone	Skirlaugh (0401) 62400
Open	Easter Saturday–Spring Bank Holiday: weekends; then daily except Monday and Friday (unless Bank Holiday) until last Sunday in September
Acreage	150
Access	To N of Sproatley on B1238 Hull (8 miles SW) to Aldbrough (5 miles NE) road
Station	Kingston-upon-Hull (7 miles)
Facilities	Guide book and information leaflet Self-service cafeteria Picnic area Gift shop
Other	House to visit Playground Nature trail Model railway Vintage agricultural and vintage motorbike museum Carriage collection Collection of Lilian Lunn miniature figures

The children's zoo here includes animals of the pet variety, such as Rabbits, Guinea Pigs, Rats and Mice, as well as Goats and a Donkey. Among the birds to be seen are Peafowl, Pheasants, Parrots, Love Birds, Macaws, Budgerigars, Cardinals and Weaver Birds, as well as waterfowl (Mallard and Muscovy Ducks, Canada and Chinese Geese).

Butser Ancient Farm

Address	Queen Elizabeth Country Park, Petersfield, Hants
Telephone	Horndean (0705) 595 040
Open	From Easter: Tuesday–Saturday 14.00–17.00; Sunday 11.00–17.00, except for lunch break. Occasional Sunday afternoons in winter
Access	From Country Park car park on E side of A3 Petersfield (4 miles N) to Horndean (3 miles S) road
Station	Petersfield (4 miles)
Facilities	Guide book Guided tours
Other	Craft demonstrations

This demonstration establishment sets out to

Left Macaws are becoming a commoner sight in British collections, often flying free and rasping their splendid cry as they do so.
Above Always a delight are Humming Birds. A Black-chinned male from South America.

The Rare Breeds Survival Trust has done much to ensure that ancient forms of domestic livestock do not die out. *Above* The incredibly small Dexter Cow, and *below* A group of Old English Longhorns.

show what farming was like in the Iron Age. (There is a book for sale here on the subject.) Its animals include Soay Sheep, Dexter Cows, an Exmoor Pony and Chickens. Particularly at weekends and Bank Holidays they aim to have some demonstrations such as potting, making bread, or smelting.

Cardiff Zoo

Address	Weycock Road, Barry, Gwent
Telephone	Barry (044 62) 4687
Open	Summer 10.30–19.00; winter 10.30–dusk
Acreage	11
Access	NW side of B4266 Barry (2 miles SE) to A48 (3 miles N) road
Station	Barry (2 miles)
Facilities	Guide book Guided tours by arrangement Snack bar Gift shop
Other	Playground

Called the Cardiff Zoo, but ten miles away at Barry, this mixed collection is not the best of its kind in Britain. There is a fairly large assortment of animals, ranging from Elephant and Tiger down to many smaller mammals as well as birds and reptiles, but there is much that could be done by way of improvement, particularly for a zoo with a capital city name.

Charlecote Park

Address	Stratford-on-Avon, Warwicks
Open	April and October weekends; May–September daily except Monday unless Bank Holiday; Thursday morning reserved for schools
Acreage	200
Access	At junction of B4086 Stratford (5 miles W) to Wellesbourne Mountford (1½ miles E) road with B4088, 4 miles S of Barford
Station	Stratford-on-Avon (5 miles)
Facilities	Guide book (to house) Refreshments (until end of September)

This property, famous for alleged associations with William Shakespeare, is owned by the National Trust. Apart from the house, visitors can pay a separate fee to enjoy the grounds, redesigned in 1760 by Capability Brown, as well as the herd of Deer in the park, together with a flock of rare Spanish Sheep, descendants of a group imported in the eighteenth century.

Cheddar Marineland Aquarium

Address	Cheddar Gorge, Somerset
Telephone	Cheddar (0934) 742 854
Open	Easter–October 09.30–21.00
Access	On W side of B3135, at NE side of village
Station	Weston-super-Mare (10 miles)
Facilities	Gift shop

Competing with all the other Cheddar attractions is the Cheddar Marineland Aquarium. In a garish manner in keeping with its surroundings it advertises a

Unique collection of underwater life from oddities of the African and Far Eastern waterways to the ferocious piranha fish of the Amazon. From the romantic coral reefs of the South Pacific we have the beautiful coral fish, seahorse [sic] and invertebrata with their brilliant and dazzling colours. Also deadly scorpion fish, triggers and Moray eels.

Inside are about 25 tanks, filled with much plastic botany but with many good exhibits, such as the beautiful Scorpion Fish, a nice Moray, exotic Anemones, Sea Horses, a good Lung Fish, living Coral and one Piranha. Both the salt and

It is remarkable that a fish should have a prehensile tail, but *Hippocampus*, the Sea Horse, is a thoroughly remarkable fish.

Opposite Handling a grape with extreme dexterity, despite the size of that bill, is the Toco Toucan.
Above A male Three-horned Chameleon, a rare inhabitant of British reptile houses.

Put a Conger Eel (*above*) in an aquarium and the chances are that visitors will stay longer by its tank than by any other. *Below* The extraordinary Pufferfish, found in the waters of the Caribbean, seen here inflated and with erect spines, and normal.

fresh water is clean and there is helpful information on the wall, although rather difficult to read. Some of it is mis-spelt and there are howlers: invertebrata are not single-celled animals. The entrance fee is modest and, even for those not particularly addicted to aquaria and their inhabitants, is probably money better spent than if it were to go on many of the goods for sale in this tourist stop-off.

Chilham Castle

Address	Chilham Castle, nr Canterbury, Kent
Telephone	Chilham (022 776) 319
Open	April–October not Mondays or Fridays
Acreage	25
Access	On S side of A252 Charing (9 miles SW) to Canterbury (6 miles NE) road
Station	Chilham ($\frac{1}{2}$ mile)
Facilities	Guide book and information leaflet

	Bar; licensed restaurant; self-service cafeteria and kiosk
	Picnic area
	Gift shop
Other	Chilham Castle
	Pets' corner
	Pony and Donkey rides
	Woodland walk
Shows	Birds of Prey flying 15.00–16.00

In the very beautiful grounds and gardens of Chilham Castle (Jacobean, containing a Battle of Britain museum) is a mixed collection of creatures, most of which are birds. These include birds of prey, Pheasants, Peafowl, Jungle Fowl and waterfowl. There are also about 30 mammals, and a large lake containing Carp and many other coarse fish that visitors may feed. Those wishing to visit Chilham should not be caught out by it being closed on Mondays and Fridays.

Chillingham Wild Cattle

Address	Chillingham, Alnwick, Northumberland
Telephone	Chatton (066 85) 213
Acreage	300
Access	On E side of Chatton (1 mile N) to Eglingham road, S from B6348 Wooler to A1 road
Station	Alnmouth (14 miles)
Facilities	Information leaflet

There is only one species here and only 55 individuals of that species. The animal looks at first glance like a domestic creature, but the collection is unique for Britain and well worth a visit. Chillingham Wild White Cattle have been living in these woods for at least 700 years, and they *are* wild. The cows will attack anyone near their calves and the calves will be subsequently killed if handled by man. The herd number fluctuates considerably – hard winters always bring it down – but this is one more feature to be expected of a wild as against a tame and nurtured community. No one knows how these Chillingham Cattle fit into the evolution of our domestic breeds, but it does seem likely that they are directly descended from the wild cattle that once roamed our islands. At all events, 14,500 people had the good sense to go and look at them in 1976.

Apart from the Chillingham animals, the most famous, there are four other herds of White Park Cattle alive today, namely the Chartley, Dynevor, Cadzow and Vaynol herds. However, it is usually conceded that the Chillingham animals are the wildest and, owing to their isolation for the past seven centuries, the purest.

Clacton Pier Dolphin Show

Address	Clacton-on-Sea, Essex
Telephone	Clacton (0255) 21115
Open	Every day except Friday
Access	Pier
Station	Clacton-on-Sea ($\frac{1}{2}$ mile)
Facilities	Guided tours and lectures
	Catering on pier (summer)
Other	Aquarium
Shows	November–March 15.00; March–June 11.30, 15.00; July, August, September 11.30, 14.30, 16.00, 19.30

The dolphinarium, opened in 1971, now has two performing Dolphins, but there are also four Sealions and four Seals, representing six mammal species in all. There are also Penguins and 55 kinds of fish in the aquarium. The collection's theme is marine animals.

Coombe Abbey Bird Garden

Address	Coombe Countryside Park, Brinklow Road, Coventry, West Midlands
Telephone	Coventry (0203) 453 500
Open	All year 10.00–dusk
Acreage	10
Access	On N side of A427 between Binley, on eastern outskirts of Coventry, and Brinklow
Station	Coventry (5 miles)
Facilities	Guide book
	Guided tours
	Bar; snack bar and kiosk (summer)
	Picnic area
	Gift shop
Other	Pets' corner
	Donkey rides
	Playground ⎱ all in
	Nature trail/woodland ⎰ park
	walk
	Abbey ruins
Shows	Falconry display

In 1972 ten acres of a large countryside park were set aside to form the Coombe Abbey Bird Garden. It now contains about 1200 birds of 100 different species. These are extremely varied, and include talking Mynahs, Macaws, Parrots and Cockatoos; rare breeds of Poultry; colonies of Black Ibis and White-backed Vulture (which

should have a new aviary in 1977); and endangered species such as Cape Barren Geese, Cheer Pheasants and Laysan Teal. Birds of prey provide a falconry display.

Coton Manor Wildlife Garden

Address	Guilsborough, Northants
Telephone	Guilsborough (060 122) 219
Open	April–October 14.00–18.00
Acreage	$7\frac{1}{2}$
Access	1 mile S of Guilsborough, to W of A50
Station	Northampton (10 miles)
Facilities	Information leaflet Tea-room (in season) Picnic area Gift shop

If you want an old English garden of great beauty and character with birds roaming at large, Coton Manor Wildlife Garden fulfils your need. It was opened in 1970 and possesses 250 birds, including Flamingos, Cranes and Macaws. In 1976 11,500 people went to see the place.

Cromer Zoo

Address	Howard's Hill, Cromer, Norfolk
Telephone	Cromer (0263) 2947
Open	All year 10.00–17.00
Acreage	4
Access	At W end of town. Howard's Hill runs between A149 to Sheringham (to N) and railway (to S)
Station	Cromer ($\frac{1}{2}$ mile)
Facilities	Self-service cafeteria Picnic patio
Other	Aquarium Pets' corner
Feeding	With purchased food

Alex Kerr, circus man, opened Cromer Zoo in 1960 after he had retired. Many animals with which he had worked were brought to Cromer and they formed the original nucleus. The collection is now run by his widow and has been broadened. As many of its animals are large and the acreage is small, the place is crowded. There are Big Cats, Hyenas, Bears, Chimpanzees, Monkeys, Wallaby, Deer and many smaller mammals. In the pool are Pelicans and Penguins.

A flock of Chilean Flamingos asleep in the morning sun.

Previous pages The exquisite form of the Blue Malaysian Coral Snake (*left*), and, showing less of its form but more of its ability to use a tree, is (*right*) the Emerald Boa.

An aviaryful of mixed Parrakeets.

Crooked Barn

Address	Welford, Barton Road, Stratford-on-Avon, Warwicks
Telephone	Bidford-on-Avon (078 988) 2213
Open	Early April—end of September 10.30—18.00 except Mondays unless Bank Holidays
Access	On S side of minor road linking Welford-on-Avon to Barton, running along S side of River Avon
Station	Stratford-on-Avon (6 miles)

Over 60 breeds of domestic fowl are kept here.

Culzean Country Park

Address	Maybole, Ayrshire
Telephone	Kirkoswald (065 56) 269
Open	Park open all year
Acreage	560
Access	W of A719 Ayr (12 miles NE) to Maidens (2 miles SW) road
Station	Maybole (5 miles)
Facilities	Guide book and information leaflet Lectures and guided tours Self-service cafeteria; snack bar and kiosk (summer) Picnic areas Gift shop
Other	Culzean Castle Playground Woodland walk Story of Culzean exhibition Walled garden

The principal attractions of Culzean Country Park are its castle, its three-and-a-half miles of shoreland and its 300 acres of woodland, but it also possesses a small aviary, a Deer park, and a pond area which has a few tame Duck supplementing the wild population. It is therefore not so much an animal collection as a beautiful place which has a few animals to complement the scene, such as the 16 species of bird.

Cuttislowe Park Aviary

Address	Banbury Road, Oxford
Telephone	Oxford (0865) 58490
Open	At all times
Acreage	80
Access	Just NE of junction of A40 with A423
Station	Oxford (2½ miles)
Facilities	Kiosk (summer) Picnic area
Other	Playground and sports facilities in park
Feeding	With own food

A new aviary was completed here in 1975 and there are now 50 species of bird and 12 of mammal in the collection. The animals form only a minor part of the attractions of this public park and the small aviary has been designed principally to interest children.

The Rhea is a smaller, South American cousin of the Ostrich.

Delamere Aviaries

Address	Hill Furze, Fladbury, Evesham, Hereford and Worcester
Telephone	Evesham (0386) 860 580
Open	10.00–dusk
Acreage	1½
Access	1 mile N of B4084 Wyre Piddle (2 miles W) to Evesham (4 miles E) road at Fladbury Cross
Station	Pershore (3 miles), Evesham (4 miles)

Apart from the birds there are a modest aquarium, a reptile house and a small collection of mounted Butterflies.

Dundee: Camperdown Wildlife Centre

Address	Camperdown Park, Dundee
Telephone	Dundee (0382) 645 444
Open	Summer 10.00–20.00; winter 10.00–16.30
Acreage	6
Access	On S side of A923 Coupar Angus (10 miles NW) to Dundee road (2 miles SE)
Station	Dundee (3 miles)
Facilities	Information leaflet Lectures and guided tours Self-service cafeteria and kiosk (summer) Picnic area Gift shop
Other	Camperdown mansion house Pony and Donkey rides Nature trail and woodland walk
Shows	Animals fed 14.30 and 16.00

Within a large public park stands the Camperdown Wildlife Centre whose purpose is primarily educational. To this end most of its collection is of the indigenous animals of Scotland. There are 435 animals here representing 20 mammal species, 36 bird species and 1 kind of reptile.

The mammals include Red and Fallow Deer, Red Squirrels, Pine Martens, Polecats, Weasels, Stoats, Brown Bears and, as foreigners to the scene, Wallabies and Kinkajou. There are also Sheep, Goats and Ponies. Among the birds are Eagles, Buzzards, Kestrels, four kinds of Owl, Ravens, Jackdaws and many others on the British list. There is a greater proportion of foreigners

Opposite Lamentably represented in zoos are the amphibia. A *Dendrobates*, the so-called Poison Arrow Frog.

among the birds than the mammals and these include various Pheasants, Peafowl, Parrots, Parakeets and Finches. Although it was opened in 1968 by the Parks and Recreation Department, the actual Wildlife Centre was only built in 1973 and its second phase is now under construction.

Dunfermline: Pittencrieff Park Aviary

Address	Dunfermline, Fife
Open	Dawn–dusk
Acreage	35 (whole park)
Access	On W side of town, immediately S of A985 to Kincardine
Station	Lower Town (¼ mile)
Facilities	Licensed restaurant and cafeteria (in park)
Other	Pittencrieff House Play area and entertainments Nature trail Museum

There is a small aviary as one of the attractions in this public park.

Easton Farm Park

Address	Easton, Woodbridge, Suffolk
Telephone	Wickham Market (0728) 746 475
Open	April–September, Wednesday–Sunday inclusive and Bank Holidays 10.30–18.00
Acreage	35
Access	On W side of village of Easton, on minor road from Wickham Market to Brandeston, W of B1116
Station	Wickham Market (2 miles)
Facilities	Guide book and information leaflet Self-service cafeteria with children's menu; snack bar and kiosk Picnic area Gift shop
Other	Pets' corner Playground Wagon rides Nature trail and woodland walk
Shows	Daily milking approx. 14.30–16.15
Feeding	With purchased food

Along with the invasion of exotic animals into our countryside has been a re-invasion by many of the farm species that used to inhabit it. The theme at Easton Farm Park (which opened in 1974) is farm animals. These include Jacob, Soay, St Kilda and Lincoln Longwool Sheep; Suffolk

Kept in many a private aquarium the Siamese Fighting Fish, here with its bubble nest, is sometimes found in the larger aquariums.

Horses; Shetland Ponies; Donkeys; Highland, Dexter and Longhorn Cattle. There are also many wildfowl.

Everyday Cows are hardly a collection of animals in the sense so frequently used in this book but there are special viewing areas for seeing 130 ordinary Cows being milked each afternoon, a sight of particular interest to young urban dwellers who may be thinking that all milk originates in factories.

Exmouth Aquarium

Address	Esplanade, Exmouth, Devon
Telephone	Exmouth (039 52) 3016
Open	During school summer holidays daily 10.00–dusk; rest of year 10.00–17.30 but closed on Monday, Wednesday and Thursday in winter
Access	Between Clock Tower and Pavilion along seafront
Station	Exmouth ($\frac{1}{4}$ mile)

There are 32 tanks of exhibits at this seaside aquarium (including one of 3000 gallons and two of 1500 gallons), and they contain 67 species of fish (local marine, tropical marine and fresh-

water), a Turtle and half a dozen Terrapins plus a few invertebrates. The most dangerous among the 120 individual fishes is the Turkey Fish (a Sea-scorpion), and among the most interesting is the Tanago Bitterling. It lays its eggs in a mussel which then acts as incubator. Sea Horses have bred here, and also Angel Sevrons. Sea Anemones are to be seen, and other tanks not on show contain live fish for sale to visitors, who can also buy shells and shell jewellery.

Exmouth Zoo

Address	Seafront, Exmouth, Devon
Telephone	Exmouth (039 52) 5756
Open	Summer 10.00–dusk; winter 10.00–17.00
Acreage	1
Access	At E end of Esplanade, just to N of start of Marine Drive
Station	Exmouth ($\frac{1}{2}$ mile)
Facilities	Guide book

Behind the beach huts, and sandwiched between a putting green and the cricket grounds, lies Exmouth Zoo. It is housed in what looks like an old cricket pavilion plus the acre or so at the

146

back. However, it does pack quite a few animals into its modest area and, according to the most recent volume (16) of the *International Zoo Yearbook*, there are 29 species and 63 specimens of mammal, 70 species of bird and 152 specimens, 19 species of reptile and 31 specimens, and 8 species of amphibia with 18 specimens. A grand total of 126 species is indeed a lot for one acre and a pavilion.

The larger animals on exhibit (in September 1976) were three Pumas, a Chimpanzee, a Barbary Ape, Tayra (a large South American Marten), many Snakes ('We may bite you') and quite a few of the bigger kinds of bird. The place was run as an adjunct to Paignton Zoo for its first five years, but since 1962 has been a separate establishment. Quite a lot of breeding is achieved here, with Kinkajou being the first to be bred in Britain. There are only two poisonous Lizards in the world, the Gila Monster and the Mexican Beaded Lizard, and both are from the Arizona/Sonora desert area of North America. It is odd to find them so near the sound of the sea, as well as all the other noises from their fellow creatures within this homely zoo.

'Which animals do you hate most?' 'Snakes,' said those questioned. 'Which animals do you never miss in a zoo?' 'Snakes,' said the same people. A Black and White Cobra.

Falconry Centre

Address	Newent, Glos
Telephone	Newent (0531) 820 286
Open	Every day except Tuesday 10.30–17.30 or dusk if earlier; closed for 3 days either side of Christmas
Acreage	12½
Access	In centre of Newent take B4216 to Huntley. Shortly, between BP garage and car park take Watery Lane to Cliffords Mesne. Continue over staggered crossroads and Centre is on left, 1½ miles from Newent
Station	Gloucester (11 miles)
Facilities	Guide book and information leaflet Lectures Guided tours (for 25 or more mid-week) Coffee and soft drinks on sale Picnic area (when hay is cut) Gift shop
Other	Falconry display within 1 hr of any visitor's arrival, weather permitting Brooder room in breeding season where young can be seen

A flying falconry display occurring within one hour of every visitor's arrival, assuming weather conditions permit, makes this place unique. Generally it is the other way about; a visitor has to time his or her arrival for some fixed event. The show itself is also most memorable. To see a Falcon, say, swooping down from some great height to pass underneath the very bench on which people may be sitting is quite unforgettable; but then so is the rest of this establishment.

It was started in 1967 by Philip Glasier, well known for his writings on birds of prey. At Newent there is now one of the largest collections of such birds anywhere in the world. In 1976 there were 250 birds here of 52 species, and 39,000 people came to see them, the flying displays and the associated museum. In many of the aviaries are young birds as the Centre is virtually the only public collection of breeding Falcons. Rearing successes have taken place with Lanner Falcons, Laggar Falcons, Goshawks, Merlins, Harris' Hawks, Red-shouldered Hawks, Ferruginous Hawks, five kinds of Eagle Owl, and others. Of particular interest is the brooder room where young birds can be seen in their early stages.

The fact that enormous prices can be acquired for certain birds of prey, particularly those good for falconry, means that deceit, theft and various other illegalities are rife in this market. Falconry clubs are sometimes blamed for their part in popularizing the sport, and even the beautiful film *Kes*, which showed how one bird transformed a boy's life, has been criticized for not making audiences aware of all the rules. There is

Excellent flying displays are given within (at most) an hour of every visitor's arrival at the Falconry Centre, Newent.

research, and provide information for all interested parties.

Birds of prey have had a rough time in recent years. They suffered greatly from the new pesticides, steadily from old-style gamekeepers, repeatedly from egg-collectors and even frequently from self-indulgent ornithologists. It is therefore amazing, to many an outsider, quite how little controlled breeding is being carried out with this group of birds. That is partly why a visit to the Falconry Centre is such a stimulant. It does breed many, but there are also all the adult birds to see, notably along the Hawk Walk as well as flying in the field just past the aviaries.

Farway Countryside Park

Address	Honiton, Devon
Telephone	Farway (040 487) 224
Open	Good Friday–September except Saturday unless Bank Holiday weekend 10.00–18.00
Acreage	70
Access	On E side of minor road from B3174 (linking A375 with A3052) to Southleigh
Station	Honiton (5 miles)
Facilities	Guide book and information leaflet Licensed cafeteria (beer, cider, wine) 11.30–14.30; countryman's lunch, cream teas and snacks Picnic area Gift shop
Other	Pets' corner Playground and children's amusements Pony rides Donkey carts; Shire Horse-drawn hay-wagon Nature trails and woodland walk Putting

In a thick fog one day in May 1971 broadcaster Frank Muir opened the Farway Countryside Park. Had it lifted he would have been able to see down to the Coly valley and across to the surrounding Devon hills, and would therefore have witnessed the excellent location of the place he was opening. Its theme is rare and present-day farm animals. Its style is to have animals and people wandering around freely within the 70 acres of land that is unsuitable for cultivation but adequate for grazing. There are various appropriate extras such as beer, cider and the Shire Horse-drawn hay-wagon, but most of the attention goes to the animals.

These include Red, Roe, Fallow and Sika Deer, Donkeys, Horses and Ponies (Shetland,

considerable legislation but almost everyone would like to see it changed, either in one direction or another. The current confusion is probably welcomed by those who make big money from selling these birds, and one answer is to bring the price down by breeding more of them. To help with this problem the Raptor Breeders' Association was founded in 1976 at Newent. Its aims are to further breeding, to have a say in legislation, to arrange bird exchanges, to conduct

Dartmoor, Exmoor, Highland, Dales and Welsh), and Cattle such as the West Highland, Belted Galloway, Longhorn, Dexter, Gloucester and Chartley. There are also several varieties of Pig, five of Goat and seven of Sheep. Naturally the precise number of species and individuals varies from year to year but there are about 500 animals including Poultry in this collection.

The pets' corner contains traditional animals such as Foxes, Badgers, Pigeons, Pheasants, Ducks on a pond, Rabbits, and several others less familiar in the past such as Peacocks, Guinea Pigs and Guinea Fowl.

Flamingo Gardens and Zoological Park

Address	Weston Underwood, Olney, Bucks
Telephone	Bedford (0234) 711 451
Open	Good Friday–end of September Wednesday, Thursday, Saturday and Sunday 14.00–20.00
Acreage	12
Access	1 mile W of A509 at Olney
Station	Wolverton (8 miles)
Facilities	Guide book and information leaflet Picnic area Gift shop

Neither kith nor kin to Flamingo Land, Kirby Misperton, or Flamingo Park Bird Sanctuary, Isle of Wight, the Flamingo Gardens and Zoological Park at Weston Underwood, near Olney, is quite a separate establishment. It does indeed possess Flamingos, in fact all six species of them, and is therefore thoroughly entitled to the name, but it also possesses many hundreds more creatures totalling 1500 in all. Its specialities, apart from the all-important Flamingos, are Cranes (the only pair of Asiatic White Cranes in captivity in Britain); Storks (European White, Hammerkop, Saddle-billed, Marabou); Geese (very many varieties); Swans (all four Arctic Swans have bred here – Trumpeter, Bewick's, Whooper and Whistling – a 'first' for this zoo); and birds of prey (such as Golden, Imperial and African Fish Eagles, Andean Condors and Lammergeier).

Once again a private collection, grown large and in need of revenue, was opened (in 1964) to the rest of us for mutual gain. Now there are over 200 species of bird in residence as well as a dozen kinds of mammal. These mammals are (almost) all of the hoofed variety, and include American Bison, European Bison (which browse, unlike the American grazers), Arabian Camel (one hump, hot sandy regions), Bactrian Camel

two humps, rocky colder areas), Llama, Guanaco, Vicuna and Alpaca (the four Camels of South America), Formosan Sika Deer, Yak and Highland Cattle. Unhoofed, but no less pleasing, are Bennett's Wallabies.

Large birds outside the dominant specialities are Penguin (Humboldt's), Pelican (Crested, Brown), Bustard (Kori, Little, Great), Emu and Two-wattled Cassowary. (The distinctive and so-called casque of this last bird is said to help it batter its way through the bush, but does not give its name to the species. Casque is a romance word for helmet whereas Cassowary is Malay.) The considerable breeding achieved here is largely carried out away from the 12 acres open to us and on a further 60 acres dedicated to that purpose. Without doubt there is space here, and the colossal aviaries emphasize the fact. In the walled garden is one cage measuring 100 feet along each of its four sides and 12 feet high.

Considering the value and the beauty of this collection, the number of visitors each year is small. Perhaps the opening restrictions, in hours per day, days per week, and months per year, give an impression to the chary that it is always closed. But it is, for example, open every afternoon of every summer weekend, and what better time for visiting this fascinating place?

Flamingo Park Bird Sanctuary

Address	Oakhill Road, Springvale, Seaview, Isle of Wight
Telephone	Seaview (098 371) 2153
Open	April and May 14.00–18.00; June–September 10.30–18.00, Sundays 14.00–18.00
Acreage	10
Access	Oakhill Road runs between B3330 Ryde (2½ miles NW) to St Helens (3 miles SE) road, and the road along the front from Seaview towards Ryde. The Sanctuary is on the E side, half-way along
Station	St John's Road (2 miles), Ryde Esplanade (3 miles)
Facilities	Guide book and information leaflet Self-service cafeteria and kiosk Picnic area Gift shop
Other	Pets' corner
Feeding	With purchased food

The theme here is waterfowl but the most striking first impression may be the supreme view over the Solent. The park, which was opened in 1971, is part pens, part lakes and pools (which

The Aleutian Canada Goose is now rare.

Practically all the inmates live in the open but there are one or two indoor dwellings, such as the British and foreign bird house, attractively planted and containing a waterfall and fish. Apart from the Solent view and the island site another firm attraction here is that so few of the birds are pinioned. The majority are free and frequently leave the sanctuary only to return in time for the next meal. Considerable tree and shrub planting has been carried out and, as the bird stock is being increased all the time, Flamingo Park will be even more attractive in the years to come.

Gatwick Garden Aviaries and Children's Zoo

Address	Russ Hill, Charlwood, Surrey
Telephone	Crawley (0293) 862 312
Open	Easter–end of September 10.30–19.00
Acreage	5
Access	At W end of Charlwood take road going W then S round church towards Russ Hill and Rusper. Gardens on W side of road
Station	Gatwick Airport (3 miles)
Facilities	Guide book and information leaflet Lectures and guided tours (by arrangement) Snack bar and kiosk Picnic area Gift shop
Other	Pets' corner Donkey rides Playground
Feeding	With own food, if shown

attract wild birds) and part animal zoo with a pets' corner, bird houses and so forth.

In all there are about 2000 birds here, even when the wild ones have flown away, and about 90 species are represented. Almost half of these are waterfowl and include Egyptian Geese, Snow Geese, Barnacle Geese, Carolina Duck (all four species have bred), Black-necked Swans, Black Swans, Bar-headed Geese, Muscovy Duck (also seen on many an English farm but they originated in South America), Laysan Teal, Baikal Teal, Fulvous Tree Duck, Penguin Duck, Maned Geese, Gadwall and many more. There are Flamingos (Chilean), Demoiselle and Crowned Cranes, Peafowl and a great intermingling between the visitors and the visited. Feeding of the birds with food on sale from the kiosk is particularly encouraged, partly because the pleasure is good for both sides.

With 10 mammal species and 100 kinds of bird the Gatwick collection is mixed, but it focuses mainly upon South American Monkeys and large bird enclosures.

Prime exhibits include the Spider Monkeys (with a group of five females and one male being one of the largest in Britain), ten Squirrel Monkeys, and a breeding family of White-fronted Capuchin Monkeys. Among the birds are Macaws (which have bred), Black Swans (who are, say the management, 'as regular as clockwork' in producing 12–16 young a year), Penguins, Flamingos, various hand-tame, free-flying birds, and many of the Parrot family from Australia. Visitors are allowed to feed the animals either with food bought on the premises or, provided it is suitable, with their own. The outdoor aviaries were first opened in 1973 but the Gardens were only truly initiated in 1976 when the Council relaxed its restrictions about the number of open days a year, and 15,000 people came that year to visit the place.

Glasgow: Linn Park Nature Centre and Children's Zoo

Address	Clarkston Road, Glasgow G44 5TA
Telephone	Glasgow (041) 637 3096
Open	All year
Acreage	4
Access	E of A727 at Netherlee, 3½ miles S of city centre, 1 mile N of Clarkston
Station	Muirend (Glasgow Urban Line) (½ mile)
Facilities	Guide book Lectures and guided tours Self-service cafeteria (summer); kiosk (open in winter as required) Picnic area
Other	Playground Nature trail and woodland walk
Shows	Feeding of animals on variable routine

Within Linn Park's 212 acres is a small zoo. This contains 6 kinds of mammal and 23 of bird, with its Highland Cattle being the dominant exhibit. There is a nature centre and information room within the mansion house and, as a rare extra, there is a nature trail for blind people. There are no admission charges.

Glasgow: Tollcross Park Children's Zoo

Address	Wellshot Road, Glasgow G32 7HY
Telephone	Glasgow (041) 778 1046
Open	All year
Acreage	96 (whole park)
Access	Along N side of A7251, 2½ miles E of city centre, 2½ miles W of junction with M74
Station	Carntyne (Glasgow Urban Line) (¼ mile)
Facilities	Guide book Guided tours
Other	Playground Nature trail

As at Linn Park, also in Glasgow, Tollcross Park now has a small section dedicated to animals. Here are 66 kinds of bird, 2 of fish (in a pool in the conservatory) and a few mammals such as Ponies and Highland Cattle. The most impressive

enclosure is the new tropical bird house. As at Linn Park there is a nature trail for blind people, and admission is free.

Glengoulandie Deer Park

Address	Glengoulandie Caravan Park, Foss, Pitlochry, Perthshire
Access	Alongside B846 from Aberfeldy to Tummel Bridge

There is a small herd of Red Deer here beside the B846 between Aberfeldy and Tummel Bridge. In the summer months these animals would normally be in the high hills, and therefore this group affords the tourist an opportunity for seeing a native breed more easily.

Guilsborough Grange Bird and Pet Park

Address	West Haddon Road, Guilsborough, Northants
Telephone	Guilsborough (060 122) 278
Open	Early March–October 11.00–19.00
Acreage	30
Access	¾ mile NW of Guilsborough, to W of A50
Station	Northampton (11 miles)
Facilities	Information leaflet Guided tours Tea-room with waitress service Picnic area Gift shop
Other	Pets' corner Pony and Donkey rides Playground Woodland walk
Shows	Feeding 15.00

This is mainly a bird collection but the dominant impression is of open space, highly suitable for picnics or doing nothing. There are a few mammals, namely 4 Fallow Deer, 2 Small-clawed Otters, 4 Pygmy Goats, 1 Vietnamese Pig, 1 Jersey Bullock and 18 assorted Horses, Ponies and Donkeys.

On the bird side there are 370 individuals, such as Snowy and Savigny Owls, Doves, Parakeets, Lovebirds, Finches, Geese and Penguins. Possibly no less important to many visitors is the fact that there are four acres of lawns, gardens, pond, pool and streams surrounded by fields and woods.

Gwydir Castle

Address	Llanrwst, Gwynedd
Telephone	Llanrwst (0492) 640 261
Open	Easter–mid-October
Access	Turn W off A496 in Llanrwst over river bridge, then left on far side, and Castle entrance is 50 yards along on left
Station	Llanrwst (1 mile)
Facilities	Guide book (to house) Café and kiosk Picnic area Gift shop
Other	House to visit Old Dutch gardens
Feeding	With own food

White Peacocks are a rare sight but five can be seen among the 80 Peafowl in the grounds of Gwydir Castle, a dwelling (with an extremely ancient history) that rose from the ashes of many fires after the late Arthur Clegg bought it in 1944. His son Richard now lives in the house and breeds these beautiful Peacocks. His collection also includes Gold and Silver Pheasants and Ducks.

Harewood Bird Garden

Address	Harewood, Leeds, West Yorks
Telephone	Harewood (097 336) 238
Open	April–October daily; rest of year Wednesday and Sunday only
Acreage	4
Access	On W side of A61 Leeds to Harrogate road, immediately S of junction with A659
Station	Leeds City (7 miles)
Facilities	Guide book Lectures (schools) Licensed restaurant (parties); self-service cafeteria; snack bar and kiosk (summer) Picnic area Gift shop Wheelchairs for hire
Other	Harewood House
Show	Penguins fed 15.30

A small part of the Harewood estate was turned in 1970 into the Harewood Bird Garden. Since then it has become one of the most important bird collections in the country and the best in the north-east of England. There are at present about 800 birds from 180 different species. The only other living animals on view are Butterflies.

The bird specialities are Penguins, which are Humboldt's, breed regularly and can be seen swimming underwater; a tropical house (opened in 1971) with Hummingbirds, Sun Birds, Tanagers, Manakins, Sugarbirds and many others; free-flying Macaws such as the Blue and Gold, the Red and Blue, and the Hyacinthine. There are also many varieties of Pheasant, such as Elliot's, Golden, Mikado, Brown-eared, Blue-eared, Swinhoe's and Hume's Bar-tailed. The largest aviary can be walked through and contains Gallinules, Quail, Cardinals, Touracos and Mynahs, including the rare Rothschild's species which is beautifully white save for a blue streak around the eyes.

Among the other Harewood birds are the Crowned Pigeon (largest of all the Pigeons), Flamingos (which live in and around an extremely handsome lake), Paradise and Crowned Cranes (with the former being a rare sight in Britain), many kinds of Parrots (representing some of the 300 species of this sort of bird), Scarlet Ibis (which at roosting time in South America can provide one of the wonders of the ornithological world), Snowy and Eagle Owls, many Jays, Magpies and Starlings, Giant Hornbills and the Sun Bittern (which scuttles so much that it may be on its way to becoming a flightless bird).

The grounds of Harewood House were improved over 200 years ago by that most famous landscape architect of them all, Capability Brown. The bird garden, even though it forms such a small part of the estate, reflects some of that man's continuing excellence.

Harlow: Pets' Corner

Address	Town Park, Harlow, Essex
Telephone	Harlow (0279) 22790
Open	March–October 11.00–18.00; November–February 11.00–1 hr before dusk
Acreage	2
Access	Immediately to S of B1048 on N side of town
Station	Harlow Town (alongside)
Facilities	Self-service cafeteria, snack bar; kiosk (summer) (all in park) Picnic area in park
Other	Aquarium
Shows	Animals fed 13.00

In the 150 acres of Town Park is a very small collection, specializing in farm and domestic creatures. The assortment includes Sheep, Calves, Lambs, Guinea Pigs, Rabbits, ornamental Poultry, Ducks, Golden Pheasants and various rodents. There are also many fish in an aquarium. Entrance is free.

Hele Rare Breeds Farm

Address	Beetor Cross Garage, nr Moretonhampstead, Dartmoor, Devon
Telephone	Moretonhampstead (064 74) 249
Open	End of May–early September 12.00–18.00
Acreage	20
Access	SW of B2313 at junction with B3344 (3 miles SW of Moretonhampstead)
Station	Exeter (13 miles)
Facilities	Refreshments Picnic area
Other	Pony and Donkey rides Exhibition of rare farm implements Farm produce for sale

Hele Farm is a Rare Breeds Survival Centre and visitors can see 30 different breeds of animals, including White Park, Shetland, Gloucester and Highland Cattle; Cotswold, Lleyn, Black Welsh Mountain, White-faced Dartmoor and Woodland, Leicester and Lincoln Longwool, Wensleydale, Wiltshire Horn, Soay, Shropshire and St Kilda Sheep; Pigs; Goats (including Galloway Forest); Horses; and Ponies. In a special paddock children can come into close contact with selected animals.

High Peak Garden Centre

Address	Bamford, Derbys
Telephone	Bamford (043 34) 484
Open	10.00–dusk
Acreage	$2\frac{1}{4}$
Access	Beside A625 from Castleton (4 miles W) to Hathersage (2 miles E)
Station	Bamford ($\frac{1}{2}$ mile)
Other	Garden centre

The garden centre demonstrated its landscaping and horticultural capabilities in preparing this garden with its streams and pools, and then populating it with waterfowl and a selection of colourful birds such as Cockatoos, Finches, Budgerigars, Lovebirds and Pheasants.

The variegated fleece and magnificent horns of a Jacob Ram, an ancient British breed.

Hopetoun House Deer Park

Address	South Queensferry, Lothian
Telephone	Edinburgh (031) 331 1348 and 1316
Open	Early May–mid-September except Thursday and Friday 13.30–17.30
Acreage	Extensive parkland
Access	Off A904, 2 miles W of southern end of Forth Road Bridge
Station	Edinburgh Waverley (11 miles), North Queensferry (5 miles)
Facilities	Guide book (to house) Teas
Other	House and gardens Museum Nature trail

The style and elegance of Hopetoun House are complemented by its deer park, with Fallow and Red Deer accompanied by St Kilda Sheep. There are also ornamental birds.

Hornsea Pottery

Address	Hornsea, Humberside
Telephone	Hornsea (040 12) 2161
Open	All year except 1 week over Christmas; Easter and Spring Bank Holiday 09.00–18.00; July–1st week in September, weekdays 09.00–19.00, Saturday 10.00–18.00, Sunday 10.00–19.00; rest of year, weekdays 09.00–17.00, Saturday and Sunday 10.00–17.00
Acreage	28
Access	Immediately S of Hornsea on B1242 to Aldbrough (5 miles)
Station	Beverley (13 miles)
Facilities	Guide book and information leaflet Bus within site Self-service cafeteria and kiosk Picnic area Gift shop
Other	Playground, trampolines and kiddie cars Pony traps Guided tour of factory Country craft centre Crazy golf
Feeding	With purchased food

To have a factory and a zoo as part and parcel of the same entertainment area is an odd combination, but it occurs at Hornsea. The guided tour around the pottery was established in 1949 and many other amenities have been added since. For example, in 1960 the mini-zoo was opened.

It contains 54 mammals and 100 birds, and these include a group of Rhesus Monkeys, Rabbits, Guinea Pigs, Pheasants, Cockatoos, Macaws, Parrots, Lovebirds, Parakeets and many smaller birds. Although the grounds total 28 acres, and attracted 650,000 people in 1976, the mini-zoo is only a small part of this large area.

Ilfracombe Tropical Wildlife Corner

Address	Bicclescombe Park, Ilfracombe, Devon
Telephone	Ilfracombe (0271) 62702
Open	Summer 11.00–dusk
Acreage	$\frac{1}{2}$
Access	On S side of town to E of A361 to Barnstaple
Station	Barnstaple (9 miles)
Feeding	With purchased food

A very small zoo but with a considerable assortment of animals within its space. Its founder–manager is Mr C. H. Trevisick, the author, broadcaster and lecturer.

Island Zoo

Address	St Catherine's Island, Tenby, Dyfed
Open	Easter–September at low tide daily 10.00–dusk
Acreage	$2\frac{1}{2}$
Access	At low tide across sand below Castle Hill
Station	Tenby ($\frac{1}{4}$ mile)
Facilities	Cafés (on beach) Picnic area
Other	Pets' corner

It is extremely odd for a zoo to have its opening hours dictated by the tides, but this one is on an island and access is only possible when visitors can walk to it. It is also odd to have a zoo housed in an old Victorian fort, but Lord Palmerston allegedly built it as a defence against Napoleon III (quite a different person from Napoleon Bonaparte, who earlier caused considerable fortification to be erected round our shores).

The collection started in 1968 and its theme, whatever the origins of its quaint location, is the presentation of smaller animals that are normally overshadowed in other zoos by larger creatures. Over 100 creatures have been brought together on this island, namely 22 kinds of mammal, 15 of

Amphibia can be appealing creatures, such as this Spotted Salamander.

bird and 6 of reptile. The mammals include a family of Stump-tailed Macaques, Otters, a Patas Monkey, Scottish Wild Cats, Marmosets, Civets, Genets and Bushbabies. Among the birds there are Barn Owls, a talking Macaw, a Cockatoo and several small tropical species. Among the island's reptiles are Iguanas, Lizards and Turtles.

Kelling Park Aviaries and Leisure Centre

Address	Weybourne Road, Holt, Norfolk
Telephone	Holt (026 371) 2235
Open	Summer 10.00–18.00; winter 10.00–dusk
Acreage	4
Access	Turn N off A148 Holt (1½ miles W) to Cromer (8 miles E) road; on E side of road
Station	Sheringham (4 miles)
Facilities	Guide book and information leaflet Bar, licensed restaurant; snack bar (summer) Picnic area Gift shop
Other	Pets' corner Donkey traps Playground Crazy golf

This is a bird garden which really merits the name as it not only has a fine assortment of birds, but in addition they live in a well laid-out garden. There are 12 species of mammal here, such as a Sun Bear, Giant Porcupines and Monkeys, but the main focus is on the 60 species of bird.

There are, for example, Flamingos, Penguins and waterfowl, as well as Cranes, Pheasants and many kinds of Parrot. Its attendance is small (it attracted only 20,000 visitors in 1976), but the collection and the garden are good.

Knaresborough Zoo

Address	Conyngham Park, Knaresborough, North Yorks
Telephone	Knaresborough (042 376) 2793
Open	10.00–dusk
Acreage	2
Access	On W side of Knaresborough, N of A59 from Harrogate
Station	Harrogate (3 miles)
Facilities	Kiosk Gift shop

It seems odd that this small Yorkshire town should have the largest snake in captivity in the world, but its Reticulated Python (originally caught in Malaysia) is over 27 feet long and so holds the (Guinness) record. The small zoo, which was opened in 1965 by a former circusman, has a general collection and animal 'shows' are a feature.

Leamington Spa: Jephson Gardens

Address	Leamington Spa, Warwicks
Open	All year 08.00–dusk except Bank Holidays and Sunday when open 10.00–dusk
Access	In town centre along N bank of River Leam to E of Victoria Bridge
Station	Leamington Spa ($\frac{1}{4}$ mile)
Facilities	Information leaflet Self-service cafeteria (summer) Picnic area
Other	Playground Putting, table tennis

As part of the Jephson Gardens there is a small area where a few birds and fish are housed, some of the birds being tropical. Admission is free.

Leigh Park

Address	Havant, Hants
Open	April–September, Saturday, Sunday and Bank Holidays 10.00–dusk
Access	Turn W off B2149 into Middle Park Way. Car park 200 yds on left
Station	Havant (2 miles)
Facilities	Refreshments Picnic area
Other	Playground Gardens Farm trail

There is a small animal collection here, including rare breeds of domestic stock.

Lilford Park

Address	Lilford Hall Ltd, Lilford, Oundle, Peterborough, Northants
Telephone	Clopton (08015) 648 and 665
Open	All year weekdays 11.00–20.00 or dusk
Acreage	200
Access	On W side of A605 Oundle (3 miles N) to Thrapston (6 miles S) road
Station	Peterborough (15 miles), Wellingborough (13 miles)
Facilities	Information leaflet Self-service cafeteria and kiosk (summer) Picnic area Gift shop
Other	Pets' corner Playground Pony rides Rowing boats for hire (in park)

Large numbers of animal collections now to be found in the British countryside were opened up in the 1960s, that prosperous time when people saw the likelihood of receiving a return for their invested capital, but the aviaries at Lilford Park were built 100 years earlier – in 1861. Today the collection possesses 76 kinds of bird plus a small variety of mammals, such as a very tame Vietnamese Pot-bellied Pig.

Among the more spectacular bird exhibits are the Flamingos, a Sarus Crane, Kori Bustards (the males look much like gateposts when displaying), Emus, various Pheasants (such as Elliot's, Cheer and Hume's Bar-tailed) and a very large collection of wildfowl. Recent breeding successes have been with Snowy Owls, Spur-winged Plovers, Red Grouse and Eagle Owls. Naturally, with such a huge acreage, by no means is it all taken up by aviaries, ponds and so on. There are ample picnic opportunities among the pine trees, the rock gardens and the various attractions that are not aviaries.

Linton Zoological Gardens

Address	Mortimer House, Hadstock Road, Linton, Cambs
Telephone	Cambridge (0223) 891 308
Open	All year except 25 December 10.00–19.00 or dusk if earlier. Last admission $\frac{3}{4}$ hr before closing
Acreage	$10\frac{1}{2}$
Access	Turn S off A604 Cambridge (11 miles NW) to Haverhill (8 miles W) road; down B1052 to Hadstock, on W side of road
Station	Cambridge (11 miles)
Facilities	Guide book and information leaflet Lectures and guided tours Cafeteria (summer, and Sunday in winter) Picnic areas Gift shop
Other	Pony and Donkey rides (Sunday and Bank Holidays

There were a few exotic animals living in the grounds now occupied by Linton Zoological Gardens before 1972 but the zoo was only opened then. This was after the land had been bought by the present management and, as every enclosure or building has been constructed during the past five years, their new zoo carries a modern look. The collection has also expanded considerably in these years and will undoubtedly continue to do so in the future.

At present there are approximately 42 species of mammal, 55 of bird, 12 of reptile, 4 of

Two kinds of Fox. *Above* The Fennec (plus cub) from the deserts of North Africa and Arabia, and *right* The Bat-eared from East and southern Africa.

amphibia and even one Bird-eating Spider. Among the larger mammals are Himalayan Bears, Llamas, Panthers, Lions, Pumas, Wolves, Donkeys, Red Deer and Wallabies. Among the middle-sized mammals are Genets, Binturongs, Civet Cats, Pig-tailed and Vervet Monkeys, Agoutis, Porcupines, Mongooses, Badgers, Foxes and Coatis. There is also a large number of small mammals. These include Angora, Golden and Chinese Hamsters; Egyptian, Albino and Mongolian Gerbils; Dalmatian, Hairless and Angora Mice; Kusu and Hooded Rats. The reptiles include Indian, African and Reticulated Pythons, Corn and Gopher Snakes, and half a dozen kinds of Turtle and Tortoise.

There is no particular theme to the mammal and reptile collections and this generalization also applies to the birds. There are about 7 sorts of birds of prey (including some prolific Indian Eagle Owls), about 15 kinds of Parrot-like birds, 5 sorts of Pheasant, 9 of waterfowl and a few waders, Hornbills and Crows.

Particular breeding successes, apart from those Indian Eagle Owls, are the Binturong, the Spotted Genet and the Galloway Goat. The Lion, Dusty, has achieved a certain notoriety by being, or so it is said, the largest of his kind in Britain. Tanya, his mate, is said to be terrified of both umbrellas and children riding on adult shoulders. The zoo is very much a family affair, looked after by Mr and Mrs Len Simmons and their three daughters. There is a Linton Zoological Society and members gain from complimentary tickets, a newsletter and general meetings held throughout the year. The zoo was little more than a field in 1972 and it has been extensively planted with ornamental trees and shrubs since its purchase.

Llandudno: Haulfre Gardens

Address	Llandudno, Gwynedd
Telephone	Llandudno (0492) 76059
Open	All year 24 hrs
Acreage	19
Access	At Great Ormes Head end of town just to NW of Abbey Road/Church Walk linking West Shore and Llandudno Bay
Station	Llandudno (½ mile)
Facilities	Self-service cafeteria

There are Canaries and Budgerigars to be seen in this public park, and there is also an aquarium.

Logan Fish Pond

Address	Port Logan, by Stranraer, Wigtowns
Access	To W of B7065, off A716 Stranraer to Drummond road and ½ mile N of Port Logan
Station	Stranraer Harbour (15 miles)
Facilities	Information leaflet
Feeding	With purchased food

In 1800 a natural tidal pool was used to keep a supply of fresh fish for Logan House. This arrangement, with its iron grille preventing the escape of the fish, has been open to visitors on a commercial basis since 1955, and is unique as animal collections go.

The basin contains 48,000 gallons of water and usually contains about 30 species of fish, such as Pollock (or Lythe), Sea Perch, Wrasse, Plaice and Cod. Salmon and Sea Trout have been included but do not take well to the conditions. The Cod are the easiest to feed and visitors are allowed to do so, from time to time, by the fish pond keeper.

London: Battersea Park Zoo

Address	Battersea Park, Albert Bridge Road, London SW11
Telephone	London (01) 228 9957
Open	Easter–September
Acreage	⅓
Access	On E side of Albert Bridge Road, immediately S of Albert Bridge
Station	Battersea Park (from Victoria) (adjacent)
Facilities	Guided tours (schools) Self-service cafeteria Picnic area
Other	Pony and Donkey rides Pony traps Playground Play park and boating lake (in park) Woodland walk (in park)
Feeding	With own food

The zoo side of Battersea Park includes Small-clawed Otters, Diana Monkeys, Maras, Peruvian Guinea Pigs and Pygmy Donkeys. Among the 80 or so birds are Orange and Scarlet Cock-of-the-Rock, and many waterfowl which congregate on and by the lake. In an enclosure apart from the zoo are Fallow Deer and Blackbuck.

London: Crystal Palace Children's Zoo

Address	Thicket Road, London SE20
Telephone	London (01) 778 4487
Open	Easter–September
Acreage	¾
Access	Thicket Road links A214 and A234 just S of Crystal Palace Park
Station	Penge West (from London Bridge) (200 yds)
Facilities	Guided tours (schools) Self-service cafeteria (summer) Picnic area
Other	Pony and Donkey rides Pony traps Prehistoric animals Play park, boating lake and woodland walk (in park)
Feeding	With own food

Apart from the many other attractions there is a zoo (admission is free) which possesses about 160 animals. Its 50 mammals include Maras (which have bred), and among its 100 birds are Kea Parrots. There are also about 10 reptiles. The most impressive animal feature at Crystal Palace is the collection of huge and lifelike (one assumes) prehistoric monsters, arranged upon an island.

London: Horniman Museum

Address	100 London Road, Forest Hill, London SE23
Telephone	London (01) 699 2339
Open	All year except 24, 25 and 26 December: weekdays 10.30–18.00; Sunday 14.00–18.00
Access	On N side of A205 South Circular Road
Station	Forest Hill (¼ mile)
Facilities	Information leaflet Lectures Snack bar (summer) Gift shop
Other	Picnic area, playground, animal enclosure and nature trail (in surrounding gardens)

Within the Horniman Museum, whose mammals and birds are all mounted specimens, is an aquarium with tanks containing living tropical and temperate freshwater fish, marine fish and some reptiles and amphibians.

London: Royal Parks

The Royal Parks of London do not possess animal collections in the conventional sense, but are interesting from the wildlife point of view and do have captive populations. There are three inner parks: St James's and Green Park (142 acres altogether); Hyde Park and Kensington Gardens (616 acres); and Regent's Park and Primrose Hill (464 acres). The three outer parks are: Greenwich (196 acres); Richmond (2469 acres); and Hampton Court and Bushy Park (1721 acres, plus another 71 for Hampton Court Green and Hampton Court Gardens).

Feral animals tend to be attracted to places where there are pinioned and tame free-flying birds, as in St James's. Consequently, a park's population at any one time can be far more than the sum of its theoretical stock. This attraction of wild forms can even happen with zoos, but obviously is commoner in wilder places like the parks. About 17 bird species actually nest each year in St James's Park, about 30 in Regent's Park, and over 50 in the greater expanse of Richmond. Pelicans are the most bizarre birds to be found on the five-acre St James's lake and, although two were there in 1687, they have since been only intermittently present. On occasion the Pelicans have been unwelcome (eating Tufted Ducks, for example) and at other times Swans have attacked them; but some Pelicans are now in residence and are fed from the lake's eastern end. In recent years about 40 species of wildfowl and one of Cormorant have also been kept in the royal parks, quite apart from all the other birds who have flown in to visit them.

Four royal parks now contain Deer, as against all of them in the past. Regent's Park and St James's lost theirs during the time of the Civil War, and Hyde Park did so around 1840. Currently Greenwich, Richmond, Hampton and Bushy parks are the possessors. The total of both Fallow and Red Deer is about 1000, with two-thirds being Fallow and with Richmond possessing more than half of the total population. Of course, the numbers have varied greatly over the years, particularly when they were being hunted (and poached, despite the penalty of death). A particular tragedy occurred in 1886–7 when the Richmond herd are believed to have suffered rabies. Some 200 of them died.

There is a variety of other mammals in residence, of which pride of place should go to the Badgers of Richmond. Within that park's woods are about eight setts. There are also Foxes, Weasels, Stoats, Grey Squirrels (about 1500 are shot each year), Hedgehogs, Rabbits and Hares; but these populations are not so much collections

Shelducklings, still without their adult colouration, making for the water. A pleasing feature of many captive waterfowl collections is that wild birds fly in to join them.

(as with the St James's wildfowl and the Red and Fallow Deer) as the natural creatures of the English countryside taking advantage of some open space, however much it may be surrounded by the homes of humans.

A good booklet called *Wildlife in the Royal Parks* is published by HMSO. This points out that it is much easier 'to watch the bucks and stags at rut and to listen to their barks and roars at Richmond than in the green glades of the New Forest or on the heather slopes of the Cairngorms'. Quite so, however many motor cars and people are equally conspicuous.

Looe Aquarium

Address	The Quay, East Looe, Cornwall
Telephone	Looe (050 36) 2423
Open	June–September from 10.30
Access	Park car on edge of town and walk along E quay of river for 200 yds
Station	Looe (¼ mile)

The small, friendly aquarium here has about a dozen tanks, all of which contain marine specimens caught nearby. Throughout the season people bring in additions and therefore the stock expands until the late autumn when everything goes back into the sea. The intimacy of the collection and the fact that visitors come in to see what they themselves may have caught during their holiday makes one think that every seaside resort should have such an exhibit. As well as the living individuals in the tanks, there is also a Shark display cabinet plus a few pickled exhibits.

Lowlands Farm

Address	Fenbridge Road, Werrington, Peterborough, Northants
Telephone	Peterborough (0733) 74477
Open	Easter–end-September
Acreage	60
Access	On E side of A15 Peterborough (2 miles S) to Glinton (1½ miles N) road
Station	Peterborough North (2 miles)
Facilities	Guide book and information leaflet Lectures Snack bar Picnic area Gift shop
Other	Pets' corner Shire Horse hay-cart Playground Nature trail
Feeding	With purchased food

The theme here is of rare farm animals. The collection is new, and there are about 100 individuals, such as Henry the Iron Age Pig, Samson the White Park Bull, and a flock of Manx Loghtan Sheep. In the children's section are suitably young Goats, Calves, etc.

Lyme Regis Marine Aquarium

Address	The Cobb, Lyme Regis, Dorset
Telephone	Lyme Regis (029 74) 2309
Open	Summer only, every day
Access	The Cobb is the harbour area SW of the town

Many a seaside aquarium does well just by stocking its tanks with local representatives, such as Bass.

As at Looe, the collecting of local fish and shore animals is a very simple and effective method of stocking an aquarium. At the end of the season the inmates can be returned whence they came. This excellent practice has been carried out at Lyme Regis since 1958.

Mablethorpe Animal and Bird Gardens

Address	North End, Mablethorpe, Lincs
Telephone	Mablethorpe (052 13) 3346
Open	Easter–autumn 10.00–dusk; winter Sunday only 11.00–dusk
Acreage	2
Access	1 mile N of town
Station	Skegness (16 miles)
Facilities	Guide book and information leaflet Snack bar (summer) Picnic area Gift shop
Other	Playground
Feeding	With purchased food

Opened in 1973, this little zoo now contains 25 kinds of mammal, 25 of bird, 1 of reptile, 1 of fish and 25 of invertebrate. Many of the inhabitants are those which are often kept as pets but specialities here are Moluccan Cockatoos, Greater Hill Mynahs and Indian Crested Porcupines, all of which bred in 1976.

Marine and Freshwater Aquarium

Address	Broadlands, Bourton-on-the-Water, Glos
Telephone	Bourton-on-the-Water (0451) 20462
Open	Easter–end of September 10.00–17.00
Access	On W side of minor road leading S from High Street towards Farmington
Station	Moreton-in-Marsh (8 miles)

So many people are driving around the Cotswolds looking for something to do that many places have responded to their need. Bourton-on-the-Water not only has its excellent Birdland and a Butterfly exhibition, but also this aquarium. In it are 500 marine, freshwater and tropical fish. These include Piranha, and Carp from the largest Carp farm in Britain. The aquarium is located in a small Cotswold house in a back street, and 62,000 people found their way to it in 1976.

Perhaps the most famous creature of South America, and certainly its most famous fish, is the Piranha. The formidable teeth exist, but are hard to see.

Matlock Bath Aquarium

Address	110 North Parade, Matlock Bath, Derbys
Telephone	Matlock (0629) 3624
Open	All year except 25 December
Access	North Parade is part of A6. Aquarium is on W side of road
Station	Matlock Bath (¼ mile)
Facilities	Information leaflet Gift shop

The hot spring here, whose water was formerly used by visitors to the Hydro, is now enjoyed by fish such as Carp, Orfe, Tench and Trout. The larger fishes are fed by hand on certain days during the summer by a skin diver in their pool.

Merley Tropical Bird Gardens

Address	Merley, Wimborne, Dorset
Telephone	Wimborne (020 15) 3790
Open	Summer 10.00–17.00
Acreage	3½
Access	Immediately to W of A349 Wimborne (1 mile N) to Poole (3 miles S) road
Station	Poole (3 miles)
Facilities	Self-service cafeteria Gift shop

Merley's three-and-a-half acres are all enclosed in a large walled garden. This contains a thousand birds, dominated by tropical representatives such as Macaws, Parrots, Parakeets, Lories, Cockatoos, Touracos, and several Pigeons including the Blue-crowned, as well as Peacocks and Pheasants. Among the 150 species are also Flamingos and Penguins.

Millport: Robertson Museum

Address	Millport, Isle of Cumbrae, Bute
Telephone	Millport (047 553) 581/2 and 756
Open	Easter–September: Monday–Friday 09.30–12.30 and 14.20–17.00; June–September Saturday also; Easter–end May 09.30–12.00 only
Access	To E of A860 coast road at SE corner of island
Facilities	Information leaflet

The museum at this University Marine Biological Station contains living as well as dead specimens, with an extensive collection of local marine animals (eight big tanks, three large sinks and four wall tanks). Live fish include Cod, Haddock, Whiting, Pollack, Saithe, Gurnard, Conger Eel, Spotted and Spot Dogfish, Plaice, Dab and Sole. There is the largest Wrasse found in the Clyde, the Ballen-wrasse, and Gold Sinny Wrasse as well as Sea Anemones. There are also Sticklebacks, Gobies, Blennies (including Butterfish), Bullhead and Suckerfish. Among the crustaceans are Lobsters (also the Norway variety), Crabs (including Spider, Shore and Sucular), Soldier Hermit-crabs and Molluscs. There are also Star-

Leonard Williams, Woolly Monkey expert extraordinary, with friends.

fish (Common, Spiny and the Brittle-star), Tube-worms, Sea-slugs and Oysters, and the museum always tries to have an Octopus as well. Summertime visitors' angling contributions are welcome at this aquarium but are not the mainstay of the collection.

Monkey Sanctuary

Address	Looe, Cornwall
Telephone	Looe (050 36) 2532
Open	Easter–September 10.30–18.00
Acreage	4
Access	Turn S off B3253 Plymouth to Looe road and continue towards coast
Station	Looe (4 miles)
Facilities	Guide book and information leaflet Lectures (approx. five daily) Fruit drinks and tea
Other	Pets' corner

Who would have thought that tens of thousands of people (70,000 in 1976) would find their way along some steep and narrow Cornish roads to meet a small group (15 in 1976) of their fellow primates known as *Lagothrix lagothricha*? But they do, and what is more, they frequently enjoy their visit so much that they tell friends, pass on the good news and make great efforts to return when time and holidays permit. They have not, they say, seen anywhere else like it – and they are right. The Monkey Sanctuary is like nowhere else; but then Leonard Williams, its founder, is not like other men.

For the visitor, having parked the car farther up the hill, the first sight is a supreme view through the trees to the English Channel. However, there is also a house exuding small walkways, as if some internal hobby had grown out of hand, and these lead to huge areas half-way between fruit cages and gigantic play-pens. Up above, linking the trees, are thick ropes and the whole contrivance is claimed to be, and convincingly, the largest outdoor and indoor Monkey enclosure linked to a tree area existing in Britain. Here the animals are king, the 15 Humboldt's Woolly Monkeys whose lifestyle is the crucial feature of this place. Most zoo cages are cell-block penitentiaries by comparison with this domain.

There are other animals, Marmots and the odd bird, but the Monkeys are the sanctuary's *raison d'être*. Everything else takes second place. Visitors are allowed to wander about and are then permitted to let the animals inspect them. Several times a day there are these 'meeting times' between Monkeys and Men, and very stimulating they are. With normal cages the humans jeer, or look, or wave at the beasts they have come to see. Here the boot is on the other paw. The people sit, and the Monkeys are let into the room (or outside if the day is fine) to climb about, play with ropes and make their inspection of yet another group of humans should they feel like doing so. On other days these same people may have been poking fun at other animals, but here they sit, calmly and almost reverentially. It is a new experience and, judging by the numbers who reach this Cornish corner, a very welcome one.

Leonard Williams, patriarch of the community (family and other helpers live here), was the first to keep a successful breeding colony of this Woolly Monkey species. (There are two other such Woolly species in the world: Smoky and Hendee's.) With most zoos their Woolly Monkeys are animals they are glad to keep alive, being non-starters – as the saying goes – in the breeding stakes. Mr Williams most single-mindedly did his very best for his precious charges and they, in return, began producing young. Between 1967 and 1976 his colony gave birth ten times, with two of these babies being second-generation offspring. Never before have Woolly Monkeys in captivity had it so good, and never before have people had it so good in seeing them.

Muncaster Castle Bird Garden

Address	Ravenglass, Cumbria
Telephone	Ravenglass (065 77) 614
Open	Easter–September 12.00–17.00 except Friday
Acreage	77
Access	On S side of A595 Whitehaven to Bootle road, 1 mile E of Ravenglass
Station	Ravenglass (1 mile)
Facilities	Guide book and information leaflet Restaurant, self-service cafeteria, snack bar and kiosk Picnic area Gift shop
Other	Muncaster Castle Playground Bus Nature trail and woodland walk Garden centre

Within the grounds and even in the courtyard of Muncaster Castle is a collection of animals, predominantly of birds but with a few mammals to keep them company. These include Himalayan Bears and Wallabies. The garden was opened in 1970 and its theme, both then and now, is birds.

The courtyard aviaries contain many small species such as Weavers, Cardinals and some of the more modest members of the Parrot family. The Chipmunks also have their home in this ancient place. In the castle's gardens there is a lake currently exploited by Flamingos and many sorts of Geese, as well as Sacred and Wood Ibis. The rarest animals here are the Pheasants, such as Cheer, Mikado, Hume's Bar-tailed and Swinhoe's. There are Hornbills, Crowned Pigeons, Rheas, Peafowl, Guinea Fowl, and Demoiselle and Sarus Cranes.

Do not be caught out by the fact that the garden only opens after noon each day and is closed on Fridays.

Normanby Hall

Address	Scunthorpe, Humberside
Telephone	Scunthorpe (0724) 720 215
Open	All year in daylight hrs
Acreage	170
Access	Alongside B1430 immediately to E of Normanby and 2 miles N of Scunthorpe
Station	Scunthorpe (2 miles)
Facilities	Guide (to house) Cafeteria (summer)

There are an aviary and deer park as additional attractions for visitors to this stately home.

Padstow Bird and Butterfly Gardens

Address	Fentonluna, Padstow, Cornwall
Telephone	Padstow (084 13) 262
Open	All year 10.30–1 hr before dusk
Acreage	2
Access	W from harbour up Duke Street, branch right into Fentonluna Lane; entrance on left (½ mile from harbour)
Station	Bodmin Road (15 miles)
Facilities	Guide book and information leaflet Snack bar and kiosk (summer) Gift shop

With only two acres at their command the Bird Gardens are bound to be small but, despite that limitation, the place contains one of the more interesting bird collections in the country. Its speciality is soft-billed birds, but there are others here. (Soft-billed means living off fruit or insects as against seeds.)

In general, the birds in zoos do not breed anything like as well as the mammals, partly because they have precise requirements that zoo-keepers fail to provide. How can a bird make a nest, for instance, if it does not have suitable material scattered around? Or a suitable place on which it can be amassed? Therefore it is doubly important that so many of the Padstow birds are not only exciting but have bred, such as the Thailand Hoopoe, White-cheeked Touraco, Great Kiskadee, Bleeding-heart Pigeon, Andaman Grackle, Emerald Dove and Forsten's Lorikeet. In all there are about 60 species of bird and more than double that number of individuals.

There is also a Butterfly collection, most of which is in cabinets, although some specimens are alive and feeding and breeding.

Paignton Aquarium

Address	The Harbour, Paignton, Devon
Telephone	Paignton (0803) 556 927
Open	Summer 10.00–22.00
Access	Alongside S side of harbour
Station	Paignton ($\frac{1}{4}$ mile)

As at many other coastal resorts the aquarium contains specimens found in the nearby sea. The major exhibits are fish, but there are also many invertebrates, that division of the animal kingdom so neglected in animal collections. This aquarium was opened in 1955.

Palacerigg Country Park

Address	Cumbernauld, Strathclyde
Telephone	Cumbernauld (023 67) 2004
Open	All daylight hrs
Acreage	700
Access	On minor road linking B803 (2$\frac{1}{2}$ miles S) Walston to Slamannan road and B8054/8039 junction (2 miles NW), on SE side of Cumberland
Station	Cumbernauld (2$\frac{1}{2}$ miles)
Facilities	Guide book and information leaflet Lectures Self-service cafeteria (summer) Picnic areas
Other	Nature trail
Shows	Feeding 14.30

The considerable development at Cumbernauld is extremely new, but Cumbernauld's Palacerigg Country Park is even newer, having been opened

in 1974. Its theme is the conservation of native species and to this end there are 43 kinds of mammal, 26 of bird and 2 of reptile in the collection. Particularly noteworthy are Pine Marten (British but how many of us have seen them in the wild?), Badgers and Wolves. The six-mile nature trail is a very suitable extra.

Pitlochry Salmon Ladder

Address	Pitlochry Power Station, Perths
Open	All reasonable times

Just off the A9 at Pitlochry is Faskally Dam where, for a small fee and at all reasonable (and seasonable) times, visitors can look through windows and see Salmon ascending the River Tummel.

Poole Park Zoo

Address	Poole Park, Poole, Dorset
Telephone	Parkstone (0202) 745 296
Open	All year: March–October from 10.00, last admission 18.00 or sunset if earlier; November–February Saturday, Sunday, Bank Holidays (except 25 December) and during local school holidays 10.00–sunset
Acreage	1
Access	Immediately S of A350 (Parkstone Road), on N side of Parkstone Bay
Station	Parkstone, Poole (1 mile)
Other	Children's corner

Considering its size there are a surprising number of residents here. Animals included are Leopard, Puma, Himalayan Bear, Monkey, Porcupine, Otter, Soay Sheep and Lion. Among the birds are Flamingo, Penguin, Mynah, Parrot and many small tropical varieties, with the total number of bird species being about 60. There is also a children's corner with Guinea Pigs and Rabbits as well as Goats and Sheep.

Port Erin Aquarium

Address	Department of Marine Biology, University of Liverpool, Port Erin, Isle of Man
Telephone	Port Erin (0624) 832 027
Open	All year: Monday–Friday 10.00–17.00; Saturday 10.00–13.00
Access	On S side of Port Erin Bay at far end of Breakwater Road towards Castle Rock
Station	Port Erin ($\frac{1}{4}$ mile)

Containing about 200 fish, and rather more invertebrates, this aquarium (free to visitors) only possesses animals collected from the nearby sea.

Powderham Castle

Address	Kenton, Exeter, Devon
Telephone	Starcross (062 689) 243
Open	Easter and Sundays only to mid-May; then daily to end of season except Friday and Saturday 14.00–17.30
Acreage	Extensive parkland
Access	To E of A379 at Kenton; beside River Axe estuary
Station	Starcross (1 mile)
Facilities	Guide book and information leaflet Tea-rooms, snack bar and kiosk Gift shop
Other	Castle, park and gardens *Elizabeth R* costumes from BBC series

As with many a stately home (this one is the residence of the Earl and Countess of Devon) animals form part of the natural setting. Powderham Park contains a herd of 160 Fallow Deer which help to enrich the place.

Prinknash Bird Park

Address	Prinknash, Cranham, Glos
Telephone	Painswick (0452) 812 727
Open	All year except Monday and Friday: April–November 10.00–18.00; November–March 11.00–1 hr before dusk
Acreage	9
Access	On W side of A46 Painswick (3 miles SW) to Cheltenham (8 miles NE) road
Station	Gloucester (5 miles), Stroud (8 miles), Cheltenham (8 miles)
Facilities	Information leaflet Guided tours (by arrangement) Self-service cafeteria Picnic area in park Gift shop
Other	Farm shop Pottery and shop
Shows	Feeding at 16.00
Feeding	With purchased food

Although it was opened only in 1974 and the acreage is modest, there are already over 700 birds in this collection and quite plainly there will soon be more. The main speciality is the larger kinds of bird such as wildfowl, Pheasants,

Peafowl and the like. Probably the most startling exhibit is the flock of free-flying Snow Geese.

The park is next to Prinknash Abbey and, as there is a restored sixteenth-century 'Haunted Monk's Fishpond' plus views of Gloucester Cathedral and the Welsh Hills, the park has an ancient feel to it. Its main area contains a lake and the open ground beside it. This is occupied principally by Geese (Bar-headed, Swan, Barnacle, Canada, Taverner), Swans (Black, Mute) and Ducks (Pintail, Red-crested Pochard, North American Ruddy, Laysan Teal, Ruddy Shelduck and Patagonian Crested).

The Pheasants include Elliot's, Hume's Bartailed, Mikado, Copper, Lady Amherst's, Yellow Golden, Silver and Reeves's. Pygmy Goats from Nigeria have bred here – namely Hansel and Gretel produced Thumbelina – and there are also Jacob Sheep to represent the mammals, but it is the birds that dominate and there are over 70 species of them within this very pretty park.

Robin Hill Country Park

Address	Downend, Arreton, Isle of Wight
Telephone	Arreton (098 377) 430
Open	March–Spring Bank Holiday 10.00–18.00; Spring Bank Holiday–August 10.00–dusk; September–November 10.00–18.00
Acreage	80
Access	1 mile N of A3056 Newport (3 miles NW) to Sandown (7 miles E) road, just to W of Arreton village
Station	Ryde (7 miles)
Facilities	Information leaflet Educational lectures Bar; snack bar (summer) Picnic area Gift shop
Other	Pets' corner Pony and Donkey Rides Playground Nature trail and woodland walk Radio-controlled boats Roman villa excavations Putting green Kite flying 'Trim Course' Whippet racing (Sunday) Commando-style assault course
Shows	Snake demonstrations most afternoons or on request
Feeding	With purchased food

The principal feature of Robin Hill is the degree of familiarity it permits between the visitors and

The Egg-eating Snake about to consume (*top*) and then (*above*) having consumed, as is only reasonable with such a name, an egg. The crushed shell is later rejected.

the visited. There is, for example, a ten-acre 'contact' walk-through enclosure where its Deer, Wallabies, domestic animals and free-flying birds are far more accessible to us than in normal cages. There is also a walk-through pond area rich with Ducks, Geese, Cranes and Storks.

In all there are about 500 animals here of a very mixed bunch. There are 40 kinds of mammal, 35 of bird, 30 of reptile, 10 of amphibia, 10 of fish and 20 of invertebrate. Rarities include the Red Squirrels which, as many of us like to think, are much more handsome than the American Greys who have so largely replaced them. Many of the animal houses are new, such as three sections of the 'Jungle House', the planted indoor aviary and the cages of many other creatures now living here in the Isle of Wight.

Sewerby Zoo

Address	Bridlington, Humberside
Telephone	Bridlington (0262) 73769
Open	All year 09.00–dusk
Acreage	80
Access	Take Sewerby road (parallel with B1255 to Flamborough, but nearer coast) NE from Bridlington; or turn S off B1255 2 miles E of Bridlington, 2 miles W of Flamborough
Station	Bridlington (2 miles)
Facilities	Guide book (for Hall and park) Information leaflet Bar, licensed restaurant and self-service cafeteria (summer) Picnic area
Other	Sewerby Hall with art gallery and museum Playground Sports and amusements in park (summer)
Shows	Feeding 16.00 (notices displayed)
Feeding	With own food

Within the complex of Sewerby Hall and park lies the zoo. It has been designed to be of particular interest to children and contains 112 mammals, 218 birds and 30 fish. The largest groups are of Formosan Sika Deer and Bennett's Wallabies. Other mammals are Porcupines, a Golden Gibbon, a Spot-nosed Monkey, Rhesus Monkeys, Llamas and various domestic creatures. The birds include Humboldt's Penguins, many kinds of Pheasant and Duck, Chilean Flamingos, Macaws, Parakeets, Lories, Weavers, Canaries, Linnets and Budgerigars.

The zoo was opened in 1946 by the Bridlington local authority, and only bird aviaries have been built in recent years. There have been some breeding successes, notably with Llamas and Penguins.

Shaldon Children's Zoo

Address	The Ness, Shaldon, nr Teignmouth, Devon
Telephone	Shaldon (062 687) 2234
Open	Weekends until Easter, then daily 10.00–dusk
Access	To W of A379 Torquay (7 miles S) to Shaldon (½ mile) road
Station	Teignmouth (1½ miles)
Facilities	Gift shop
Other	Pets' corner Aquarium Donkey rides
Feeding	With own food

This is a minute zoo but a new extension is planned. Its theme is small mammals and the 40 animals here include Marmosets, other Monkeys, Squirrels, Pygmy Goats, Donkeys and Mynahs.

Skegness Dolphinarium

Address	Tower Esplanade, Skegness, Lincs
Telephone	Skegness (0754) 2523
Station	Skegness

There was one performing Dolphin at Skegness in 1976, and it is hoped that there will be at least one in future during the summer season.

Somerleyton Hall

Address	Nr Lowestoft, Suffolk
Telephone	Lowestoft (0502) 730 224
Open	Easter–mid-October Sunday and Thursday, also Bank Holidays and Tuesday and Wednesday in July and August: 14.00–18.00
Acreage	12 open
Access	On N side of B1074 Fritton (2 miles NW) to Lowestoft (4 miles SE) road
Station	Lowestoft (4 miles)
Facilities	Guide book and information leaflet Snack bar Picnic area Gift shop
Other	House to visit Playground Nature trail

The rare domestic breeds on show are one Highland and two Dexter Cows, and both rams and ewes of Jacob, St Kilda, Soay, Black Welsh Mountain and Orkney Sheep.

Southam Zoo

Address	Daventry Road, Southam, nr Leamington Spa, Warwicks
Telephone	Southam (092 681) 2431
Open	Easter–October 10.00–dusk
Acreage	7
Access	On N side of A425 to Daventry
Station	Leamington Spa (7 miles)
Facilities	Information leaflet Kiosk Picnic area Gift shop
Feeding	With purchased food

This is a compact zoo but still contains large animals such as Bengal and Sumatran Tigers, a group of Chimpanzees, Leopards, Bears, Panthers, Lions, several kinds of Monkeys, and Alligators. In all there are 186 creatures representing 43 species of mammal, 52 of bird and 1 of reptile. Particular breeding successes have been with Binturong (not frequently seen in British zoos but they seem to breed well), Servals, Chimpanzees and Spider Monkeys. Among the birds are many waterfowl, birds of prey and various small exotics. There is also a pets' corner and, further to delight the children, the Chimpanzees are permitted to put on their own show on special days.

Southport Aquarium

Address	Marine Parade, Southport, Merseyside
Telephone	Southport (0704) 32553
Open	Easter–end of September 09.30–20.30
Access	Marine Parade runs along the seafront
Station	Southport Chapel Street (½ mile)
Shows	Snakes fed (Sunday)

The reptiles here includes Snakes, small Crocodiles, Geckos, Iguanas, Lizards and Terrapins. The 52 species of fish are principally of the freshwater variety, including some Blind Cave specimens. There are also Axolotl and Frogs.

Southport: Hesketh Park

Address	Southport, Merseyside
Telephone	Southport (0704) 34024
Open	09.00–dusk
Acreage	⅓
Access	To NE of town on E side of A565 to Preston
Station	Southport
Facilities	Guided tours (organizations) Restaurant (summer); snack bar Picnic area
Other	Pets' corner Playground Woodland walk Feeding With own food (not bread)

Owned by the local authority (and therefore free), Hesketh Park contains a bird collection. There are about 40 species, such as talking Mynahs, Leadbeater's Cockatoo, African Parrots, Peafowl, Pheasants and the many extra inhabitants of the heated bird house. There is another aviary at Southport, in the Botanical Gardens at Churchdown.

Spetchley Park

Address	Spetchley Park, Worcester
Telephone	Spetchley (090 565) 224
Acreage	110
Access	Immediately S of A422 Worcester (3 miles W) to Broughton Hackett (2 miles E) road
Station	Worcester (3 miles)
Facilities	Guide book and information leaflet (to garden) Self-service cafeteria (Sunday only 14.00–18.00)

It is almost axiomatic that good British parkland contains Deer, and their lack is most distressing whenever they are absent. At Spetchley Park there are 90 Red Deer, 50 Fallow Deer and also exotic wildfowl. Visitors would undoubtedly come to the gardens and park even without these residents, but they are assuredly an asset to the estate.

Spring Hill Wildfowl Park

Address	Forest Row, East Sussex
Telephone	Forest Row (034 282) 2783
Open	All year except 25 December 10.00–18.00
Access	In middle of Forest Row on A22 turn off between Swan Hotel and church into Priory Road; after ½ mile turn right opposite school
Station	East Grinstead (5 miles)
Facilities	Information leaflet Cafeteria for light teas, coffee, minerals Picnic area Gift shop
Shows	Feeding of birds late afternoon

The most remarkable feature of the Spring Hill Wildfowl Park is the way that the birds roam at will, with visitors having to pick their way between them. This involvement has not stopped a considerable amount of breeding and pens are normally used to help the birds rear their offspring. Notable successes have been with Abyssinian Blue-wing Geese, Hawaiian Geese, Red-breasted Geese and, even more exceptional, Ostriches.

There are many officially endangered species here such as five breeds of Pheasant, four of Geese and two of Duck. In all there are over 100 species of bird, which also include Flamingos, Cranes, White and other Peacocks. Apart from the five outstandingly rare Pheasants, there are 15

other kinds. The collection was privately run until 1974 when it was opened to visitors. In 1976 over 40,000 of us took advantage of the opening.

Stagsden Bird Gardens

Address	Stagsden, Beds
Telephone	Oakley (023 02) 2745
Open	All year 11.00–19.00 or dusk
Acreage	8½
Access	200 yds up Turvey Road in Stagsden village N from A422 Astwood (2½ miles SW) to Bedford (5 miles E) road
Station	Bedford (4½ miles)
Facilities	Guide book Snack bar (summer); kiosk Picnic area Gift shop

In 1961 the owner of the Stagsden collection brought home to Britain some Hume's Bar-tailed Pheasants. They had never before been imported alive into the western world from their home in Burma, and the following year they were successfully bred here in Bedfordshire. The gardens were opened to visitors in 1965 but the arrival and then the breeding of those Bar-tailed Pheasants still sets the tone of the place: it specializes in rare birds and every effort is made to breed them.

In all there are now 1000 individuals of 150 species. Apart from the several species of rare Pheasant there are many old breeds of poultry and rare waterfowl. A particular success was in breeding the Satyr Tragopan which normally lives high up in the Himalayan forests. There are also homing Budgerigars, talking Mynahs and Parrots.

Sundown Pets Garden

Address	Treswell Road, Rampton, Retford, Notts
Telephone	Rampton (077 784) 274
Open	All year 10.00–dusk
Acreage	10
Access	Turn E off A638 1 mile S of East Retford; take minor road to Rampton (7 miles); turn N in village for ½ mile towards Treswell
Facilities	Information leaflet Tea garden Picnic area Gift shop
Other	Playgrounds
Feeding	With own food

Many animal collections seem to tolerate children rather than welcome them, but the Sundown Pets Garden is quite blatantly a place where Mum, Dad *and* the kids are all equally well received. The animal collection predominantly offers pets and farm creatures. These include Lambs, Pigs, Goats, Donkeys, Monkeys and Foxes as well as Parrots, Pheasants and Peafowl. In all there are about 200 animals in this children's zoo (which was opened in 1969).

However, it is well appreciated that children will turn to other things at the drop of a play area, wigwam, large fort, Viking ship, swing bridge, rotating barrel, or trampoline, all of which are here at Sundown. The management does not have exact attendance figures but merely claims 'a large number of satisfied visitors'.

Teignmouth Aquarium

Address	The Den, Seafront, Teignmouth, Devon
Telephone	Teignmouth (062 67) 3383
Open	Summer 10.00–20.00
Access	The Den is immediately W of the pier
Station	Teignmouth (¼ mile)

This aquarium has now been open for 20 years and, like the one at Torquay, does not restrict its exhibition to local marine fauna. These include Sharks, Rays and Moray Eel, but tropical marine fish are also represented, with a good collection of coral. Reptiles to be seen here include Cayman and Crocodiles, as well as Turtles.

Thorney Wild Life Park

Address	Thorney, Peterborough, Northants
Telephone	Thorney (073 18) 221
Open	Summer 10.00–dusk
Acreage	45
Access	On W side of B1040, 200 yds S of A47 Peterborough (7 miles W) to Guyhirne (8 miles E) road
Station	Peterborough (7 miles)
Facilities	Guided tours (by arrangement) Self-service cafeteria, snack bar, kiosk Gift shop
Other	Amusements Railway

The decade of the 1960s saw a greater proliferation of animal collections in Britain than at any other period. This park was opened in 1968 and a very considerable collection is now amassed near the site of Thorney Abbey (founded in 1038) and Abbey House (built in 1660). It includes many of the largest mammals as well as a large number of the more dramatic birds. As with so many of the animal collections in this country, a circus family (the Robertses) was involved in its establishment.

Torquay Aquarium

Address	Beacon Quay, Torquay, Devon
Telephone	Torquay (0803) 24439
Open	Summer 10.00–20.00
Access	At far end of Beacon Quay, on E side of harbour
Station	Torquay (2 miles)
Facilities	Gift shop

This aquarium has been open for over 20 years but during the 1970s has been extensively rebuilt. It claims it is the largest aquarium in the west and, whereas many of the aquaria at seaside resorts only exhibit local fauna, and rely on locals and visitors to supply the exhibits, this one is of sufficient importance to have had a TV documentary film made of some of its exhibits being collected in the Bahamas. It is most extensive on the tropical marine side but freshwater fish are well represented as are local marine specimens. Among new arrivals in 1976 were Loggerhead Turtles and Jackson Penguins.

Waddesdon Manor

Address	Aylesbury, Bucks
Telephone	Waddesdon (029 665) 211 282
Open	Last Wednesday in March–last Sunday in October
Access	Immediately S of A41 Bicester (10 miles W) to Aylesbury (6 miles SE) road, at W end of Waddesdon village
Station	Aylesbury (6 miles)
Facilities	Guide book and information leaflet Restaurant for afternoon teas except Monday, unless Bank Holidays, and Tuesday
Other	Manor House and grounds

The animals living at Waddesdon Manor are eclipsed by the splendour of the house and its grounds. Nevertheless, there is an exciting aviary, built in the nineteenth century in an eighteenth-century style, which was opened to visitors in 1966. It is semi-circular, divided into cages and possesses a mixed assortment of Toucans,

Wellplace Bird Farm

Address	Ipsden, Oxon
Telephone	Checkendon (0491) 680 473
Open	Easter–October Saturday and Sunday from 10.00, weekdays from 13.30; October–Easter Saturday and Sunday from 10.00
Acreage	$4\frac{1}{2}$
Access	2 miles E of A4074 Wallingford (3 miles N) to Reading (13 miles SE) road and 1 mile E of Ipsden, on S side of minor road to Henley
Station	Goring and Streatley (5 miles)
Facilities	Information leaflet Kiosk Picnic area Gift shop
Other	Pets' corner Donkey rides
Feeding	With purchased food

Although over 100 species of bird live here, totalling about 1000 individuals, the place is by no means restricted to them. There are also about 50 mammals which include Monkeys, Badgers, Otters, Servals, Raccoons, Llamas, Squirrels and Foxes, as well as Ponies, Sheep and Donkeys. Of the birds there are Cockatoos, Parrots, Rheas, Flamingos, Pelicans, Cranes, Pheasants, Peafowl, waterfowl and many smaller varieties. The farm was opened in 1968.

Rothschild's Mynah (or Grackle), white save for blue around the eyes, lives only on the island of Bali and is an officially endangered species. A few are to be found in British aviaries.

Touracos, Jays, Woodpeckers, Starlings and members of the Parrot family.

It is particularly appropriate that it should contain Rothschild's Grackle (or Mynah). This white bird, whose restricted habitat is the Island of Bali, is extremely rare but was named after a member of the Rothschild family who built this house. Although in the middle of England the mansion is in the French Renaissance style, was designed by a French architect, and even had the gardens laid out by another Frenchman. After the house had been completed a small group of Japanese Sika Deer were introduced into the grounds and these are still represented here. They and the birds are rather more to complement the house and all its attractions than for their own sake, but they look none the worse for that.

West Wales Farm Park

Address	Blaenbedw Isaf, Plwmp, Llandyssul, Dyfed
Telephone	Rhydlewis (023 975) 317
Open	May–September 10.00–18.00
Acreage	50 acres for park
Access	$1\frac{1}{2}$ miles S of Plwmp on A487 Aberayron (9 miles NE) and Cardigan (12 miles SW) road, on W side of minor road to Rhydlewis (3 miles S)
Station	Carmarthen (30 miles)
Facilities	Information leaflet Guided tours and lectures (by arrangement) Snack bar and kiosk Picnic area Gift shop
Other	Pets' corner Pony rides Horse-drawn cart rides Playground
Shows	Sheepdog demonstrations (occasional)

Another collection whose theme is rare and indigenous breeds of farm livestock. There are 70 different species here, such as White Park, Belted Welsh Black and Old Gloucester Cattle. It only opened in May 1977 but, even so, most species were expected to breed during the opening year.

Weston Park

Address	Shifnal, Salop
Telephone	Weston-under-Lizard (095 276) 207 and 385
Open	April–September 11.00–19.30 except Monday and Friday, unless Bank Holidays
Acreage	350
Access	On S side of A5 Oakengates (8 miles W) to M6 Junction 12 (8 miles E) road
Station	Shifnal (6 miles), Corford (6 miles)
Facilities	Guide book and information leaflet Bar occasionally open; licensed restaurant, self-service cafeteria, snack bar, kiosk (special prices for children) Picnic area Gift shop
Other	House to visit Pets' corner Pony rides Pony traps Playground Architectural trail Nature trail and woodland walk Studio pottery Garden centre
Feeding	With own food

Although most visitors will come to Weston Park because of the house, grounds and all the other attractions, there is a pets' corner (opened in 1966) and there are Fallow Deer and rare breeds of Sheep roaming within the park.

Weston-super-Mare: Mini-Zoo and Aquarium

Address	Marine Lake, Weston-super-Mare, Avon
Telephone	Weston-super-Mare (0934) 23221
Open	April–October from 10.00
Access	At N end of beach beside road from town towards Birnbeck Island
Station	Weston-super-Mare Central ($\frac{3}{4}$ mile)

Within this small zoo and small aquarium are a few mammals, birds, reptiles, amphibia and fish. Among the fish are tropical marine and freshwater specimens as well as some caught in the nearby sea. The collection was opened in 1961 and attracted 50,000 visitors in 1976.

Whitson Zoological Park

Address	Whitson Court, Nr Newport, Gwent
Telephone	Newport (0633) 72515
Open	10.30–18.00
Acreage	20
Access	Follow minor road S from B4004 Newport ring road
Station	Newport (5 miles)
Facilities	Guided tours (by arrangement) Snack bar (summer)
Other	House to visit (by appointment) Playground
Feeding	With zoo food

Whitson Court is a John Nash house, built in the late eighteenth century. Within its grounds is a mixed assortment of animals, such as Monkeys and Bears, some birds, a few reptiles and a large number of tropical fish.

Widcombe Bird Gardens

Address	Culmhead, Blagdon Hill, nr Taunton, Somerset
Telephone	Blagdon Hill (083 342) 268
Open	March–October 10.30–18.00
Acreage	20
Access	To N of minor road running W from B3170 (linking A303 with Taunton) towards Wellington, on S side of Blagdon Hill
Station	Taunton (6½ miles)
Facilities	Guide book Café (light lunches and cream teas); kiosk Picnic area Gift shop
Other	Pets' corner Playground Paddle boats Woodland walk

The theme and the dominating factor of this collection is general bird life. Of the 1000 animals resident here there are 170 species of bird represented and only 12 of mammal.

The birds are very mixed and include wildfowl, Pheasants (Elliot's, Cheer and Swinhoe's being the rare ones), Peafowl, Owls, old breeds of Bantams, Macaws (which talk) and many tropical birds including Sonnerat's Jungle Fowl. Visitors are allowed to feed them in the lake area, a concession which applies in many other establish-

Superb leapers among the branches, and hoppers when on the ground, the Bushbabies (or Galagos) are nocturnal animals not seen well in captivity unless the daylight hours have been reversed. A Senegal Bushbaby.

ments for wildfowl. Most animals can suffer when fed unsuitable home food but, judging from Ducks resident in urban parks, even a 100 per cent diet of stale bread seems to permit vigorous life. The Widcombe garden, with its shrubs and trees, is particularly striking and there is a woodland walk that takes great advantage of fine trees. The modest number of mammals include Sika Deer, miniature pantomime Ponies, Llama, Sheep and Goats.

Wildlife Park and British Nature Centre

Address	Westbury-on-Trym, Bristol, Avon
Telephone	Bristol (0272) 625 112
Acreage	10
Access	Signposted off A4108 into Westbury-on-Trym and into back streets
Station	Bristol (3 miles)

In 1965 David Chaffe opened this wildlife centre within a delightful wooded valley (of the Trym) that had somehow survived reasonably intact among the bricks of Bristol. Its theme was to be conservation. Since then, one assumes, it has had financial difficulties as the cages are in poor repair, the notices hard to read and not every animal looks in good shape. The sight of a dozen Oyster-catchers in a muddy cage, or of swathes of

weeds in other enclosures, or of unkempt pools is not the greatest advertisement for conservation. One rare delight was a Raven who, when all was quiet, would suddenly call out 'Walter!'; but he too called from a cage luxuriant with nettles.

Mr Chaffe's plans for 1977 were to sell the lease, move some of his collection elsewhere, and continue with his lecturing. So the wildlife centre may acquire a new look before very long.

Wold Pottery Bird Garden

Address	Routh, nr Beverley, Humberside
Telephone	Leven (0401) 42236
Open	All year except 25 and 26 December: summer 10.30–17.00; winter 10.30–dusk. Pottery open Monday–Friday
Acreage	2½
Access	A1035 Beverley (4½ miles SW) and Leven (2 miles NE) road; turn E in Routh village where signposted Meaux, Wawne, Sutton. Pottery is 250 yards on S side of road
Station	Beverley (4½ miles)
Facilities	Information leaflet Ice cream Gift shop

The Wold Pottery was 20 years old when, in 1974, it was decided to associate a small bird garden with it. This had previously been a personal hobby and was opened so that people could see the collection. It currently contains about 165 birds of 15 species. These include ornamental Pheasants and White Peafowl, Quails, Cockatiels, Parakeets and Laughing Thrushes, as well as colourful Bantams wandering at their will. The particularly rare Pheasants include Swinhoe's, Elliot's and Himalayan Monals.

Worldwide Butterflies

Address	Over Compton, Sherborne, Dorset
Telephone	Yeovil (0935) 4608
Open	All year except 25 December
Acreage	3
Access	N side of A30 Yeovil (3 miles W) to Sherborne (3 miles E) road, immediately E of Little Chef restaurant
Station	Sherborne (3 miles), Yeovil (3 miles)
Facilities	Guide book Guided tours Kiosk (restaurant nearby) Gift shop

Not a single vertebrate, the normal inhabitant of every zoo, lives here. Instead each living creature is an insect, and 99 per cent of them belong to just one group, the order Lepidoptera. Plainly such a minority interest, located down a rough lane that starts abruptly from a dual carriageway, will have no more than a few fanatics knocking at its door. After all, Butterflies and Moths spend most of their lives either as eggs, or creeping caterpillars, or mere pupae before, flitting here and there, they flutter swiftly – by most standards – to their graves. Perhaps a thousand lepidopterists visit it each year? Well, in 1976 over 50,000 people found their way to Worldwide Butterflies.

How right they were! It is a fascinating place. Once again, as is such a refrain in this book, one man's hobby grew and grew until it seemed a sane thing to let in people to see the work. Robert Goodden became interested in Butterflies when he was four. At eight he requested employment from a Butterfly farmer. At 16 he applied again, was accepted and left after 18 months to start his own business. He began in a Charmouth attic. After five years, longing for more space, he moved to a corner of the family estate, brought his breeding Butterflies with him, and then opened up (in 1973) to visitors. Although he runs the largest mail order Butterfly business in Britain, sending pupae, ova, larvae, mounted adults, habitat cages, killing bottles, relaxing fluid, anti-vermin crystals, breeding units and all manner of equipment to all manner of countries, it is visitors who will be the main source of money from now on. Once again it is our pockets that are helping to promote yet another animal collection.

Nevertheless, there is much to see and we get our money's worth. The major exhibit is a tropical jungle, pulsing with exotic specimens throughout the year. As many Butterflies live only for about six weeks there can be problems not experienced by other zoos whose stock, by and large, lives for years. There is a considerable museum-type display area, which also contains breeding cages. Outside this central building are the main breeding grounds with many lightweight, transportable structures that house, according to season, the burgeoning populations. Naturally wintertime is not peak period in the Butterfly and caterpillar business.

In 1978 Worldwide Butterflies will take another leap forward when it moves into Compton House, the nearby part-Elizabethan and part-Victorian dwelling that was the centrepiece of the old family estate. To have the biggest show of living Butterflies in Britain is one thing, but to have a mansion's front rooms as the major display area is quite another. Needless to say, the huge walled garden and the tall Victorian greenhouses will be dedicated to raising the appropriate plants for hordes more Lepidoptera. Worldwide Butterflies is only just beginning.

Yafford Mill

Address	Nr Shorwell, Isle of Wight
Telephone	Brighstone (0983) 740 492
Open	Easter–October
Acreage	25
Access	On S side of B3323 Brighstone (1½ miles W) to Shorwell (¼ mile E) road
Station	Ryde (12 miles)
Facilities	Guide book and information leaflet Snack bar and kiosk (summer) Picnic area Gift shop
Other	Pets' corner Pony and Donkey rides (weekends) Playground Nature trail and woodland walk Water mill Collection of agricultural bygones and horse-drawn machinery
Feeding	Ducks, with own food

The beautiful, ancient, working watermill is not only the dominant feature here but sets the tone of the place. Essentially the clock has been wound back and the animals on show are also, so to speak, ancient, beautiful and in working order.

The collection's theme is rare-breed farm animals. To this end there are, for instance, a flock of Portland Sheep, as well as the Ronaldsay, Dorset Horn and Jacob varieties; Berkshire, Tamworth and Gloucester Old Spot Pigs, and Highland, Welsh Black, Sussex, South Devon and Galloway Cattle. In a similarly traditional manner there are also Rabbits, Seals, Shetland Ponies and waterfowl, many of which are rare.

4 Town Zoos

Aberdeen Zoo

Address	Hazlehead Park, Aberdeen
Telephone	Aberdeen (0224) 39369
Open	Summer 10.00–20.30; winter 10.00–dusk
Acreage	3
Access	2 miles on W side of city immediately S of A944 to Huntly
Station	Aberdeen (2 miles)
Facilities	Guided tours by arrangement Kiosk Gift shop
Other	Children's section Playground

For such a large city this is a very small zoo, being less than three acres, but perhaps it is more surprising that it was only opened in 1966. An original aim of the Aberdeen and North of Scotland Zoological Society, which owns the zoo, was to specialize in indigenous fauna, but the current collection is much wider. In all there are about 200 mammals and 400 birds, including local creatures such as Wild Cats, Pine Martens, Seals, Deer and Squirrels, and exotics such as Chimpanzees, Monkeys, Wallabies, Pumas, Kinkajous, Guanacos and Small-clawed Otters (which come from southern Asia and are smaller than the European kind). The zoo opened with the assistance of the City of Aberdeen and promotes its educational activities enthusiastically.

Blackpool: Municipal Zoological Gardens

Address	East Park Drive, Blackpool, Lancs
Telephone	Blackpool (0253) 65027
Open	Summer 10.00–18.00 (last admission 17.30); winter 10.00–16.00
Acreage	32
Access	Immediately to E of Stanley Park on eastern outskirts of town, and N of approach road from M55
Station	Blackpool North (1 mile)
Facilities	Guide book and information leaflet Lectures (for schools) Bar, licensed restaurant, self-service cafeteria, snack bar, kiosk (summer) and vending machine (winter) Train within zoo Picnic area Gift shop Pushchairs for hire
Other	Children's zoo
Shows	Sealions fed 11.00 and 15.30; Penguins fed 11.30 and 15.00

Previous pages With Keeper Morton at London Zoo (in 1966) is Chi Chi, the Giant Panda who was to die in 1972.

It is easy to have a prejudice, particularly at a coastal resort, that any zoo founded by the council will look commercial and show little sensitivity about the animals. It is also easy, and very pleasing, to be completely wrong. The first 32 acres of the new Zoological Gardens opened in 1973 by Blackpool Corporation are a delight.

The impression at this zoo, however inaccurate it may be, is that there was lots of money to spend and the freedom to spend it in new and exciting ways. The overall picture, which is certainly accurate, is of well-thought-out enclosures, widely spaced apart with lots of grass and newly planted trees scattered in between. Plainly, the area was just flat fields before the zoo-men moved in and, with a total absence of natural landscaping, they did their best artificially. Each excavated pool provided the material for a hill and, although the area is still flat, there is no longer a feeling of total flatness. The zoo's designers have done the job well and will do it better in the future. Not only will further enclosures be made but another 68 adjacent acres have been earmarked for use, when time and money permit, by this corporation zoo.

Certainly many of the current enclosures are striking. Chamois walk about on one of the newly fashioned rocky hills, and one wonders why this supreme European alpinist is so rarely seen in zoos. Some Gibbons inhabit islands planted, as it were, with a scaffolding of bamboo. The Sealions have an ocean of a pool in which to swim. The Bison and Zebra have vast paddocks, and fences in this zoo are at a minimum, with ha-has and low walls serving instead wherever possible. However, the most extraordinary enclosure is the air-house bird-house. The fabric, as with all such pressure domes, is kept up solely by air. If plenty of internal space is the chief requirement this is a cheap and simple method of obtaining it. From the aviary point of view it means an interesting light (the material is partly translucent), a flight area unencumbered save by the trees and plants growing within, and an amazingly novel sensation for the visitors walking through it. Particularly strange is to see the feet and shadows of, usually, Seagulls walking externally on the roof. A masterly enclosure.

The air-house inhabitants include Scarlet Ibis (brilliantly scarlet, unlike many seen elsewhere), Sacred Ibis, Glossy Starling, various Pigeons and Herons, Fire Finch, Virginian Cardinal, Egret, Pin-tailed Whydah and Kiskadee. There are good pictures to help identification, but no discrimination between sizes. (Notice-boards are often poor in zoos and, where useful paintings or pictures do exist, all the birds, for example, are generally drawn with the same overall dimensions, from Cranes to Hummingbirds.)

Rare breeds of domestic animals are being increasingly put on show for our benefit. *Above* A Chartley bull, *left* A Bagot Goat, both at the Cotswold Farm Park in Gloucestershire.

Animals elsewhere are Lion, Tiger (both rather unimaginatively displayed for this zoo, with just grass and a log or two), Orang, Chimpanzee, Gorilla, Bactrian Camel, White Rhinoceros, Arabian Gazelle (very rare in the wild but happily becoming more abundant in our zoos), Squirrel Monkey, Black-headed Capuchin, Brazilian Tapir, Llama, Barbary Sheep (with another of the new rocky hills to climb on), Flamingo, Marmot (or Prairie Dog), Jackass Penguin, Red Kangaroo (the biggest of all marsupials), and Tree Kangaroo. There is a very large community of these animals here, and they do indeed climb, however much such non-hopping activity might seem alien to a Kangaroo. But evolution, having permitted or caused this Australian family to proceed apace merely by leaps and bounds, then caused or permitted some of those hoppers to become four-footed again and more adept at climbing trees.

There is a total of 692 animals in this collection, being 50 kinds of mammal, 125 of bird and 2 of reptile. Only about 50,000 people visited this zoo last year, with several millions visiting Blackpool's other attractions. But, if the zoo continues to excel and expand, people will perhaps talk of first visiting the zoo and then, if they have time, seeing what the Golden Mile has to offer.

Blackpool Tower Aquarium

Address	Promenade, Blackpool, Lancs
Telephone	Blackpool (0253) 25252
Open	Easter–end of October 10.00–23.00
Access	Within Tower on front (entry fee to Tower admits to Aquarium and other entertainments)
Station	Blackpool North (¼ mile)
Facilities	All within Tower

Within the complex of the famous Blackpool Tower is one of the major aquariums in Britain. There are 70 tanks containing 2000 specimens of 200 species, with particularly fine displays of coral fishes. The aquarium is likely to become the best marine collection in the country, if it has not

Blackpool Corporation recently opened a magnificent new zoo. Its inmates include two Chimpanzees and a Lowland Gorilla, seen here at the refreshment hour.

More like some Moorish palace than a building in which to house fish, the Brighton Aquarium is now 100 years old and, thanks to Dolphins, still drawing crowds.

already done so. There used to be a zoo within the Tower but its status has been considerably modified since the Blackpool Zoological Gardens were opened up in 1973 in an infinitely more suitable setting.

Bolton Metropolitan Borough Aquarium

Address	Central Museum and Art Gallery, Le Mans Crescent, Bolton, Lancs
Telephone	Bolton (0204) 22311
Open	All year Monday–Saturday 09.30–17.30
Access	Opposite Town Hall in city centre
Station	Bolton Trinity Street (¼ mile)
Facilities	Information leaflet Leaflet and guided tours Coffee bar Arts information/sales kiosk
Other	Museum and art gallery

Freshwater fish, both temperate and tropical, provide the majority of the exhibits. Although called an aquarium it possesses 5 bird species, along with 3 of amphibia, 11 of reptile, 3 of invertebrate and 50 of fish. Most of these fish are European species and some of them breed here, notably the Cichlids. Admission is free.

Brighton Aquarium

Address	Marine Parade, Brighton, East Sussex
Telephone	Brighton (0273) 64233/4
Open	All year from 09.00
Access	Immediately to E of Palace Pier on front
Station	Brighton (½ mile)
Facilities	Guide book Bar, self-service cafeteria and kiosk Gift shop
Other	Dolphinarium
Shows	Dolphins (at intervals all day)

A century old, superbly placed immediately to the east of the Palace Pier, and colonnaded within like some Moorish bazaar, the Brighton Aquarium is a remarkable establishment. It must have been seen by many millions in its time, and certainly has a very considerable assortment of tanks running down both sides of its huge hall, but the current impression is that the Dolphins rather than the old exhibits are pre-eminent. There is far more of a rush at the ticket desk

Overleaf American Bison, the Buffalo that used to be one of the most abundant hoofed animals in the New World. At the beginning of the nineteenth century there were 60 million of the species; just 80 years later there were only 541. This is part of the Woburn herd.

Above Brighton Aquarium very nearly pulled off an important 'first' when a Bottle-nosed Dolphin was born in October 1976. Unfortunately it died 10 days later.
Right Bristol Zoo has a good breeding record. It was the first European collection to produce a baby Chimpanzee, in 1934.

whenever a Dolphin performance is approaching than at any other time.

So, to start with those Dolphins, there are five of them, they live in a pool 80 feet long, 30 feet wide and 10 feet deep, and they put on a show several times a day. The dolphinarium is more lush than most, with a loudspeaker commentary and considerable play with coloured lights. Everyone was very surprised when one of the three females resident here gave birth on 20 October 1976; but the offspring died ten days later. Despite there being about 40 Dolphins in Britain there has never been a successful rearing (which is partly why dolphinaria have such a poor name among conservationists), but the Brighton birth, although unsuccessful, is believed to have been the first that was also conceived in Britain.

Other mammals in this collection are Sealions and Harbour (or Common) Seals. Their pools are nothing like so spacious, but they too give displays in their fashion at feeding time. Birds are represented by a group of Penguins, who can also be seen swimming underwater, and reptiles by that ponderous but highly successful aquatic group, the Turtles. Over 90 per cent of the tanks are occupied by fish, both freshwater and marine. The legacy of being a hundred years old is apparent here, as most of the tanks are modest in size with fairly small viewing windows, but even the collection is not particularly exciting, being uninterestingly lit and with much imitation botany. In the main the tanks' inhabitants are conventional and the very size of the Brighton Aquarium can lead the visitor to expect a better show. However, there are those Dolphins.

Bristol Zoo

Address	Zoological Gardens, Clifton, Bristol
Telephone	Bristol (0272) 38951
Open	All year except 25 December 09.00–17.00 or 19.00 according to season; Sunday from 10.00
Acreage	12
Access	On S side of B4468 along S side of Clifton Down
Station	Bristol Temple Meads (2½ miles)
Facilities	Guide book and information leaflet Bar, snack bar and kiosk; licensed restaurant with children's menu; self-service cafeteria (summer) Picnic area Gift and camera shops
Other	Aquarium
Shows	Penguins fed 12.30 (Sunday 12.00); Sealions fed 11.45 and 15.30; Big Cats fed 16.00 (winter 15.00)

Hard upon the heels of the founding of London Zoo arose 220 citizens of Bristol, each armed with £25, to buy and equip 12 acres of their own city. The Bristol, Clifton and West of England Zoological Society was formed in 1834 and Bristol Zoo has been going ever since. It is one-third the size of the zoo area in Regent's Park and receives about half as many visitors. Its reputation is considerable, partly due to some very important zoo 'firsts' as well as other achievements.

For example, at a time when Gorillas used to die in zoos fairly speedily, Bristol's Alfred stayed

Even in the drought of 1976 Bristol Zoo, a 12-acre haven within the urban development on every side, was a delight.

alive from 1930 until 1948. (London Zoo's long-lived Gorilla, Guy, only arrived in 1947 but is still going strong.) The Chimpanzee Adam, born at Bristol in 1934, was the first of his kind in Europe to be conceived and born in captivity. The zoo has also done well in the breeding of White Tigers, Okapi (it is rare enough just to see them), Black Rhinoceroses (five times), Giraffes (the same group has kept itself going since 1947), Orang-utans, Gibbons and Gorillas. The birth of two Lowland Gorillas in 1971 was the first such event in Britain for this species, and came 15 years after the first Gorilla had ever been born anywhere in captivity.

Almost more important than the animals at Bristol are the gardens. Many a zoo, particularly to the listless on a hot day, can seem to be highways of tarmac interspersed with tired grass, vague trees and cages. Bristol, on the other hand, even in the drought of 1976, can look a delight. There are good trees, well planted. There is a semi-circular herbaceous border of stunning beauty. There are beds filled with plants always at their peak, and acres of well-kept grass. The

principal lake is most refreshing, and makes one wonder how any zoological garden can be laid out without a handsome sheet of water. The Bristol landscaping was carried out by Richard Forrest of Acton, an important man of his time; and he, one feels, would not be displeased at the inheritance. There are great cedars, weeping beeches, redwoods, and many more, all helping to provide a sound backdrop for the animals. (Chester is the other main zoo that, judging from the displays on show, puts as much effort into botany as into zoology. Paignton is also important in this regard.)

The Bristol animal collection contains 750 individuals of 70 mammal species, 150 bird species and 30 reptile species. Well worth seeing are the Okapi (the Giraffe's only relative and unknown to science before 1901), the White Tigers (only six other collections in the world have them), the new Great Ape House (although more cramped than some), Malayan Tapirs (whose colouring is so much more striking than the commoner Brazilian kind), Crowned Pigeons (first bred in Britain in Bristol), and Dotty the Ring-tailed Lemur,

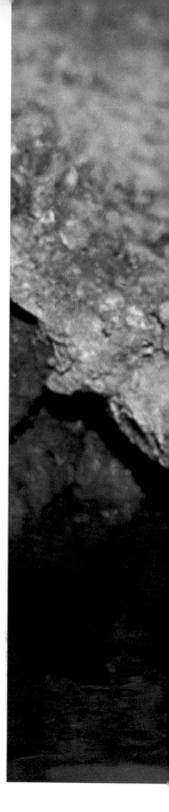

Opposite Chester Zoo is supreme both for its animals and its plants. *Above* A Lowland Gorilla, and *below* A general view that puts to shame most other zoos.

Above Quite the most gaudy of all the Ducks is the Mandarin. A male in prime condition at Slimbridge.

Another of Bristol's successes. It is currently one of the very few zoos in the world with a breeding group of White Tigers.

well known from appearances on television. There is a nice Flamingo pool, an interesting aquarium and a good atmosphere in the tropical bird house.

One trouble with any zoo, and particularly with an old one – Bristol has admitted ordinary visitors longer than any other British collection – is that modern zoo-keeping techniques differ so greatly from those of just two or three decades ago. Far quicker than human housing can go out of date, animal housing can look wrong, antiquated, cruel and unworkable almost the moment it has been erected. Within the span of one zoo director's time an enclosure can go from exciting to awful. For example, the Bear pits at Bristol are not in keeping with the place. It was originally extremely novel to have no bars between a large mammal and its human visitors, but a deep trench full of litter or unsightly water is now no better than bars. Bristol, like every other urban zoo, has its slums and is well aware of them. As today's new buildings will become tomorrow's

slums so speedily, there is much to be said for putting up houses that are cheap to erect and easy to pull down. But, in the main, urban zoos still build solidly whereas their country cousins, on the whole, prefer more temporary shelters that can be put up and later destroyed without excessive time, trouble or expense.

Even though Bristol Zoo is completely urban, surrounded by houses or roads on all sides, and even though 12 acres is not huge (being equivalent to a square with sides of 240 yards), there is a feeling of considerable space here. London's St James's Park is over seven times bigger, and Kew Gardens is 25 times as large, but Bristol Zoo seems far bigger than it is. The flowers help. So do the trees and the lake. And so does the fact that the animals, by and large, are ranged round the periphery leaving the centre relatively clear. Those 220 Bristol citizens of 1834 should feel they bought themselves a bargain for the 25 sovereigns they each contributed.

Chessington Zoo

Address	Leatherhead Road, Chessington, Surrey
Telephone	Epsom (03727) 27227
Open	March–October 09.30–18.30; November–February 10.00–16.00
Acreage	65
Access	On W side of A243 Leatherhead (5 miles S) to Hook (2 miles N) road
Station	Chessington South (½ mile)
Facilities	Guide book and information leaflet Bar, snack bar and kiosk (summer); licensed restaurant and self-service cafeteria Picnic area Gift shop Pushchairs for hire
Other	Aquarium Pets' corner Playground and funfair Train Model village Circus (seasonal, afternoons)
Shows	Great Apes fed 11.30; Leopards and Pumas fed 12.00; small mammals fed 13.00; Penguins and Pelicans fed 14.00; Lions, Tigers and Hyenas fed 15.00; Sealions fed 16.00; Monkeys fed 16.30

All Sloths have three toes on their hind feet, and either two or three on their front feet. The Two-toed Sloth from Brazil.

Take a ride on the Big Wheel here at Chessington and instantly you can get to grips with this place. To the north is London. On every other side is the confusion of the green belt. Below you is the circus, model village, funfair (with innumerable sideshows), ghost train, miniature railway, a five-acre sports field, Punch and Judy, swings and roundabouts, boating lake, dodgems, prehistoric monsters, rose gardens, playgrounds, a lot of people (over 800,000 a year) and many animals.

The collection is by no means a small adjunct, as it might be with some other funfair–zoo enterprises. Despite all the entertainment extras the animal section occupies about half of the total acreage, and is therefore on a par with the size of the zoo in Regent's Park. The number of species and of individuals is less than in London, but more than in many another urban zoo. In all there are 1225 individuals at Chessington, representing 101 species of mammal, 182 of bird, 27 of reptile, 5 of amphibia and 48 of fish.

The size of the collection means that quite a few animals are seen here in Surrey that are not commonly found elsewhere, such as the Striped Hyena, Marabou, Jabiru and Woolly-necked Storks, Nilgai (the large Indian antelope), Beaver (they are making more of a come-back into our zoos every year), Paca (a good-tasting rodent from South America), Agouti, Sloth Bear,

Lechwe, Yak, Malayan Bear, several sorts of Vulture, Hippopotamus (a familiar beast, but not a common sight in zoos), Black-footed Penguin, Blackbuck, Brush-tailed Porcupine and a considerable number of fish.

There are a few new enclosures, such as those for Otters, Black Swans, Beavers, Raccoons and some Monkeys. The Flamingo pond was also recently renovated. The Great Ape House, said to be the only one of its kind in southern England, was completed in 1967. Unfortunately, despite these labours, no enclosure is particularly striking and animals like the Barbary Sheep, which have a modest mountain and a fair amount of space, do rather better than the Apes. One wonders if there would have been twice the money to spend on each animal if there had been half as many.

Chessington and Whipsnade opened in the same year. Both are in the country within easy reach of London. Both have similar numbers of animals (Chessington is up on species, down on individuals) but almost 300,000 more people visit Chessington in a year even though (or because) the actual zoo section is a twentieth of the size of Whipsnade. Presumably the fair–circus makes all the difference, even though these other attractions mean leaving more money behind. Animals are the big draw – they still call it Chessington *Zoo* – but there must be great pulling power in all those extras. It is easy to wonder which way the zoos will jump in the coming years. Will they bring in more extras to help with the animals? Or will they concentrate upon fulfilling their primary role, the care and maintenance of the creatures that they own?

There are 150 kinds of Pheasant in the world, all from Asia (save one) and many are in peril in their native areas. The Pheasant Trust is helping to keep endangered species alive in Britain. *Overleaf* The Golden Pheasant, *Chrysolophus pictus*.

Chester Zoo

Address	Chester
Telephone	Chester (0244) 20106/7/8
Open	All year 09.00–dusk
Acreage	550 including farmland
Access	Turn NW towards Wervin off A41 Chester ring road, 1 mile S of junction with A5116 or 1½ miles NW of junction with A51. Zoo is immediately on left side of road
Station	Upton-by-Chester (1 mile), Chester General (2 miles)
Facilities	Guide book and information leaflet Licensed restaurant and self-service cafeteria with children's menu; snack bar and kiosk Picnic lawns Gift and camera shops Pushchairs for hire
Other	Aquarium Waterboat
Shows	Sealions fed 14.40, 15.40 and 16.40 (except Friday); Lions fed 15.00 (except Friday); Bears fed 15.15; Polar Bears fed 16.00

Who would have thought that Chester would have the second largest zoological collection in Britain? The answer must be only those people who have met George Mottershead, either when

George Mottershead, a man who appreciates his plants as much as his animals.

he started a plant nursery at Crewe, or when he first introduced animals there and began charging an entrance fee, or when he paid £3500 for a house and nine acres at Upton a few miles outside Chester and moved his collection there. Or when he opened up in 1931 just as Whipsnade and Chessington were also starting. Or started building; or collecting more animals, and more and more land. Every occasion would have shown Saul George Mottershead in action, living in his zoo (since 1920 he has always lived within the middle of his interests), making ends meet and prospering his collection however, whenever and wherever possible. That is why Chester has the second largest collection, the second largest gate (over 900,000 visitors a year) and 550 acres, including the surrounding farmland, now so suitable for the 3000 or more inhabitants.

There are 135 species of mammal, 292 of bird, 84 of reptile and it is difficult to know where to begin. Perhaps the *Chester Zoo News*, a monthly publication, is as good a place as any. For instance, to give a flavour of the place, here are some figures from the issue of September 1976. Mammals bred since the last report: 2 Wapiti; 2 Common Zebras; 1 Arabian Gazelle; 1 Red Lechwe; 2 Common Leopard cubs; 2 Nilgai; 1 Hamadryas Baboon. Also 1 Formosan Sika Deer, the mother having arrived pregnant. The following birds have bred: 2 Tiger Finches; 2 Jungle Mynahs; 3 Silverbills; 3 Cut-throat Finches; 6 Guiana Parrotlets; 3 Sacred Ibises; 7 Lesser Patagonian Conures; 2 Scaly-breasted Lorikeets; 1 Red-eared Waxbill; 1 Kookaburra; 1 Paradise Whydah; 3 Quaker Parakeets; 3 Laughing Doves; 3 Nanday Conures; 7 Peach-faced Lovebirds; 3 Fischer's Lovebirds; 1 Black-headed Sibia and 1 Rhea. (It even sounds well if sung to the music of 'A Partridge in a Pear Tree'.)

Gardening notes are included in the same *News*, and one must never forget that Mottershead started off as a nurseryman. Certainly, Chester Zoo has never been allowed to forget. 'In the middle of August we start rooting cuttings of the various bedding plants for next year. This makes it a busy time in the greenhouses as we like to get our required numbers rooted by the middle of September. 80,000 to 100,000 plants will be required for the display next summer.' And what a display it is. As much as any single other feature the 'bedding out' makes this zoo.

Every visitor to Chester must come away with a feeling that this or that enclosure is the very best. Perhaps it is the Great Ape area where Orangs, Chimpanzees and Gorillas (of two kinds) lord it on their respective islands beyond each moat. Or the Lion paddock where there are representatives of the 700 Lions born at Chester in the past 25 years. Or the Pachyderm house, the

The Tropical House at Chester is a delight, a noisy hothouse of a place set within a simple agricultural-type construction.

largest of its kind in the world. Or the Sealion pool. Or the sights from the waterbus. Or the free-flight aviary cunningly built out of scrap wiring and pylon angle-irons from the electricity board. Or, as the preference of many, the extraordinary tropical house.

Its most extraordinary feature is that it is quite excellent without really being extraordinary in any way. The actual structure is straightforward, being mid-twentieth-century agricultural in style. Many of the numerous cages within are equally elementary, being cube-shaped or just ordinary-shaped with wire or glass at the front and walls at the side. What makes everything so good is the sound, the smell, the atmosphere, the very feel of the place. Much of the noise comes from a waterfall, one of the simplest natural wonders of the world. Most of the smell comes from the hothouse growth of all the plants, trees, shrubs. And much of the atmosphere comes from the inspiring fact that you know it cannot have cost a great deal and you would love, given a good run on the horses, to do the same yourself: get a shed, pack it with vegetation, supply it with running water, and then fill the gaps with animals.

There is quite a bit of walking to do in this zoo, but you are always walking past water (every waterway was made to suit the zoo), past trees (virtually all, save for a few giants around the original house, have been planted since the new owner moved in), and past plants and animals. There are no amusements because the belief at Chester is that amusements and animals should not be mixed. There are extra fees for entrance into the aquarium and the tropical house, but these are very small and help to control those who enter. The roads are wide, being more like highways than paths for people (particularly near the Monkey house), but much business is conducted here. There are, for example, 232 staff and on a summer's day there will be thousands of visitors. (Even the car park can, and has to, take 3000 vehicles.)

It has all happened within the working span of one inexhaustible man. What a proud person George Mottershead should be.

Colchester Zoo and Aquarium

Address	Stanway Hall, Colchester, Essex
Telephone	Colchester (0206) 330 253
Open	All year except 25 December 09.30–approx. 19.00 according to weather and season
Acreage	40
Access	On S side of B1022 Tiptree (5 miles SW) to Colchester (3 miles NE) road
Station	Colchester (3 miles)
Facilities	Guide book and information leaflet Self-service cafeteria, snack bar and kiosk (summer) Picnic area Gift shop Pushchairs for hire
Other	Stanway Hall and grounds Aquarium Model railway Nature trail and woodland walk Exhibition centre
Shows	Feeding throughout day

Neatly and genetically arranged is this Colchester trio. Mate a Zebra (top) and a Donkey (centre) and the result (bottom) is a Zeedonk, top half apparently pure Donkey and bottom part apparently pure Zebra.

Considering that it only opened in 1963 Colchester Zoo has an enormous collection. It is a comprehensive community, with about 450 mammals, 300 birds, 200 reptiles, 150 amphibia, 200 fish and 100 invertebrates. In so far as it has specialized there is a particularly large assortment of primates (Chimpanzees, Orang-utans, Gibbons, Mandrills, Spider Monkeys, Lemurs, Woolly Monkeys) and Big Cats (Siberian and Bengal Tigers, Cheetahs, Pumas, Panthers).

The collection is still expanding and in the last five years various new houses have been built, such as an open-view enclosure for Orangs, a Chimpanzee complex, the Siberian Tiger enclosure and a nocturnal house. Breeding successes have been with several of the primates, and with Owls, Camels, Bison, Panthers, Caracals, Llamas and Zeedonks (which, as the word implies, are half-Zebra, half-Donkey). Particularly rare animals, apart from those already mentioned, are the Giant Tortoises, White Rhinos and Giant Condors.

The zoo's considerable acreage is on undulating ground interspersed with clumps of woodland and lake. Many of the houses are quite large, such as the aquarium and the Reptile house, and over 400,000 people visited this substantial zoo in 1976.

Opposite The formidable courtship display of *Pavo muticus*, the Green Peafowl.

Colwyn Bay: Welsh Mountain Zoo

Address	Colwyn Bay, Clwyd
Telephone	Colwyn Bay (0492) 2938 and 31660
Open	Summer 09.30–19.00; winter 10.00–16.00
Acreage	37
Access	On S side of Old Highway to W of B5113 Llanrwst (13 miles S) to Colwyn Bay (1 mile N) road
Station	Colwyn Bay (1 mile)
Facilities	Guide book and information leaflet Lectures and guided tours (educational) Snack bar and kiosk (summer) Picnic area Gift and camera shop
Other	Children's zoo Nature trail and woodland walk
Shows	Sealions fed 12.00 and 15.20; Penguins fed 10.10; falconry displays 11.45 and 15.00

It is hardly a mountain zoo, in that it stands on a fairly gentle slope just above a town. It is also not

An Asian Tawny Eagle about to take off during the flying demonstrations given at the Welsh Mountain Zoo, Colwyn Bay.

the Colwyn Bay Zoo, as such a title would imply a collection set amidst the assortment of seaside entertainments. Nevertheless, *Y Sŵ Fynydd Gymreig, Bae Colwyn* (the Welsh Mountain Zoo, Colwyn Bay) is – whatever its proper name – an enchanting place that does much for the resort lying below its thickly wooded acres.

Its appeal lies both in its hillside of a location and its sense of intimacy. With 37 acres it is bigger than the London Zoo at Regent's Park, but it seems more compact save for some huge paddocks with great Welsh views and the forest area with its leafy paths. It seems to be, and is, a family business. Robert Jackson founded it in 1963, but died six years later when a tree fell on him while he was fishing. His family, a wife and three young-adult sons, decided to carry on, and have done so ever since.

Some potential visitors may not relish the steep and narrow roads leading to and from the zoo, but Wales would be a different (and sadder) place without such driving tests. Others, with push-

chairs or wheelchairs, may dislike the idea of a steep zoo; but most of the zoo's paths are flatter than might be expected from a general look at its hillside. The actual car park is within the zoo on the only piece of flat ground in the area, and parking outside is quite impossible.

Highlights at this zoo include the falconry displays (two Tawny Eagles were being used in 1976, with windy days – not unknown here – being the best); the sight of the Lions from the Safari Restaurant; the view from the (new and good) Penguin pool to the magnificent Conway Valley; the Sealion display when three females unashamedly put on a circus performance when acquiring their fish; the bird of prey mews; and, among the many reptiles, the Rhinoceros Iguana, which is 100 per cent Iguana but has protrusions on its snout not unlike those possessed by a young Rhinoceros.

Endangered species (as officially defined) living here are Przewalski's Wild Horse, the Syrian Brown Bear (smaller and lighter in colour than

194

other Brown Bears), and the Bald Eagle. This is the national bird of the United States, white-headed and most elegant, but not often seen in the wild as it has dwindled in numbers despite protection by Federal law. (At least the Welsh national Dragon can never go extinct. Nor, for that matter, can the British Unicorn.) Other rarities include American Crocodiles and Andean Condors. So far the Condor eggs here have either been infertile or the male would not let the female sit on them. It would be supreme if this South American giant of a bird could be induced to rear young successfully in a cage set beneath the trees of a Clwyd hillside, and establish a British 'first' for the species. As the Rhinoceros Iguanas have also started laying eggs they too may create another British 'first'.

The total number of species here is 25 mammal, 55 bird, 35 reptile, 8 amphibia and 5 fish. There is much to be seen, but do not miss – if the day and the bird are both right – the sight of an Eagle plummeting down with wings almost closed from 1000 feet or so. It is unforgettable. Anyway, *Croeso i'r Sŵ Fynydd Gymreig* (where some of the labelling and half the guide book is in Welsh), and have a good day. Over 170,000 did so in 1976.

A very rare sight in Britain, and rare even in its native North America (it is the national emblem of the United States) is the Bald Eagle. A pair at Colwyn Bay.

Coventry Zoo Park

Address	Whitley Common, Coventry, Warwicks
Telephone	Coventry (0203) 301 772
Open	10.00–dusk
Acreage	8
Access	S of A423 (Coventry 1 mile NW) to Princethorpe (6 miles SE) road, alongside B4115
Station	Coventry (1 mile)
Facilities	Guide book and information leaflet Guided tours Licensed restaurant, self-service cafeteria, snack bar and kiosk (summer) Picnic area Gift shop
Other	Pets' corner Pony rides Playground
Feeding	With purchased food

The particular rarity here for British zoo-visitors is the Heidesnucki Sheep, a rare Danish breed, but the zoo's other inhabitants include the traditional big cats (Lions, Leopards, Pumas and Tigers, all of which have bred), Elephants, Bears, and half a dozen species of Monkey as well as Chimpanzees. Birds on show include Peacocks, Finches, Budgerigars, Parrots, Macaws, Doves, Pigeons, Chinese Silkfowl, and many Ducks and Swans.

Dudley Zoo

Address	2 The Broadway, Dudley, West Midlands
Telephone	Dudley (0384) 52401
Open	10.00–17.00
Acreage	40
Access	In centre of town, just N of main shopping area
Station	Dudley Port (2 miles)
Facilities	Guide book and information leaflet Bar, licensed restaurant, snack bar; self-service cafeteria and kiosk (summer) Picnic areas Gift and camera shops
Other	Aquarium Pets' corner Pony rides Playground Chair-lift Train Nature trail
Shows	Animals fed every $\frac{1}{2}$ hr 14.00–17.00

Start building a castle in the tenth century. Have its existence mentioned in the Domesday Book. Add to the castle as the years go by, and then watch as Cromwell fires upon the place from a nearby hill. Watch also as a huge industrial complex springs up on every side, with a city centre just 100 yards away. Suffer considerable tunnelling as the hill on which the castle stands is excavated for limestone. And then, in 1937, be amazed when someone decides to turn the whole place, hill, castle and former mine, into a modern

Dudley Zoo was Britain's most modern zoo in the 1930s. Now many of its structures, such as the Bear enclosure, are protected from alteration, and every single tree within its grounds is subject to a preservation order.

zoo. All zoo origins are odd but the history and location of Dudley Zoo are odder than most.

The ruins of Dudley Castle sit, as proper castle ruins should do, at the apex of a pimple of a hill dominating the surrounding landscape. The zoo, as most zoos certainly are not, has been built on the steep slope of this circular hill. The industrial town of Dudley begins at the foot of the hill where development was more feasible. It is a unique arrangement, with many benefits from the extraordinary situation. Firstly, no other urban zoo can claim to be quite so centrally placed. Secondly, the continuous slope has given great scope to cage design. Thirdly, as visitors wander slowly upwards in a circular fashion, they steadily achieve a more exciting view. Finally, as ultimate reward, there is the haven of Dudley Castle. Its courtyard, free from animals and peacefully secluded, is a restful spot for picnics, for a kind of tranquillity rarely to be found within 100 yards of an urban centre. As the zoo keeps on pointing out in its publicity material, the visitor here gets two for the price of one, the zoo *and* the castle it contains.

Of course, it also contains all its animals, namely 300 mammal individuals, 280 birds, 73 reptiles, 20 amphibians, and 300 fishes. Prominent among them are Arabian Gazelle (Dudley was the first European zoo to have a large herd, and has bred them), Red Kangaroo (also breeding), Lynx, Orang-utan, Flamingo (Cuban, Greater and Chilean), Polar Bear (have bred here), Giant Tortoise, Wolf (a very alert and interesting pack), Bengal Tiger (bred for the first time in 1975), Brazilian Tapir (the young have white streaks along their bodies), Audad (or Aoudad, Udad, Arui, Fechstal, Maned Sheep, or just Barbary Sheep; they are all the same animal and are the only wild sheep in Africa), Spotted Hyena, Crested Porcupine, Axis Deer, Lowland Gorilla (never been seen to mate), Guanaco and Otter. Of course, with over 1000 individuals to choose from, every visitor may come up with a different set of prominent preferences.

The reptile house is good (and free). Its Boa Constrictors have bred, an uncommon occurrence in captivity. The four Mississippi Alligators were presented to Dudley to form a breeding nucleus, this zoo having been selected by the American donors. There is a 15-foot Reticulated Snake, a Two-banded Monitor that can be taken on a lead around the zoo, Snapping Turtles, Mangrove Snakes and many more. The water, which looks clean, is in fact changed daily, another rare zoo occurrence. Entrance to the aquarium is also free as all extra charges were abolished a few years ago in exchange for an additional sixpence at the gate. The aquarium's best room is the old castle

Dudley has had more than its share of problems. There used to be a dolphinarium here which, containing Dolphins and a Killer Whale, brought in the crowds, but there was trouble over planning permission for the new pool. The animals therefore had to go, and the Whale appropriately died four days before the move was due. The castle brooding over the scene has had, as is customary for castles, a turbulent history throughout its centuries. It seems as if this new and old Dudley Zoo, the main animal collection of the West Midlands, has inherited some of that unrest. There are and have been difficulties, but the collection is a good one, great advances have been made in breeding in the past five years and the zoo deserves encouragement. Over 400,000 visitors did their best to give it in 1976.

Edinburgh Zoo/Scottish National Zoological Park

Address	Murrayfield, Edinburgh
Telephone	Edinburgh (031) 334 9171
Open	April–September 09.00–19.00; October–March 09.00–17.00 or dusk if earlier
Acreage	80
Access	On N side of A8 Edinburgh to Glasgow road, 2 miles W of city centre
Station	Edinburgh Haymarket (2 miles)
Facilities	Guide books and information leaflet Lectures Guided tours (educational) Licensed restaurant with children's menu; self-service cafeteria (summer) with children's menu; kiosks Picnic areas Gift shops Pushchairs for hire
Other	Children's zoo Aquarium Pony rides Pony traps Nature trail
Shows	Aquarium creatures fed 16.30 summer, 15.00 winter; Apes fed summer 17.30, winter 15.45; Grey Seals fed 15.00; Lions, followed by Tigers, except Tuesday, Thursday and Friday, fed summer 16.00, winter 15.30; Penguins fed summer 15.45 and 18.00, winter 14.30; Sealions, followed by Pelicans and Storks, fed summer 15.00, winter 14.30; Reptiles fed Wednesday and Sunday, summer 11.00–12.30 and 16.00–16.30, winter 15.30–16.00 Penguin Parade summer 15.30, weather permitting

crypt, seemingly tailor-made for tropical fish tanks. The rarest exhibit is probably the Lung Fish that has grown from nine inches to three feet since its arrival beneath these battlements.

Along with the merits of Dudley's location are some disadvantages. Atmospheric pollution does not help. And although the view may survey four counties this also means that winds from practically every point of the compass can be impressive. The conical hill is good for some visitors but, although the main path spirals gently upwards, it can be tiring for others. To help, there is a chair-lift (which does cost a little extra) enabling the elderly, for example, to walk down rather than up. Proximity to the city centre means that vandalism is a problem. And being 40 years old brings another difficulty. In its day Dudley was Britain's most modern zoo, and the architects brought much of their Whipsnade and Regent's Park experience to bear upon it. For instance, they made considerable and exciting use of reinforced concrete. This now means that many enclosures, including even a kiosk, are scheduled monuments protected from alteration. Every single tree within the zoo grounds is subject to a preservation order. Consequently, as any zoo management worth its rations is wishing to change, improve, or destroy the old that is no longer suitable, the job becomes infinitely harder, if not impossible, when a love for preservation is killing new ideas.

Edinburgh Zoo possesses the largest and most reproductive captive group of Penguins anywhere in the world. Gentoos and Rockhoppers are the principal producers.

Started in 1909, the Zoological Society of Scotland (which became Royal in 1948) used to be an urban zoo growing increasingly weary of its inheritance, of old cages, many committees and traditional procedures. Today it seems to have the zest of a new establishment. Much building is going on. New land has been bought. The committees have been reduced. Local authority money has been acquired, from Edinburgh, from Lothian, from Scottish Education. A new team is doing wonders.

Edinburgh Zoo is on a fairly steep, south-facing slope rising from the Corstorphine Road. It is surrounded by a golf course, a corporation park, a footpath, Scotia Academy (for boys), a Post House Hotel, the Corstorphine Hospital, and the main road from Edinburgh to Glasgow. Therefore it is all the more surprising that new land could be acquired, but the zoo now is wedge-shaped. Its frontage with the road is quite narrow, but the zoo gets fatter and more impressive the farther a visitor climbs the 300 feet or so to reach its summit. As Edinburgh Zoo is now over twice the size of the Regent's Park Zoo, possesses fewer animals and receives fewer visitors, there is towards the top a feeling of spaciousness more akin to some country estate than yet another urban collection. For example, there is a new paddock to be stocked with African plains animals (Zebra, Ostrich, Lechwe, perhaps Giraffe) that looks and is enormous for a city zoo.

The proudest possession of the Royal Zoological Society of Scotland is the flock of Penguins,

the largest and most viable group anywhere in captivity. It is world famous, largely for its breeding abilities. A King Penguin was first reared to maturity here in 1919, and Kings are now reared (virtually) every year. Gentoo Penguins are produced in greater numbers (33 in 1976), but the story is not always plain-sailing. For example, according to the Annual Report for 1975, the Gentoos laid 80 eggs, 37 of which were hatched, and 27 were reared; the Kings laid 13 eggs, of which two were hatched and only one survived; the 16 Rockhoppers produced two eggs, both of which were stolen. (Pheasants, wildfowl and Tumbler Pigeons also lost their eggs that year.) Nevertheless, despite the ups and downs (which also happen to natural colonies, or rookeries), the flock is self-sustaining at about 90 birds. None have been bought in since 1963 and very many have been sold. Visitors should not miss this community, particularly when it is busy incubating or making its summertime parade through the park.

The collection totals 380 mammals, 600 birds (including those Penguins), 300 reptiles, 30 amphibians, 400 fish, and 20 invertebrates. Particularly exciting individuals are: the Beavers, which breed two or three young every year; the Capybaras, which had young in 1976; Cassowary, which bred first in 1967, a British 'first', and those chicks have since bred; and Snowy Owls – 15 young have been reared by one pair. The good new enclosures include the Lion house (1976), which makes use of the excellent outside area (built in 1914) but gives them an inside and an outside with much more scope both for management and viewing. The new Monkey house (1973) is a good mixture of grass, paving stone, glass, interesting furnishings and hiding places for the inmates, a factor often omitted in many a modern Monkey house. The new Cheetah enclosure (1976) actually permits these animals to bound a bit, a pastime they pursue with commendable beauty. Right at the top of the zoo, another rare sight for an urban collection, is a wild Badger sett. Considerable use has been made of the Government's job creation scheme in building the new paddocks, fences, moats, and so forth (but the Badgers worked on their own).

Education is pursued vigorously. The zoo feels that a major animal collection not coupled with a teaching programme is a failure to use an important resource. Phases 1 and 2 of a new education centre were completed in 1973 and 1976 at a cost of £44,000. There is room for the very young, and straw bales and logs to sit on. There is a lecture theatre seating 220. Innumerable publications are printed, some expressly for the Gannet Club, an organization for the young. Within the education area is a natural history bookshop, said to be the finest in Scotland. Around the zoo are many notice-boards, both at a height for adults to read and lower down for children, that also emanate from the education area and are probably the

The Double-wattled Cassowary, a large, flightless bird now breeding at Edinburgh.

best of their kind in Britain. (The Wildfowl Trust notices are almost as good, but most zoo notices fail to come anywhere near these top two.) Education is not a platitude at Edinburgh, mouthed when the occasion seems to demand it, but an active, money-seeking, money-getting and well-managed enterprise. It means also that the guide book is not a few glossy pages interlaced with the same old facts (as in so many places), but 45 pages well worth the purchasing.

For those zoos enmeshed in their history, or suffering top-heavy management, or rigidly encased within a city, their keepers and directors could well profit by a visit to Edinburgh Zoo. After all, 700,000 more normal people visited the place last year, each profiting in his or her own fashion. The number is not bad for a city of half a million.

Glasgow: Calderpark Zoo

Address	Uddingston, Glasgow
Telephone	Glasgow (041) 771 1185/6
Open	All year 09.30–17.00 or 19.00, depending on season
Acreage	45
Access	Immediately NE of junction of A74 with M74, 8 miles E of city centre
Station	Uddingston (2 miles)
Facilities	Guide book and information leaflet Lectures Guided tours (educational parties) Self-service cafeteria with children's menu (summer); kiosks Picnic areas Gift shop Pushchairs for hire
Others	Playground and showground

Calderpark, a comparative newcomer among urban zoos, was not opened until 1947. Nevertheless, it was a good site and a considerable collection of animals. It is managed by the Zoological Society of Glasgow and West of Scotland, receives local authority grants (these being more forthcoming in Scotland than in England), can expand on to neighbouring land if need be, and is visited by about 130,000 people a year.

Group animals at the zoo include: White Rhino; Cheetah; Zebra (Grant's); Père David's Deer (sometimes also called Milou or Milu, and about the size of Red Deer); Black Panther (the father originally came from Dublin, and one of the young females recently born at Glasgow has been appropriately exported back to Ireland); Jaguar; Lar Gibbon; Ring-tailed Lemur (all

Lemurs are good, but the Ring-tailed are about the most striking); Rhinoceros Iguana; Blue-tongued Skink; Beaded Lizard; Potoroo (sometimes called the Rat Kangaroo); Fruit Bat; Leopard Cat; Polar Bear; Giant Hornbill; Two-wattled (or Doubled-wattled) Cassowary; and Mexican Iguana.

The Panthers are particularly interesting breeding successes. They are not a different species from the Leopard, merely a melanistic form of it. Panthers occur most frequently in the forests of southern Asia (Mowgli's friend Bagheera was one) but they can also turn up in zoo litters. In the 15 months prior to writing Glasgow has reared a total of ten Leopard cubs, some normally spotted, but some black. Melanistic Lions are also possible but exceedingly rare. At Glasgow, as was recorded in *Zoolife*, the Calderpark publication, a Lion cub was born recently 'with a large black patch running up the inside of his right leg and across his chest'. If this aberration also occurs in that male's future offspring, and if Glasgow can selectively breed its Lions for blackness, the zoo will then possess a very interesting (and valuable) race of this species.

Other recent breeding successes have been Binturong (the shaggy-haired, tree-dwelling form of Civet); Ring-tailed Lemurs; White-throated Capuchin (one of the four Capuchins, all of which live in Central and South America); Potoroo (as with other marsupials it is a long time before the young leave their mother's pouch); Fruit Bat; Zebra; and Bactrian Camel.

Considerable building has been achieved recently: a primate house, an Elephant and Rhino house, and a Camel and Zebra house. An aquarium is being built. But Calderpark fell on bad times in recent years and the new management is struggling to improve the place. Unfortunately, there is much to be done.

Leeds City Museum Aquarium

Address	Leeds City Museums, Municipal Buildings, Leeds, West Yorks
Telephone	Leeds (0532) 31301
Open	Tuesday–Friday 10.00–18.30; Saturday 10.00–16.00
Access	Opposite Town Hall in city centre, just N of A64 through city
Facilities	Souvenirs for sale

Entrance to this aquarium, which was opened in 1969, is free. There are ten tanks which include two dedicated to tropical marine animals, one to

Axolotls, and one to marine fauna of the Yorkshire coast. The others are of a more general nature. There are four vivarium tanks containing Snakes, Lizards, Salamanders, Turtles, American Bullfrogs and Marine Toads.

The London Zoo

Address	Regent's Park, London NW1
Telephone	London (01) 722 3333
Open	All year except 25 December: 09.00 (March–October) and 10.00 (winter)–18.00 (Sunday and Bank Holidays 19.00) or dusk if earlier
Acreage	36
Access	On S side of Prince Albert Road, at northern end of Regent's Park. Waterbus from Little Venice to zoo in summer
Station	Camden Town (Underground) ($\frac{1}{4}$ mile)
Facilities	Guide book and information leaflets Lectures and guided tours (schools) Bar, snack bar and kiosks; licensed restaurants and self-service cafeteria with children's menu Picnic area Gift and camera shops Pushchairs for hire
Other	Aquarium Children's zoo Pony, Donkey and Camel rides (see below) Pony and Llama traps (see below) Playground
Shows	Sealions fed (not Friday) April–September 12.00 and 15.30, winter 14.30; Penguins by children's zoo fed 14.30; reptiles fed Fridays only 14.30; Pelicans at Mappin Terrace Pool fed 14.45; Eagles fed (not Thursday) 15.15 Elephants' bathtime 11.30, weather permitting Donkey rides at children's zoo Easter–October (except Sunday) 13.15–15.45, weather permitting Camel, Llama trap and Pony trap rides Easter–30 September (except Sunday) 13.45–15.45, weather permitting

The London Zoo in Regent's Park merits all the superlatives. It is our oldest and most famous. It gave the name 'zoo' to the world. It has possessed some of the best-known animals, such as Jumbo the Elephant, and Ming and Chi-Chi the Giant Pandas. It currently possesses the largest collection of animal species within the British Isles. It receives more visitors than any other zoo. It is best placed, being within a park and yet just a couple of miles from the centre of England's capital. It receives most of the gifts that are presented to Britain, such as Edward Heath's Panda pair. It is quite the heaviest zoo, having enclosures of

High days and holidays at the London Zoo. *Above* On August Bank Holiday 1922 there were 47,578 visitors. *Below* On 7 April 1950, Good Friday, the crowds flocked to see Brumas, and over a million *extra* visitors that year came to see the baby Polar Bear.

Three styles of bird enclosure. *Above* Part of the metallic confusion of the Snowdon construction within Regent's Park. *Left* An Egret surveying the simpler furnishings at Chester. *Below* 1930s' reinforced concrete still looks good in the Penguin Pool at Regent's Park. Behind is the very solid Elephant House.
Opposite 1836–1977. London Zoo's Giraffe house, designed by Decimus Burton, still incorporates much of the old shape as it is a scheduled monument.

Giraffes — Granny=Dears. & other Novelties

awesome bulk. It sired Whipsnade, the first of its kind in the country. It has bred many 'firsts'. It has more animals not seen anywhere else in Britain than any other zoo. It has received most benefactions. It publishes more literature than any other British zoo. It has more scheduled monuments (save, perhaps, for Dudley). It has not maintained a position of supremacy among the world's zoos, but it is No. 1 in Britain.

> The Stilton, sir, the cheese,
> the O.K. thing to do,
> On Sunday afternoon,
> Is to toddle to the Zoo

sang the Great Vance in 1867. He was referring, of course, to Regent's Park, and a century later could still be singing that tune.

London Zoo is also the most expensive of any urban zoo but, if the entrance fee is divided into the numbers of animals that can be seen, it is a relative bargain. Discounting such creatures as ants, locusts and bees, there are over 9000 animals within the park's 36 acres. These include 187 kinds of mammal (try thinking of 187 the next time you are in a traffic jam), 457 of bird, 115 of reptile, 49 of amphibia, 246 of fish, and 117 of invertebrate. (Many a zoo, happily charging, say, 50p entrance fee, has some 50 kinds of animal on show as against London's 1171.)

Since 1974 the Giant Panda Chi-Chi's replacements at Regent's Park have been a pair called Ching-Ching and Chia-Chia (in tub), a gift from China to the British people. Only in Peking, so far, has this species ever bred in captivity.

Having an ancient history is not necessarily desirable when it comes to managing a zoo, and London Zoo started its post-war career with an appalling assortment of slums (as against the German zoos which were largely, and conveniently, destroyed). At Regent's Park a most extensive building programme was subsequently initiated, and the new look now dominates the zoo. Compared with other British zoos the buildings were expensive, were influenced more by architects ('the most dangerous animals in any zoo', some say) and were apparently built to last, even though the previous buildings stayed up far too long and ideas change swiftly about the needs of every animal house. One wonders how much it would cost even to knock down the present Elephant–Rhino edifice. One also wonders, when looking at the Snowdon Aviary, whether pointed corners and large-diameter tubing were ever thought suitable for flying and perching birds. However, without doubt, today's Regent's Park

looks newer, more expensive and more open than at any other time in the past 30 years.

The animals are also breeding well. About 70 per cent of the animals now living within hooting, roaring and screaming distance of Camden Town were born there. This proportion could be made greater by a simple if unwelcome expedient; namely removing a good many of the veterans who have been at Regent's Park for years, long before captive breeding became important, and who have persisted into this current and more obstetric era. Particular breeding successes have been with Orangs, Giraffes, Przewalski's Horses and Chimpanzees. Salome appeared in 1976, the fifteenth Gorilla to have been seen at Regent's Park in 89 years and the first to have been born here. Other Regent's Park firsts in 1976 were Chilean Flamingo, Rockhopper Penguin and Margay (a South American Cat), but other births included Lar Gibbon, Gelada Baboon, Bactrian Camel (the two-humped sort),

Kangaroo, Wallaby, Bat, Civet, Phalanger (a furry marsupial), Tamarin, Lemur, Loris (the birth provided the first certainty that the parents were of different sexes), Jackson's Hornbill, Red-billed Hornbill, Sarus Crane, Imperial Pheasant, Potoroo and Bushbaby. It is somewhat typical of London Zoo that even some of its births are of animals not only very rare in other zoos but possibly unknown to most of us.

London's prime exhibits are Ching-Ching and Chia-Chia, the Giant Panda successors to Ming, Lien-Ho and Chi-Chi. After the much-publicized failure of Chi-Chi to mate with Moscow's An-An, and bearing in mind that no one outside Peking Zoo has ever bred this species (and then only very occasionally), it would be fantastic if London could pull off this most dramatic and crowd-pulling of all births.

Although London's new enclosures tend to look unlike those elsewhere, such as the glass and mesh Big Cat house, the high-rise bunker of an Elephant pavilion, the Mappin terraces (amazing for 1913) that are part chimney, part goat-mountain and part aquarium-roof, and the lattice structure much employed by the Apes and Monkeys, it is the Moonlight World that is the most striking. It is so completely different. The ground floor of this Charles Clore Pavilion for Mammals is an interesting mishmash of relatively straight-forward dwellings, but the floor beneath it contains the zoo's nocturnal house. So much animal activity takes place at night that, by reversing the lighting, we at least begin to understand how much we normally miss. Residents here include the Loris, Potto, Bushbabies, Douroucouli (a New World species, also known as the Night-ape or Owl-monkey), Civets, Genets, Fennec Fox, Flying Fox (no relation) and other Bats.

The aquarium (separate entrance fee) is huge and, although opened in 1924, is better by far than many built since. It has freshwater, seawater and tropical halls. Outstanding animals are the Piranha, Dragonfish (can also be lethal but via their poisonous spines), Sea Horses (how bizarre for a fish to have a prehensile tail), Pufferfish, Fan Worms, Lung Fish, Electric Eels, Climbing Perch, Mudskipper, Archer Fish, Sturgeon and many more, 246 species being a lot of fish. There is also the Children's Zoo (another entrance fee) where children and animals may get to grips with each other at closer quarters than is possible with most of the inmates elsewhere. The Chimpanzees' tea party used to be held here but has now been cancelled on the grounds that animals, however much they put on performances of their own and might have actually enjoyed the occasion, should not be exploited in this fashion.

The Zoological Society of London, which is heavy with committees, considers that its func-tion is as was laid down 150 years ago, namely that it should advance science. Its theme, currently, is said to be 'Conservation, Education, and the Advancement of Zoology and Animal Physiology'. The idea of a zoo being a place of entertainment therefore receives short shrift, save as a lead towards education. It is difficult to conduct much science on captive animals on show to the public (although post-mortems are always useful, such as the very thorough investigation of Chi-Chi after she had died), but it is possible to educate, to provide courses at different levels, to run a Young Zoologists Club, to conduct adult meetings, to father publications such as the *Journal of Zoology* and the *International Zoo Yearbook*, to host meetings, and to promote zoology wherever possible. Regent's Park does all these things and more.

It is a mixed blessing being sited within a city's royal park. Other committees can breathe down the zoo's neck, urging that buildings and general maintenance should also be to their liking. On the credit side is the fact that Regent's Park is likely to receive presents from Buckingham Palace. In 1976, Brazil's President gave the Queen six Toucans, two Anteaters, one Giant Armadillo, one Two-toed Sloth (all Sloths have the same number (three) of hind toes; it is their front toes that differ in number) and two Black-necked Swans. All of these animals were then passed to Regent's Park, save for the Swans which went to Slimbridge. The prime advantage of being so centrally placed is the excellence of the catchment area. Not only does a fifth of the British population live nearby, but London is a dominant tourist trap from home and abroad. Along with Trafalgar Square and Marks &

A weigh-in of Giant Tortoises at London Zoo. Currently they are tipping the scales at about 380 lb, with the largest being 420 lb.

Spencer, the zoo is on many a visitor's list. In the between-war and largely pre-car days Regent's Park would sometimes receive two million visitors a year. In the post-war years, when our cars went largely overseas, the two-million mark was often touched, and three million was reached in 1950, the year that Brumas was born, London's first Polar cub. Currently, with so many animal viewing possibilities out of town, Regent's Park is doing well by achieving 1,700,000 visitors a year, the highest figure for any animal collection. But then this zoo is the home of so many superlatives.

Manchester: Belle Vue Zoo Park

Address	Hyde Road, Manchester
Telephone	Manchester (061) 223 1331
Open	10.00–dusk
Acreage	35
Access	On S side of A57 Hyde Road, 3 miles E of city centre (car park is opposite side of road)
Station	Manchester Piccadilly (2½ miles)
Facilities	Guide book Bar, licensed restaurant, self-service cafeteria, snack bar and kiosk (in amusements area) Gift shop
Other	Aquarium Children's zoo Playground, amusements and funfair Miniature railway

This extremely old commercial zoo, opened to general visitors in 1836, used to be in the countryside lying to the south-east of Manchester. It has since been overtaken by considerable urban development, by the subsequent decay of much of that development, and by extra commercial pressures even within its territory. The Belle Vue complex contains a speedway, ghost train, beer hall, roller-skating, water-chute – and all the animals. Nevertheless, it has maintained its position as a premier zoo within the country.

It is premier largely in the sense of possessing a great quantity of animals which represent a wide variety of species. There are the three Big Apes, very many kinds of Monkey (more than at London), Lions, Leopards, Tigers, Pumas, several Bears, Camels, Zebras, Elephants, Sealions, Rhinos, quite a few small mammals, Penguins, Cranes, Pelicans, Cassowaries, Wolves, Wallabies, several ungulates, Pygmy Hippos, Tapirs, Ostriches, Rheas and many inhabitants of the aviaries and the aquarium and reptile house. In

The old-style Bear pit (*above*) epitomizes the old-style menagerie, but many of today's Bear enclosures are the weakest point of an urban zoo. *Below* A Himalayan Bear at Belle Vue.

terms both of numbers and of species it is particularly rich.

In terms of buildings it has plainly had money to spend from time to time. The Pygmy Hippo building may currently have a heavy, fruity atmosphere, but the structure is novel and gives visitors an interesting angle over its inmates. The

Monkey house is substantial and does possess a very considerable number of cages. The Zebras have an interesting adobe-style enclosure. The Ape house must have cost a bit. There is also a nice walk-way up in the trees over some well-made dinosaurs.

But the zoo, and therefore the animals, seem to have lost much of the original zest. Perhaps the association with amusements has been too hard to bear. (If zoos and amusements are mixed no one can complain if people treat animals as amusements. Similarly, if the amusements make more money, more money will be spent on them, and less on the animals.) Perhaps vandalism has helped to exhaust the management. Perhaps pollution has not helped. (The Polar Bear was whiter than the Brown Bear, but nowhere else did this comparison come to mind.) Belle Vue has even had regular firework displays in its time, about as unsuitable an activity for a zoo as could be found this side of an actual war. It certainly points up that conflict of priorities. Or possibly the lack of conflict, with the amusements winning almost every time.

The urban zoos, however cramped, used to be the only places where we could see exotic animals. Now there are scores of bigger, cleaner and more suitable wildlife areas within the countryside, and we can reach them by the open road that is now at our command. It must be hard for an urban zoo to shut up shop, call it a day and send its animals to the countryside which is where – at Belle Vue – it all began. Whatever the rights and wrongs of the case, and whether or not the Manchester animals still bring in a pound or two, these thoughts did come most readily during a visit to that zoo.

Manchester: Cannon Aquarium and Vivarium

Address	Manchester Museum, Oxford Road, Manchester
Telephone	Manchester (061) 273 3333
Open	10.00–17.00
Access	Oxford Road runs parallel with, and to W of, A34
Station	Manchester Piccadilly ($\frac{1}{4}$ mile)
Facilities	Guide book
Show	Feeding on Friday afternoon

Within Manchester Museum and equally free is the Cannon Aquarium and Vivarium. Unlike most places of its kind the fish and the reptiles are evenly matched numerically, there being 30 reptiles of 19 species as against 40 fish of 12 species. Prominent reptiles are adult American Alligators, Indian Pythons, Dwarf Crocodiles, and Yellow Rat Snakes and Rainbow Boas, which have bred for five years and for two years respectively. Even the Alligators have produced eggs, which is an exceptional event, but no living young as yet.

Merseyside County Museums: Aquarium and Vivarium

Address	William Brown Street, Liverpool
Telephone	Liverpool (051) 207 0001
Open	Monday–Saturday 10.00–17.00; Sunday 14.00–17.00
Access	100 yards NW of Lime Street Station in city centre
Station	Liverpool Lime Street (100 yards)
Facilities	Guided tours (by arrangement)

Approximately 2000 animals live in the Merseyside Aquarium and Vivarium, and they represent 160 fish species, 9 reptile species and 8 kinds of amphibia. The star attractions are Sea Horses, Turtles, Piranhas and Snakes. The fish are both tropical and temperate freshwater, as well as marine. Admission is free.

Morecambe and Heysham: Marineland Oceanarium and Aquarium

Address	Stone Jetty, Central Promenade, Morecambe, Lancs
Telephone	Morecambe (0524) 414 727
Open	Summer 10.00–19.00; winter 10.00–17.00
Access	Stone Jetty is midway between Morecambe's two piers
Station	Promenade (immediate)
Facilities	Guide book and information leaflet Guided tours (schools, winter) Licensed restaurant with children's menu, and self-service cafeteria (summer)
Shows	Dolphins: May, June, September, October 11.00, 14.00, 15.00 and 16.15; July and August 11.15, 15.00, 16.15 and 18.00 Sealions: May, June, September and October 11.30 and 14.30; July and August 10.45 and 15.45

The Morecambe Aquarium is one of the best in Britain. It has been combined with an outdoor dolphinarium where Hattie, Sadie, Cleo and Rockie perform during the summer. There are other outdoor pools for Sealions (who also give performances) and for Seals and Penguins. The aquarium is indoors and possesses 40 tanks containing fish of 200 species. There are also reptile species here of Monitors, Iguanas, Tegus, Alligators and Turtles.

Marineland is run by Morecambe and Heysham Corporation, but is not free. Although the displays cease during the winter all the animals can still be seen at that time. Over 150,000 people were entertained here during 1976.

Morecambe and Heysham: Winged World

Address	Heysham Road, Heysham, Lancs
Telephone	Heysham (0524) 52392
Acreage	25
Access	Part of New Heysham Head Entertainment Centre at Lower Heysham, on W side of A589 Morecambe (2 miles N) to Heysham road
Station	Morecambe Promenade (2 miles)
Facilities	Guide book and information leaflet Bar; self-service cafeteria, snack bar and kiosk (summer) (all in Entertainment Centre) Picnic area (in Entertainment Centre) Gift shop
Other	Children's zoo Playground (in Entertainment Centre)

The future of this exhibit, opened in 1966 by the Morecambe and Heysham Corporation, is in doubt. If it has to close not only the north-west but the whole of Britain will lose a major bird collection, notably of the tropical soft-billed varieties in which it has always specialized. As the collection has also achieved quite a breeding reputation the failure to maintain this distinction will be another form of loss. Therefore, it is to be hoped that the Corporation will be able to maintain its Winged World.

The birds are all housed in one large building, which is divided into three areas. Two of these contain normal glass-fronted display sections but the third, possessing some larger birds, has open-fronted cages. Antwerp Zoo, so often a leader with new techniques, was the first to open up a passageway of an aviary where the visitors were in darkness while the birds were in well-lit enclosures. There was no glass but the birds were

loath to fly from their brightness into the darkness beyond. This novel system was incorporated into the new aviary at Heysham Head.

Another Winged World speciality is to keep only the rarer kinds of bird. For example, recent breeding successes with relatively uncommon species have included Blue-crowned Motmot, Green Wood Hoopoe, Kiskadee Flycatcher, Rufous-chinned Jay Thrush, Painted Bush Quail, African White-fronted Bee-eater and African Woodland Kingfisher. There are about 250 birds in the collection. In another section are a few mammals of the children's-zoo type as well as some reptiles. It is not known how many visit the collection, being just a part of the Entertainment Centre, but it is known that it would be a significant loss if it were to close.

Newquay Zoo

Address	Trenance Park, Newquay, Cornwall
Telephone	Newquay (063 73) 3342
Open	Easter–October 10.00–dusk; winter 10.00–16.00
Acreage	9
Access	Immediately to E of A3075 to Redruth (16 miles) on SE side of town
Station	Newquay ($\frac{1}{4}$ mile)
Facilities	Guide book Guided tours (on request) Self-service cafeteria (summer) Picnic area Gift shop
Other	Pets' corner
Feeding	With own food

This is the largest zoo in Cornwall and was started by the local Council in only 1969. The collection is very mixed and the animals are generally of the conventional zoo kind. The zoo itself has been well landscaped and animal accommodation is, on the whole, in large areas.

Among the mammals are Lions, Monkeys, Leopards, Bears, Deer, Sealions, Bison, Wallabies and Llamas. For the birds there are two lakes, stocked with Ducks, Geese, Flamingos and Pelicans, as well as a walk-through aviary containing many tropical varieties. There is also a Penguin pool. Reptiles are represented by Pythons, Crocodiles, Caymans, Terrapins, Lizards and Turtles.

The Cornish Choughs are not extinct but they are said to be so in the West Country. Newquay Zoo has a special Chough aviary from which, if all goes well, these birds will be released appropriately into the Cornish countryside.

Paignton Zoological and Botanical Gardens

Address	Totnes Road, Paignton, Devon
Telephone	Paignton (0803) 557 479
Open	All year except 25 December from 10.00
Acreage	75+
Access	On S side of A385 Totnes (5 miles W) to Paignton (½ mile E) road
Station	Paignton (½ mile)
Facilities	Guide book and information leaflet Lectures Guided tours and woodland walk (for members of Peacock Association) Bar; licensed restaurant and self-service cafeteria with children's menus, snack bar and kiosk Picnic areas Gift shop Pushchairs for hire
Other	Aquarium Pets' corner Playground Remote-controlled toy boats Miniature putting (summer) Photographer Nature trail (by arrangement)
Shows	Animals fed throughout day
Feeding	With purchased food

It initially sounds a good idea having a zoo at a major seaside resort, with all those people looking around for something to do, but the zoo suffers from the British custom of taking holidays during a narrow band of time. July, August and September are peak months, and only then do the crowds flock. The Paignton Zoological and Botanical Gardens expect to make a profit for three-and-a-half months in each year and a loss at other times. Admittedly, no zoo gates do well in wintertime, but those relying upon our quarterly migration to see the sea do even worse. Ticket sales can be worse still on the really fine days when no one thinks of anything beyond sitting on the beach. If there is a national recession, the establishments living near the bone can suffer particularly, and Paignton has been having to raise charges, cut expenses, stop building new exhibits and dispose of 'considerable numbers of animals'. This is a shame as Paignton is home for a major collection of exotic creatures as well as the site for botanical gardens of impressive splendour. Despite the cutbacks, and an annual attendance of less than 300,000, it still possesses about 1100 animals, which include 230 mammals, 450 birds (it is the birds and small mammals, notably 'the least attractive exhibits', that have in the main gone), 130 reptiles, 45 amphibians, 215 fish and 40 invertebrates. The botanical side is as remarkable as ever. It is not so much the bedding out of plants, as at Chester, but the relentless growing of trees and shrubs that strikes a Paignton visitor. There are also the tropical and sub-tropical houses, rich with plants (and birds), that are no less crucial to this garden zoo.

Whenever there is a particularly good collection where one would not have expected an outstandingly great zoo, as at Paignton, it is usually correct to presume some diligent fanatic has been at work. The Paignton man was Herbert Whitley who founded the gardens in 1923. He was an eccentric of the British style (unwilling, for example, to license his car but nipping over the road from house to zoo after checking the situation). On his death in 1955 the zoo's ownership passed to the Herbert Whitley Trust. As a result the zoo now claims that it is the only one in Britain owned by a body whose prime interest is education. It is also claimed, in the Souvenir Map and Guide, that Paignton has the greatest variety of animals in the country, save for the collection in Regent's Park, and is the most beautiful zoo of all.

Its endangered species include Chimpanzee, Tiger, Leopard, Indian Elephant, Wild Horse, Black Rhino, Formosan Sika Deer, Red Lechwe, Swinhoe's and Hume's Pheasant, Rothschild's Grackle, Nile Crocodile, Broad-fronted and Smooth-fronted Crocodile, American Alligator, False Gharial, Indian Python and Blomberg's Toad. The particularly good groups include Abyssinian Colobus Monkeys, Lar Gibbons (with an island of trees virtually to themselves, gener-

A pleasing feature of living in tropical climates is the sight of Geckos running up and down the walls. Not often seen is the Leopard Gecko.

Young Anacondas, a few days old, at the bottom of a bin. The Anaconda is the largest constrictor snake of South America.

ally best seen from the miniature railway), and Golden Conures.

The fact that education is put first with breeding second does not mean that only lip-service is paid to breeding. In the past two years, in particular, there has been considerable success in the rearing of young animals, due to selective buying of young pairs. The education interest means that common animals, easy to keep and well known, are often maintained in preference to rarities about which little is known, or needs to be known, in schools. Vandalism is a problem here, both from humans and animals. Principal animal offender is the Badger, which can undermine

fences, permit escapes and eat, for instance, the Peafowl. Main human vandals are believed to be holidaymakers, who seem to adopt a more playful set of standards when away from home.

In this zoo there is apparently a belief that animals should be above the visitors, looked up to rather than down at, and the technique provides some interesting enclosures. There are also novel diamond-shaped tree groups in the paddocks, designed to prevent the animals from ever becoming invisible. The labels are only fairly good which, as they provide the simplest method of teaching people, should perhaps be better in an education zoo. A bonus is that trees and shrubs have generally been named. Most places forget them altogether and certainly the Paignton visitor will come away from this zoo with a great regard for the vegetable kingdom on display along with all the animals. If attendance is dropping the memory of those trees and shrubs will surely help to bring people back again. There is much to be said for Whitley's creation, not least during the nine months of the year when the lemmings have moved elsewhere.

Plymouth Aquarium

Address	Marine Biological Association, Citadel Hill, Plymouth, Devon
Open	All year except Sunday, Good Friday and 25 and 26 December 10.00–18.00
Access	Just to N of the Hoe at SE corner of city
Station	Plymouth ($\frac{3}{4}$ mile)
Facilities	Guide book

The Marine Biological Association is one of the major bodies investigating marine life around our shores. Therefore, as is to be expected, its aquarium (open to the rest of us for almost a century) is of a high standard. It specializes in marine specimens caught in the Plymouth area, and certainly possesses one of the best collections of temperate seawater fish in Europe. With a research unit next door it is also to be expected that the aquarium carries out more breeding than most, and the young Dogfish encased in their mermaids' purses are always an intriguing sight.

Plymouth Zoological Gardens

Address	Central Park, Plymouth, Devon
Telephone	Plymouth (0752) 51375
Open	All year: summer 10.00–18.00; winter 10.00–sunset
Acreage	6
Access	Zoo is on N side of Central Park, which is immediately N of Plymouth Station
Station	Plymouth ($\frac{1}{2}$ mile)
Facilities	Guide book Snack bar (summer) Picnic area Gift shop
Other	Donkey rides
Shows	Big Cats fed 14.15; Sealions fed 15.00
Feeding	With own food

Most animals only spend a year or so within this zoo because it operates to a considerable extent as quarantine centre. It was opened by Jimmy Chipperfield in 1962, four years before Longleat began, and many of the animals for his safari parks spend a statutory time in Plymouth before being moved to the wider and more open spaces elsewhere. An urban zoo is quite likely to be a distance from farm animals and is therefore more suitable for the requirements of a quarantine centre.

The Plymouth animals include 20 kinds of mammal, 15 of bird, 2 of reptile and 2 of amphibia, many of which, such as the Lions, Tigers, Leopards, Pumas, Elephants, Camels, Llamas, Guanacos, Zebras, Giraffes, Deer, Antelope, Rhinos and Hippos are often to be seen in safari parks up and down the country. Inevitably the animals here are seen in more confined conditions as the parks they go to are often hundreds of acres in size whereas Plymouth Zoo is only six.

Scarborough Zoo and Marineland

Address	38 St Nicholas Street, Scarborough, North Yorks
Telephone	Scarborough (0723) 66401
Open	Easter–November 10.00–dusk
Acreage	7
Access	To W of (and above) Town Hall at N end of South Bay
Station	Scarborough ($\frac{1}{4}$ mile)
Facilities	Guide book and information leaflet Guided tours Cafe Mississippi paddle boat for picnics Gift shop
Other	Aquarium Dolphinarium Pets' corner Playground
Shows	11.00, 12.30, 14.15, 15.30, 17.00, 18.30, 19.30 and 20.00 (see below for details)
Feeding	With purchased food

This is a zoo with a difference. Parties are conducted round it so that visitors can, in a tour lasting one-and-a-half hours, see a Dolphin performance, a Chimpanzees' tea party, a farmyard (where children are given milk to feed to the animals), a Sealion display (children are given fish for them) and finally, the march of the King Penguins.

The collection's speciality is therefore of animals which are able to put on a bit of a show. But there are others here as the total population is of 23 kinds of mammal, 10 of bird and 30 of fish. Among the animals not mentioned so far are Raccoons, Baboons, Dingoes, Lions, Flamingos and, in a special enclosure of their own, Dinosaurs.

Although the tour is a satisfactory way of seeing many of the exhibits, visitors are also allowed to wander round on their own. Half a million saw this zoo in 1976.

Skegness: Natureland Marine Zoo

Address	North Parade, Skegness, Lincs
Telephone	Skegness (0754) 4345
Open	All year: summer 10.00–19.30; winter 10.00–16.00
Acreage	1
Access	At N end of town, between North Parade and sea
Station	Skegness (1½ miles)
Facilities	Guide book Guided tours for parties (by arrangement) Snack bar (summer) Gift shop
Other	Pets' corner
Shows	Sealions, performing Seals and Penguins fed summer 11.00, 12.00, 15.00, 16.00 and 18.00; winter 11.30 and 15.00 Baby Seals fed (with commentary) summer 10.00, 12.00, 14.00, 16.00, 18.00 and 19.30
Feeding	In pets' corner, with purchased food

Between the bowls and the amusements lies the Natureland Marine Zoo which does specialize in marine creatures, notably Sealions, Seals and Penguins. As Skegness is just up the coast from the Wash, an important Seal area, and as many of the pups are blown ashore during strong winds, a number of these abandoned animals are saved and brought to the zoo. Although Sealions are always ready to give exhibitions, it is much rarer to find a performing Seal as here at Skegness.

Within the Tropical House is a very mixed bunch, such as Imperial Scorpions, Owls, Pythons, Crocodiles, Caymans, Terrapins, Giant Snails and fish. There are even storms here every five minutes, complete with thunder, lightning and rain. Elsewhere are Flamingos, Hummingbirds, Tanagers, Sugarbirds, White-eyes, Mynahs and Parrots, a pets' corner, a wildfowl pool, a North Sea tank (one of the largest in Britain) and various smaller tanks in the aquarium.

There is also a Floral Palace, with three markedly different sections, that contains free-flying tropical birds.

Southampton Zoo

Address	The Common, Southampton, Hants
Telephone	Southampton (0703) 556 603
Open	Summer 10.00–18.00; winter 10.00–16.30
Acreage	2½
Access	At S end of The Common, on W side of The Avenue (A33 to Winchester)
Station	Southampton (1 mile)
Facilities	Snack bar Gift shop

This compact zoo, part of the Chipperfield empire, often acts as a holding unit for animals on their way to or from a safari park. Most of its mammals are large, such as Tiger, Lion, Leopard, Jaguar, but there are also various Monkeys and others even smaller. There are a few reptiles and birds but, as with Plymouth – another Chipperfield domain – there is little hint of the freedom and the enclosed vastnesses to be found in the various safari kingdoms.

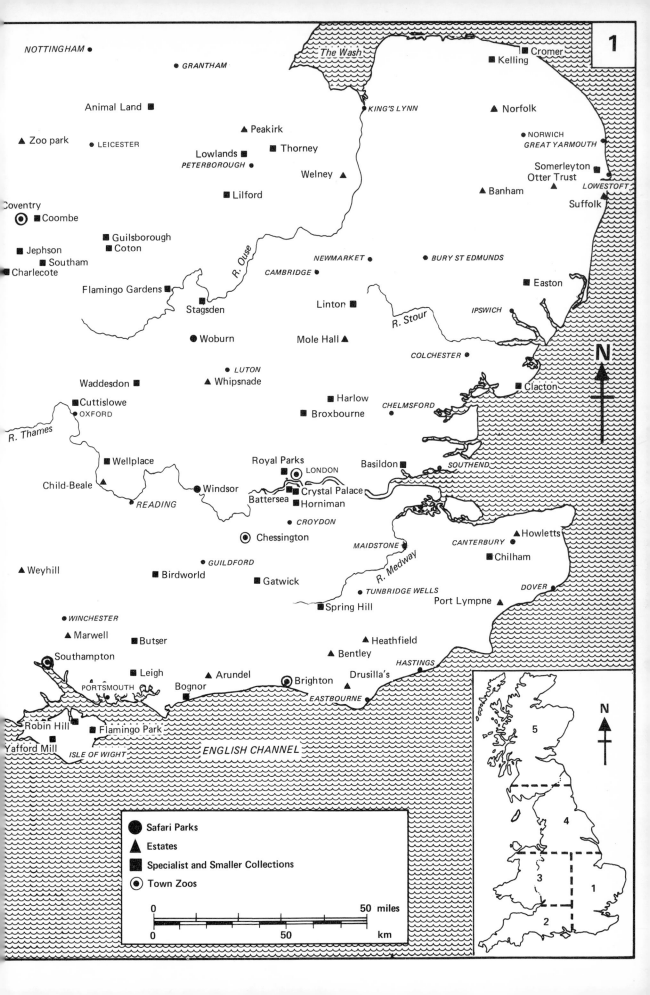

NOTTINGHAM ●

● GRANTHAM

The Wash

■ Cromer
■ Kelling

Animal Land ■

▲ Zoo park   ● LEICESTER

KING'S LYNN ●

▲ Norfolk

▲ Peakirk

● NORWICH
GREAT YARMOUTH

Lowlands ■   ■ Thorney
PETERBOROUGH ●

Somerleyton
Otter Trust ▲
LOWESTOFT

Welney ▲

■ Lilford

▲ Banham

Suffolk
▲

Coventry
◉ ■ Coombe

R. Ouse

NEWMARKET ●

● BURY ST EDMUNDS

■ Easton

■ Jephson
■ Southam
■ Charlecote

■ Guilsborough
■ Coton

CAMBRIDGE ●

Flamingo Gardens ■

■ Stagsden

Linton ■

IPSWICH ●

R. Stour

▲ Welney

Mole Hall ▲

COLCHESTER ●

● Woburn

Waddesdon ■

● LUTON
▲ Whipsnade

■ Harlow   CHELMSFORD

■ Cuttislowe
● OXFORD

■ Broxbourne

■ Clacton

R. Thames

■ Wellplace

Royal Parks
◉ LONDON

Basildon ■

SOUTHEND

Child-Beale ▲

● Windsor

READING

● Crystal Palace
Battersea ● Horniman

● CROYDON

▲ Weyhill

◉ Chessington

● GUILDFORD

MAIDSTONE

R. Medway

CANTERBURY ●

▲ Howletts

■ Chilham

■ Birdworld

■ Gatwick

TUNBRIDGE WELLS ●

DOVER

Port Lympne ▲

● WINCHESTER

Spring Hill

▲ Marwell

■ Butser

▲ Heathfield

Southampton ⓒ

■ Leigh

▲ Arundel

▲ Bentley

HASTINGS

● Brighton

Drusilla's

PORTSMOUTH

Bognor

EASTBOURNE

Robin Hill ■
■ Flamingo Park

Yafford Mill

ISLE OF WIGHT

ENGLISH CHANNEL

1

N

Legend

● Safari Parks

▲ Estates

■ Specialist and Smaller Collections

◉ Town Zoos

0 _____ 50 miles

0 _____ 50 km

N

5

4

3   1

2

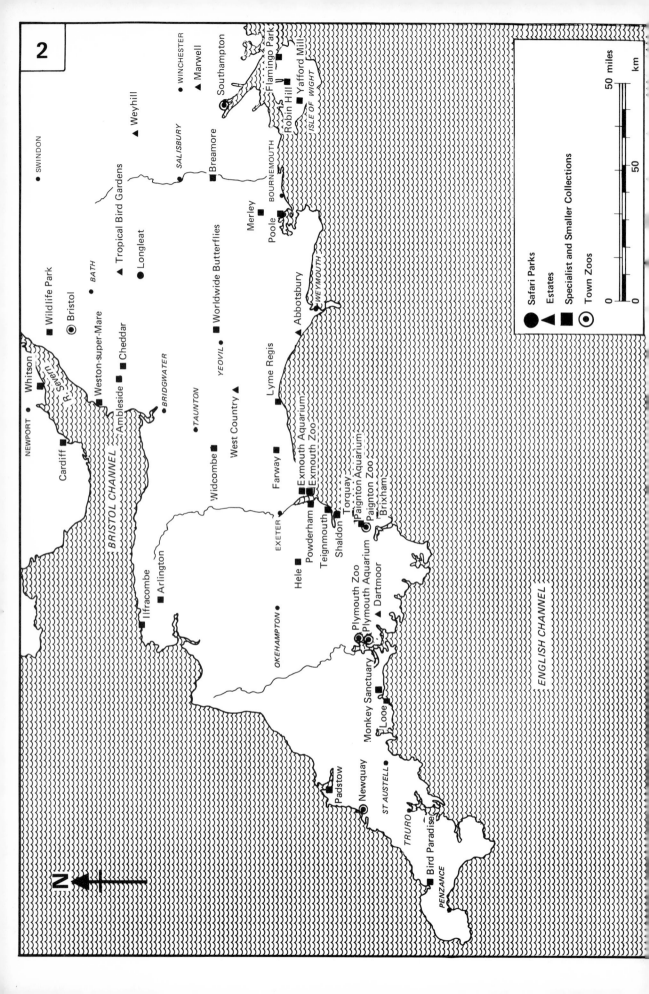

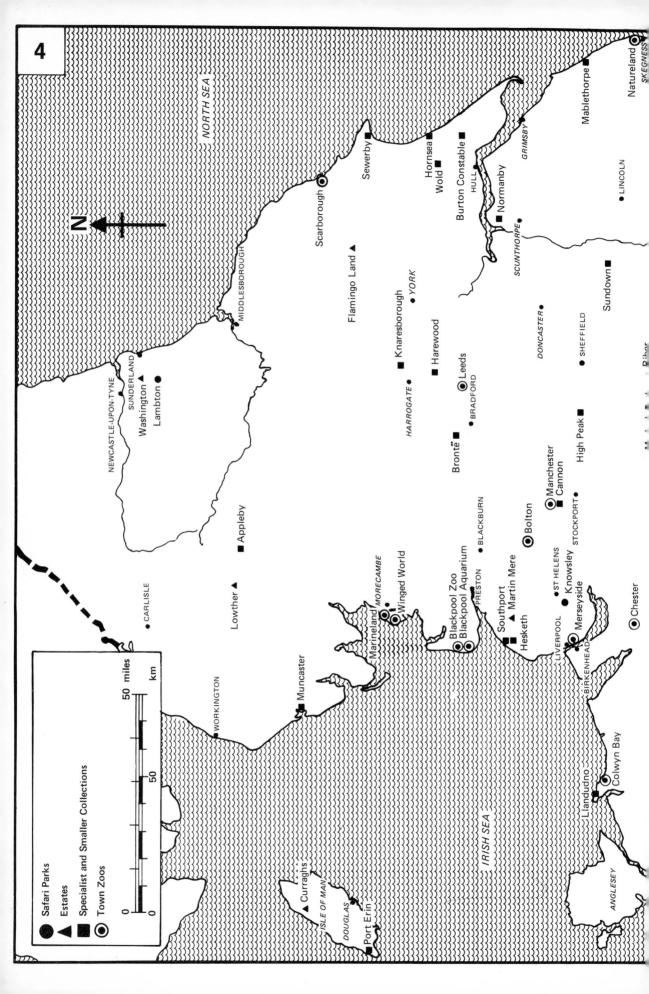

4

NORTH SEA

N

MIDDLESBOROUGH

NEWCASTLE-UPON-TYNE

SUNDERLAND ▲
Washington ▲
Lambton ●

■ Appleby

Lowther ▲

● CARLISLE

WORKINGTON

Muncaster ■

50 miles

km

50

ISLE OF MAN

DOUGLAS

Port Erin ●

Curraghs ▲

Safari Parks ●
Estates ▲
Specialist and Smaller Collections ■
Town Zoos ◎

IRISH SEA

ANGLESEY

Llandudno ■
Colwyn Bay ●

Chester ◎

BIRKENHEAD

LIVERPOOL

Knowsley ◎
Merseyside

● ST HELENS

▲ Hesketh

Southport ■
Martin Mere ▲

Blackpool Zoo ◎
Blackpool Aquarium ◎

Winged World ◎
Marineland ◎

MORECAMBE

PRESTON ●

● BLACKBURN

Bolton ◎

STOCKPORT ●

Manchester ◎
Cannon ■

High Peak ■

● SHEFFIELD

DONCASTER ●

Bronë ■

HARROGATE ● ●
Leeds ◎
BRADFORD ●

Harewood ■

Knaresborough ■

YORK ●

Flamingo Land ▲

Scarborough ◎

Sewerby ■

Hornsea ■
Wold ■

Burton Constable ■
HULL ●

Normanby ■

SCUNTHORPE ■
●

GRIMSBY ●

Sundown ■

● LINCOLN

Mablethorpe ■

Natureland ◎
SKEGNESS

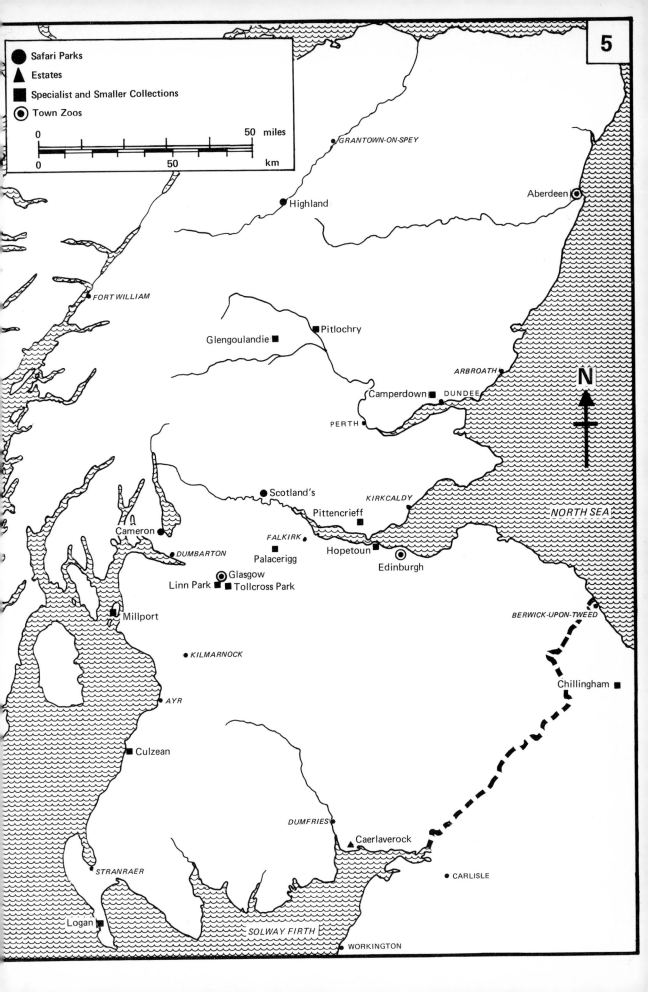

5

Legend:
- ● Safari Parks
- ▲ Estates
- ■ Specialist and Smaller Collections
- ◉ Town Zoos

0   50 miles
0   50 km

● GRANTOWN-ON-SPEY

Aberdeen ◉

● Highland

FORT WILLIAM

Glengoulandie ■   ■ Pitlochry

ARBROATH ■

Camperdown ■   DUNDEE

PERTH ●

N

● Scotland's

KIRKCALDY

Pittencrieff ●
■

NORTH SEA

Cameron ●

FALKIRK ●

DUMBARTON ●   Palacerigg ■   Hopetoun ●

◉ Glasgow   Edinburgh ◉

Linn Park ■ ■ Tollcross Park

Millport ●

BERWICK-UPON-TWEED

KILMARNOCK ●

Chillingham ■

AYR ●

Culzean ■

DUMFRIES ●

Caerlaverock ▲

STRANRAER ●

● CARLISLE

Logan ■

SOLWAY FIRTH

WORKINGTON ●

Collections Believed to Have Closed Recently

Animal Training School and Dolphinarium, South Elmsdale
Bideford Zoo
Bird Land, Cromer
Black Mountain Bird Garden, Llanddeusant
Cleethorpes Adventure Land and Zoo
Cliftonville: Queens Hotel Dolphinarium
Clopton Bird Gardens and Fish Centre, nr Thrapston
Cornish Seal Sanctuary, St Agnes
Dreamland Safari Zoo, Margate
Isle of Wight Dolphinarium
Nuneaton Zoological Gardens
Pan's Garden, Ashover
Pinevalley (Devon Wildlife Park), nr Okehampton
Porthcawl Dolphinarium
Rhyl Dolphinarium
Verulamium British Wildlife, St Albans
St Asaph Zoo, North Wales
Sherwood Zoo Park, Hucknall
Southend Dolphinarium
Stanley Zoo, Harperley Hall, Tantobie, Newcastle-on-Tyne
Stansted Wildlife Park, Essex
Tropicana Aquarium and Mini-Zoo, Rhyl
Tropical Bird Garden, Bishops Tachbrook
Wellingborough Zoo Gardens

Acknowledgments

Ardea London: 10 below left (photo Adrian Warren), 11 top left, 11 below right (photo Kenneth W. Fink), 42 below left (photo Kenneth W. Fink), 67 (photo K. J. Carlson), 68 below right (photo Dennis Avon and Tony Tilford), 91 (photo Clem Haagner), 128 left (photo R. J. C. Blewitt), 128 right, 159, 166 above and below (photo Alan Weaving), 170 (photo Kenneth W. Fink)
Associated Press: 186
Stephen Benson: 134 above, 153, 177 *above and below*
C. K. Brain: 16 left and right
Brighton Aquarium: 182 left
British Tourist Authority/Woburn Abbey: *180–1*
Camera Press: 2–3 (photo Philip Arnold), 22–3 (photo Philip Arnold), 42 above (photo Philip Arnold)
Bruce Coleman Limited: 10 above left (photo Des and Jen Bartlett), *48* (photo Hans Reinhard), *81 above* (photo Jane Burton), *81 below* (photo H. Rivarola), 92 (photo Graham Pizzey), 93 (photo Allan Power), 96 (photo Jane Burton), *129*, *132–3* (photo Des and Jen Bartlett), *133* (photo Bob and Clara Calhoun), *137* (photo Jane Burton), 138 below (photo Jane Burton), *140–1* (photo S. C. Bisserot), *144* (photo S. C. Bisserot), *188–9* (photo Hans Reinhard), *192* (photo G. B. Frith)
The Daily Telegraph: 8 below
John Doidge: 118 top left
Dudley Zoo: 196–7
Mary Evans Picture Library: 203 above, 206 above
Falconry Centre, Newent: 148
Fox Photos: 11 below left and middle right, 19 above and below, 38, 107 below
Robert Goodden: *84, 85, 88*
K. W. Green: *36, 184 above and below*
J. H. D. Hooper: 12 above
Alan Howard: 97 above
Leslie Jackman: 160
Kenneth Jagger: 120–1, 142, 143 above and below
Jarrold Colour Publications: 24, 27 above, *33* (photo Richard Tilbrook), *40* (photo Richard Tilbrook), 88–9 (photo Richard Tilbrook)
Keystone Press Agency: 80 above, 125, 193
Lilli Koenig: 157 left
George Lower: 135
Mansell Collection: 8 above, 15 above
Marwell Zoological Park: 94 above
Karl H. Maslowski: 155
Mercury Press Agency: 47 (photo David Kendall)
National Geographic Society: 182 right
M. Patel: 31
Press Association: 201 below
Popperfoto: 10 centre, 12 below, 116, 124, 187
Punch: 13
The Scotsman: 198
Philippa Scott: 105 below, 106, 150, *184–5*
Paul Shillabeer: 199
Anthony Smith: 15 below, 21 left, 25 above, 27 below, 32, 34 below, 39 left and right, 50, 53 above, 56 above and below, 60 centre and below, 66 above, 71, 74 top left and right, below left and centre, 78–9, 80 below, 83 above and below right, 87, 98, 101, 109 above, 111 below right, 118 below left and right, 119 top left and right, and below, 126 above right and below left and right, 127, 134 below, 162, 178, 179, 183, 190, 191, 194, 202 above left and right, and below, 203 below, 206 below
Twycross Zoo: 117
Philip Wayre: 99 above
Weidenfeld and Nicolson Archive: 10 above left and right, 11 centre left, 20
D. J. Wheadon: 111 above
Dave Williams: 123, 195
Zoo Park, Twycross: 117
Zoological Society of London: endpaper, 4, 10 below right, 11 above right, 21 right, 30 above and below, 36–7, *41*, *44–5*, 53 below, 62–3, 72 below, 77 above, 113 above and below, 114 below, 126 above left, *136*, 138 above, *140*, 146, 147, 157 right, 161, 172, 174–5, 201 above, 204, 205, 209, 210

Numbers in *italics* refer to colour pages.
Picture research by Jill Southam.
Maps drawn by Design Practitioners.

The author and publishers have taken all possible care to trace and acknowledge the copyright of all the photographs reproduced in this book. If any errors have accidentally occurred the publishers will be happy to correct them in future editions, provided that they receive notification.

Index